DATE DUE

JAN 0 6 1989	

Shakespeare's Heroical Histories

Shakespeare's Heroical Histories

Henry VI and Its Literary Tradition

David Riggs

Harvard University Press

Cambridge, Massachusetts, 1971

Distributed in Great Britain by Oxford University Press, London

Publication of this book has been aided by a grant
from the Hyder Edward Rollins Fund

Library of Congress Catalog Card Number 75–152701

SBN 674–80400–7

Printed in the United States of America

To Sue

Preface

Since many of the passages quoted in my text are cited from early printed books, or from diplomatic editions such as the Malone Society Reprints, the following procedures have been adopted. The spelling of all play titles (except Bale's *King Johan*) has been normalized, according to the form given in Samuel Schoenbaum's revised *Annals of English Drama*. Contracted speech headings have been silently expanded; so have any contractions that are merely the printer's abbreviations (such as "thẽ" for "them"). Whenever I have quoted directly from an early printed book, or a microfilm copy of one, the entry number from Pollard and Redgrave's *Short-Title Catalogue* (*STC*) is given with the first reference in the notes. This has been done because many of the works cited — especially in chapter 2 — are translations into English from Latin and French: these can vary greatly from edition to edition, and they are often difficult to locate. The references given in the List of Works Cited are, however, brief citations, and they do not include the variant editions that are occasionally listed in the notes. I have used Andrew S. Cairncross' texts (published in the New Arden Shakespeare) for all three parts of *Henry VI;* for *Richard III* I have used the recent edition of G. Blakemore Evans; all other citations from Shakespeare refer to G. L. Kittredge's edition of the *Complete Works*.

The Greek word *topos* and its Elizabethan equivalent "topic" both appear in my text: while they are, strictly speaking, interchangeable, I have generally used the Elizabethan coinage when referring to manuals of rhetoric used in Elizabethan schools. When I describe a play as "popular," the reference is to its auspices of production, not to the enthusiasm with which it was received.

I wish to thank the President and Fellows of Harvard University for a Frank Knox Travelling Fellowship which enabled me to spend a year at the Shakespeare Institute of Birmingham University, the staff of the Houghton Library at Harvard for many kindnesses extended during the writing of this manuscript, and the Department of English at Stanford University for funds that helped to cover the costs of preparing the final copy.

viii   Preface

I have a large and general obligation to the teachers, students, and
friends with whom I studied Elizabethan drama during ten years at
Harvard University. These are too numerous to permit a full catalogue
here, and in any case the kinds of assistance that they offered are not
easily summarized. A few points of indebtedness should, however, be
acknowledged here. My attempt to relate the history play, and particularly Marlowe's *Tamburlaine,* to the social crises of Elizabethan England
owes a great deal to some lectures given by Professor Michael Walzer
of the Harvard University Department of Government; and my concluding efforts to formulate the problem of public as opposed to private
identities as it relates to the passage quoted from *The Prince* on page
152, grew directly out of a lecture given by Professor Stanley Cavell of
the Harvard University Department of Philosophy. For advice and en-
couragement of all sorts, extending over many years, I wish to thank
Professors Harry Levin and Herschel Baker, who supervised the doc-
toral dissertation on which the three central chapters are based, and
Professor Daniel Seltzer, who introduced me to most of the questions
that are treated here, and to many of the answers besides. Professors
G. Blakemore Evans, Neil Rudenstine, and Stephen Barney all read the
original manuscript and suggested how I might improve it. Later, my
colleagues at Stanford, Herbert Lindenberger, Lawrence Ryan, Wesley
Trimpi, and JoAn Chace were kind enough to go over the last draft, and
to assist in a number of final revisions.

D.R.
Stanford University
Stanford, California

Contents

Contents

Shakespeare's Heroical Histories

1 Premises of Heroical-Historical Drama, 1587–1592

Yes, trust them not; for there is an upstart crow, beautified
with our feathers, that with his *tiger's heart wrapp'd in a
player's hide* supposes he is as well able to bombast out a
blank verse as the best of you; and being an absolute
Johannes fac totum, is in his own conceit the only Shake-scene
in a country. O that I might intreat your rare wits to be
imployed in more profitable courses; and let those apes imitate
your past excellence, and never more acquaint them with your
admired inventions.

(Robert Greene, *Greene's Groats-worth of Wit*, 1592)

When Robert Greene warned his old acquaintances among the playwrights to beware of an "upstart crow, beautified with our feathers," he
launched the enterprise of Shakespeare criticism — appropriately enough
— by initiating one of its perennial arguments. In its broadest applica-
tion, the argument comes to involve the entire problem of Shakespeare's
relationship to Elizabethan literary culture; but it begins with a few
unkind remarks about one of the early plays and its indebtedness to
the popular drama written by the "university wits" of the later 1580's.
Speaking with reference to *3 Henry VI,* Greene suggests that an unlet-
tered novice could never have written such a play were it not for the
prior achievement of himself, Marlowe, Nashe, Peele, and the rest, who
supplied the "colors" (of rhetoric), the "blank verse," and all the other
"admired inventions" that go to make up a literary language. What is
more, he strongly insinuates that what this actor-turned-playwright has
achieved is merely a facile imitation of that language. In "his own
conceit," he may be "the only Shake-scene in a country," but in fact he

2 Shakespeare's Heroical Histories

is just another of those apes who live off other men's past excellence.
Understandably, scholarship has sought to discount these ill-natured
criticisms, either by attributing them to some obscure personal grudge,
or by dismissing them as altogether irrelevant. The origins of the trilogy
are now explained, as a rule, on the premise that Shakespeare began
by borrowing the interpretive procedures of the Tudor historians, for
which he found dramatic precedent only in *Gorboduc* and a few "moralities of state," such as Bale's *King Johan* and the anonymous *Woodstock.*
Virtually all the recent book-length studies of the histories begin with
chapters on Elizabethan historiography, and they proceed on the assumption that these dramatists "appropriated the themes of history and
chose their materials in the same way as the professional historians. The
process was largely intuitive." [1] The problem here, as with any exercise
in historical criticism, has to do with the nature of the tasks that "intuition" can be expected to perform; and in this regard I would submit
that Greene's view of the matter is still better informed than many of
the rejoinders it has elicited. It is, after all, rather surprising that critics
who are considerably more thoughtful than he should so readily accede
to the odd idea that the young Shakespeare went outside the professional
stage for his working models, even where the dramatic speech is so
plainly derivative that generations of scholars were prepared to dismiss
the plays from the canon altogether. If, of course, it were true that only
professional historians could be said to possess an informed, systematic
philosophy of history, there would be a built-in case for Shakespeare's
reliance on them. But it is far more likely, as I hope to show, that he,
like the university playwrights, was furnished with a cohesive, literate
approach to history well before his exposure to the chronicles of Holinshed and Hall.

Accordingly, the study that follows undertakes to show that Shakespeare did indeed set out to imitate a kind of heroical history play
that Greene and his contemporaries had already brought to fruition; only
I shall argue that Shakespeare imitated those playwrights not out of
artistic desperation, but rather as a fellow practitioner in a humanistic
tradition that he quickly came to understand better than any of them.
What Greene, with his acute critical myopia, saw as an isolated case
of plagiarism might better be envisioned as the midpoint of several con-
centric circles. Immediately beyond the particular instance of *Henry*

VI and its fund of rhetorical clichés there is the continuous repertory of popular historical drama from, say, *Tamburlaine* to *Richard III,* within which one can at least begin to ascertain the special meanings that those clichés would have held for Shakespeare and his audience. Then, circumscribing this local dramatic tradition, there are the presiding theories of "heroical" poetry and humanist historiography, which originate in classical criticism, enjoy a wide revival in the *quattrocento,* and eventually infiltrate most of the Elizabethan attempts to define historical literature. Finally, there are the accepted procedures of classical rhetoric, which regulated any educated Elizabethan's approach to history and literature, and which help to explain the verbal strategies and the conceptions of character that are common to all these plays.

My account of this complex legacy begins — in the middle of things — with matters of literary theory and theatrical practice, and then proceeds, in the two chapters that follow this one, to analyze the rhetorical and dramatic antecedents of Shakespeare's earlier histories. The latter part of the book will deal with *Henry VI* and its place in Shakespeare's development. The purpose of such a survey, very briefly, is to see the trilogy not as the erratic beginning of a remarkable career, but rather as the sustained effort of one playwright, drawing on the resources of a long and varied humanistic tradition, to assess a literary ideal by setting it within the recent history of his own society.

For the most part, then, this study moves in a loosely chronological way through those phases of Elizabethan literary culture that parallel, as it happens, the distinctive stages of Shakespeare's early career: the education in rhetoric offered by the Tudor grammar school; the education in popular drama offered by the London theater of the late 1580's; and the gradual emergence of Shakespeare as a highly successful dramatist in the early 1590's. Such a chronology can be deceptive. In particular, it should always be kept in mind that the lines of influence operated, as it were, simultaneously within the playwright's imagination. Hence, this introductory essay is largely devoted to developing a set of assumptions about history and literature that are broad enough to anticipate the materials dealt with in subsequent chapters, and yet are clearly relevant to the actual business of making an Elizabethan history play. I have tried to ensure that these are not just my own assumptions by using, whenever possible, passages in which a practicing playwright draws, or

4 Shakespeare's Heroical Histories

suggests, some connection between a traditional conception of heroic literature or humanist historiography on the one hand, and an Elizabethan history play on the other. If these do not provide a comprehensive theory of the genre they should at least evoke some of the special criteria that the early histories would have been expected to fulfil. Eventually, to approach the *Henry VI* plays by way of the conventional *topoi* and rhetorical procedures that order their most important meanings will be, I hope, to reveal a kind of continuity within the trilogy that has not been observed in previous criticism. Here again, though, the primary object is to locate the plays as firmly as possible in their traditional contexts; that is, to elucidate their place in Shakespeare's prolonged mediation between heroic ideals and those ethical and political realities that the study of history should always bring to consciousness.

This broad network of influences and relationships has not received much attention within Shakespeare criticism. In the specific case of *Henry VI,* students have charted two distinct highroads, both of which, without lingering in the trilogy any longer than seems necessary to uphold the playwright's artistic integrity, lead directly to *Richard III.* One group, which may be represented by Edmund Malone, S. T. Coleridge, and John Dover Wilson, would, in effect, cast the entire problem of antecedents and influences back on Greene's doorstep by attributing to Shakespeare only the "Shakespearian" scenes, speeches, and even individual lines, while endeavoring to "clear [him] of all responsibility for the dull, miserably commonplace, and often unmetrical verse" to be found in these plays.[2] Where the poetic idiom sounds like second-rate Marlowe, Peele, Nashe, or Greene, it is concluded that one of them, rather than Shakespeare, is responsible. Since this theory necessarily involves certain conjectures about the composition of *Henry VI* and the provenance of its text, even a brief consideration of it must be deferred to chapter 4. I would observe at the outset, however, that the potential fallacies in this line of reasoning are formidable, particularly when one considers the high priority placed on observing decorum, as opposed to self-expression, in Renaissance literature; and in fact it will be argued here that many (if not all) of the varied styles in *Henry VI* can be explained on just that principle.

An alternative way of reading the trilogy, which has been set forth by E. M. W. Tillyard and others who are versed in Tudor historiography, would argue that specific scenes and speeches are not really at issue here anyway.[3] What does matter, in this view, is the playwright's grand conception of providential history and hierarchical order, which looms into view beneath the fog of rhetorical clichés just often enough to ensure that the whole could only have been imagined by Shakespeare. This idea has been reiterated many times, and there is much to recommend it. If providential history may be identified with the element of moral teleology that Shakespeare, like most Elizabethans, professed to see in the succession of reigns that led to the union of Lancaster and York, then there is, beyond question, a providential theme in *Henry VI* which is duly consummated in *Richard III*. The problem is that this providential design is visible, for the most part, only as a bare outline of the events that Shakespeare selected from the chronicles. Hence, expositions of the "Tudor myth" in *Henry VI* tend to be schematized plot summaries in which the leading character (England) is literally without dramatic existence, while her most eloquent spokesmen (Exeter, Alexander Iden, the nameless Father and Son) generally hover somewhere on the periphery of the story. Few critics have ventured to explain, for example, how the joking about Joan's sexual misconduct, or the Talbots' concern with their family "name," illuminates the ways of Providence in *1 Henry VI*; and yet these matters assume great importance in several scenes that are absolutely central to the play. In other words, despite the playwright's readiness to endorse, on occasion, Elizabethan dogma about the moral necessity of hierarchical loyalties, it by no means follows that *Henry VI* exists merely to illustrate the providential ratification of that dogma.

The uncertainties that beset the critic here point towards a problem that must have confronted the dramatist as well: how can a theatrical form largely derived from *Tamburlaine the Great* and the humanistic traditions that stand behind it be used to present a highly ethical interpretation of fifteenth-century English history? Such a question can hardly be answered without some reference to the position of these plays in relation to their sources and antecedents. It requires of criticism that it begin, in effect, by asking what kind of play it was possible for Shakespeare to write in 1590. One returns to Greene's question — Was the upstart crow really the master of his materials? — but on something like Shakespeare's terms: Where did those materials come from? What dramatic possibilities did they afford? And how could an artist of a temperament rather different from any of the University playwrights turn them to his own purposes? The end in view here is not still another synoptic definition of that elusive genre, the Elizabethan history play, but rather a selective picture of the form as it passed into Shakespeare's hands; "selective" because, if only to reduce the subject to manageable proportions, it will be necessary to distinguish between what were live options for a professional playwright in 1590, and what were not. Several of the stage historian's usual favorites, such as Bale's *King Johan, Woodstock,* and *The Troublesome Reign of King John* have been largely excluded from the account. Their place in the genesis of the Elizabethan history has been discussed many times over, and the interested reader would do better to consult the authorities on the subject; further, this study is concerned more with certain literary prototypes as they evolved on the early Elizabethan stage than with the transmission of Tudor polemic into the public playhouse; and finally, as I shall argue at the conclusion of this chapter, the connections that have been drawn between the "moral" history and the Shakespearian kind are still vague enough to leave alternative lines of inquiry open and available. A far more interesting play, Marlowe's *Edward II,* has been omitted because of its relatively late date, and because a full treatment of it would necessarily go beyond the scope of the problem at hand. The format of my survey will be analytical rather than historical. The reader who wishes a more coherent and chronological account of the way in which the kinds of historical drama to be discussed here came into being is asked to wait until the subsequent chapters. The point of departure for this one will be some remarks that indicate what an Elizabethan audience of about 1590 would have expected to see and hear when "history" was put on the stage.

One final word of explanation seems called for. In view of the influential argument that F. P. Wilson has made for treating the English history play as Shakespeare's peculiar discovery, my hypothetical date of 1590 may appear arbitrary in the extreme.[4] I can only reply that I have taken the absence of a secure chronology more as an invitation to speculation than as a discouragement to criticism, and so have endeavored to proceed in the spirit of *Marlowe and the Early Shakespeare.* Except in the case of Marlowe's *Tamburlaine,* I have kept clear of any hypotheses that depend on specific verbal parallels or a definite instance of one playwright influencing another. In fact, I hope that such questions will seem less pressing as it becomes more apparent that all the dramatists under consideration were working within a common literary tradition.

Heroical Poetry and Humanist Historiography

When Elizabethan playwrights troubled to write about their "histories" they found virtues that later readers have tended to ignore. Where modern scholarship looks for an allusive, didactic commentary on Renaissance politics and the ways of Providence, Shakespeare's contemporaries were more likely to begin by expressing their enthusiasm for a visual and rhetorical display of heroic deeds. Any number of scattered utterances in plays, pamphlets, and critical treatises could be cited in this regard, but the idea of historical literature that underlies most of them is perhaps best introduced by Thomas Heywood's agreeably fantastic account of its origin and progress:

In the first of the *Olimpiads,* amongst many other active exercises in which *Hercules* ever triumph'd as victor, there was in his nonage presented unto him by his Tutor in the fashion of a History, acted by the choyse of the nobility of Greece, the worthy and memorable acts of his father *Iupiter.* Which being personated with lively and well-spirited action, wrought such impression in his noble thoughts, that in meere emulation of his fathers valor (not at the behest of his Stepdame *Iuno*) he perform'd his twelve labours: Him valiant *Theseus* followed, and *Achilles, Theseus.* Which bred in them such hawty and magnanimous attempts, that every succeeding age hath recorded their worths, unto fresh admiration. *Aristotle* that Prince of Philosophers, whose bookes carry such credit, even in these our universities, that to say *Ipse dixit* is a sufficient *Axioma,* hee having the tuition of young *Alexander,* caused the destruction of Troy to be acted before his pupill, in which the valor of *Achilles* was so naturally exprest, that it imprest the hart of *Alexander*, in so much that all his succeeding actions were meerly shaped after that patterne, and it may be imagined had *Achilles* never lived,

Alexander had never conquered the whole world. . . . Why should
not the lives of these worthyes presented in these our dayes, effect
the like wonders in the Princes of our times, which can no way bee
so exquisitly demonstrated, nor so lively portrayed as by action. . . .
A Description is only a shadow received by the eare but not
perceived by the eye: so lively portrature is meerely a forme seene
by the eye, but can neither shew action, passion, motion, or any
other gesture, to moove the spirits of the beholder to admiration:
but to see a souldier shap'd like a souldier, walke, speake, act
like a souldier: to see a *Hector* all besmered in blood, trampling
upon the bulkes of Kinges. A *Troylus* returning from the field in
the sight of his father *Priam* as if man and horse even from the
steeds rough fetlockes to the plume in the champions helmet had
bene together plunged into a purple Ocean: To see a *Pompey* ride
in triumph, then a *Caesar* conquer that *Pompey:* labouring *Han-
niball* alive, hewing his passage through the Alpes. To see as I
have seene, *Hercules* in his owne shape hunting the Boare, knocking
downe the Bull, taming the Hart, fighting with Hydra, murdering
Gerion, slaughtring *Diomed,* wounding the *Stimphalides,* killing the
Centaurs, pashing the Lion, squeezing the Dragon, dragging *Cer-
berus* in Chaynes, and lastly, on his high Pyramides writing *Nil
ultra,* Oh these were sights to make an *Alexander.*
To turne to our domesticke hystories, what English blood seeing
the person of any bold English man presented and doth not hugge
his fame, and hunnye [honey] at his valor, pursuing him in his
enterprise with his best wishes, and as beeing wrapt in contempla-
tion, offers to him in his hart all prosperous performance, as if
the Personater were the man Personated, so bewitching a thing is
lively and well spirited action, that it hath power to new mold the
harts of the spectators and fashion them to the shape of any
noble and notable attempt. What coward to see his contryman
valiant would not bee ashamed of his own cowardise? What English
Prince should hee behold the true portrature of that [f]amous
King *Edward* the third, foraging France, taking so great a King
captive in his owne country, quartering the English Lyons with the
French Flower-delyce, and would not bee suddenly Inflam'd with

so royall a spectacle, being made apt and fit for the like atchieve-
ment. So of *Henry* the fift.[5]

There are two significant lines of emphasis in this little fiction, one
of which has to do with the uses of poetry, and the other with the
uses of history. Taking the history play, first of all, as essentially a
literary artifact, Heywood is most interested in the moral and psychological possibilities of "lively and well-spirited action." The play given
before Hercules must indeed have epitomized those possibilities, for it
was only one "amongst many other active exercises," or athletic games,
performed at the first of the Olympiads; here (if here only) the playwright did not have to worry about the limits imposed on his muse by
the "wooden O." The immediate psychological "impression" of the
action directly produced the desired consequence ("emulation of his
fathers valor") in the "audience," which in turn left its memorial to
posterity in the twelve labors. In setting forth this paradigm of lively
action transmuted into didactic literature, Heywood takes for granted
several commonplaces of Renaissance criticism that would have been
familiar to his Elizabethan readers. With the help of a few phrases from
Sir Philip Sidney's *Apology for Poetry,* the underlying premises might
be briefly summarized as follows. Just as the distinctive value of all poetry
arises from its ability to move the emotions as it instructs the reason,
so the highest form of poetry is the "heroical," which is "not onely a
kinde, but the best and most accomplished kinde of Poetry. For as the
image of each action styrreth and instructeth the mind, so the loftie image
of such Worthies most inflameth the mind with desire to be worthy, and
informes with counsel how to be worthy." [6] The "heroical" has this
enormous potential for moving and instructing the audience because, in
its original form, it is the pure embodiment of physical action rising to
the level of a moral spectacle. In the ideal type of the Herculean hero,
which Eugene Waith has traced through several Renaissance plays,
the "mythic" display of active exploits (the twelve labors) represents the
triumph of physical courage over its baser parts (just as the twelve
labors show Hercules destroying corrupt tyrants, monsters, and bestial
men) and its reconstitution, in Kenneth Clark's fine phrase, as "moral
energy, triumphing through physical means." [7] By extension, this refinement of physical power into "moral energy" offers a paradigm for the

process whereby any "lively and well-spirited action" comes to acquire
a conceptual significance, and so begins to realize its didactic potential.
The moral premise and its didactic corollary are both epitomized in
the rhetorical figure of the "aspiring mind," a common *topos* in expositions of *fortitudo*,[8] which signifies the raising of personal courage above
whatever is merely physical, or "base," and its re-embodiment in what
Heywood calls the "patterne" (Sidney calls it the "loftie image") of
energetic moral purity, which fashions its "impression" in the "noble
thoughts" of the spectator.

Under the guise of extolling the antiquity of the history, then, Heywood actually is setting forth what he conceives to be its highest
possibilities. Its purpose is nothing less than to preserve and transmit
the Herculean "patterne" of heroic virtue by continually re-enacting it
in "lively and well-spirited action" before an audience of worthy aspir-
ants. Hercules himself is aptly presented as the prime "mover," after
his father Jupiter, in this continuing paradigm. As Puttenham notes, he
was a "hero" in the original sense of the word, which refers to those
"great Princes and dominators of the world" who "came to be accompted
gods and halfe gods or goddesses (*Heroes*)." [9] Hence, as the intermediary
between the wholly divine but also "worthy and memorable" acts of
his father Jupiter, and the great warrior-princes of Greece and Rome,
he stood in a unique position to deliver the pure, godlike image of
heroical perfection into the domain of human literature and history
(represented here by Achilles and Alexander). From the moment it enters that domain, moreover, its persistence depends, as Sidney and Heywood would both agree, on the poet's unique ability to recreate "the loftie
image of such Worthies." Within the Elizabethan playhouse, actually
to move a "bold Englishman" to a Herculean pitch of excellence, with
its attendant scorn for all that is base and vile ("murdering *Gerion,*
slaughtring *Diomed,* wounding the *Stimphalides,* killing the Centaurs"),
would, of course, pose a whole series of problems that Heywood does
not pause to consider. Shakespeare takes up the technical difficulties
in the choruses to *Henry V,* and much of this essay will be concerned
with some of the ethical ones. Heywood does make it clear, however,
that just as the playwright's "historical" subject matter lay initially in
the realm of epic, so his primary responsibility, as a poet, was to portray

the hero who could move his audience to admiration and emulation as he fulfilled his personal destiny through physical action. What is rather less apparent from the passage given above, but no less important in the full context of Heywood's discussion, is that the maker of "histories" considered as an historian can operate within the same framework of literary values; only here the emphasis shifts away from the matter of poetic artifice and its affective potentialities, and towards the procedures by which "worthy" examples are selected, arranged, and entered in the registers of fame. The important figures in this case are the "tutor" and, more especially, Aristotle, whose prestige Heywood would clearly like to enlist on behalf of his profession. The kind of historical imagination that these shadowy figures are supposed to possess is, of course, thoroughly grounded in the outlook of classical humanism. Once again, a few key assumptions — commonplaces that Livy, Tacitus, Plutarch, or Erasmus would have unthinkingly endorsed — may be rapidly summarized.[10] History justifies itself as a form of knowledge when it deals with whatever is permanent in the flux of time; or, more narrowly, when it is able to identify the "agents" (that is, the kinds of men) that ordinarily cause historical events to happen. Its epistemological claims depend, therefore, on such a priori definitions of human character as were codified in manuals of rhetoric: "arms and studies," for example, or "magnificence." It becomes, moreover, a form of moral knowledge and an instrument of humanistic education when the historian uses his faculty of "eloquence" to beautify his materials, and so to preserve for posterity the memory of the worthiest examples. Thus, "the best of the Historian is subject to the Poet," to borrow Sidney's phrases once again; for the historian, as he remarks elsewhere in the Apology, "cannot be liberall (without hee will be poeticall) of a perfect patterne." [11] So, in his chapter "Of historicall poesie," Puttenham observes that there

> was nothing committed to historie, but matters of great and ex-
> cellent persons and things that the same by irritation of good
> courages (such as emulation causeth) might worke more effec-
> tually, which occasioned the story writer to chuse an higher stile
> fit for his subject, the Prosaicke in prose, the Poet in meetre.[12]

As he preserves the worthiest examples of individual fortitude from the ruins of time, the humanist historian lays the groundwork for the heroical poet; and as he draws upon his eloquence to elevate and vivify those examples, he may enter into a region where the Aristotelian differentiae between history and poetry begin to disappear altogether. Even at this point, his literary predilections do not necessarily interfere with his obligation to isolate the chronological forms of events. It is precisely in the sequence of heroic "impressions," or images, that Heywood professes to discern the outlines of an inclusive historical process. Alexander's "actions" were so modelled on the "patterne" of Achilles that "it may be imagined had *Achilles* never lived, *Alexander* had never conquered the whole world." Here again, the playwright could continue to celebrate "perfect patterns" of individual greatness without entirely losing sight of a temporal continuum that supersedes and includes them. As Odysseus remarks to Achilles, "emulation hath a thousand sons" (*Troilus and Cressida*, III.iii.156).[13]

This collaboration between literary and historical traditions was, to be sure, of a potentially unstable nature. The poet was always free to elect the more purely fictive structures of tragedy and heroical romance. The historian was always subject to demands for more narrowly specified and systematic explanations of human character than would ordinarily obtain in the heroic age of Hercules and Achilles (he still had to account, in one way or another, for *all* the sons of emulation). Those demands were, moreover, growing more insistent throughout the Renaissance, and eventually they gave rise to the "new science" of history, in which the positivistic and documentary dimension of the historian's imagination was sundered from its traditional literary basis, and vested with the pre-emptive title over the whole enterprise that it still, in the main, enjoys. During the later sixteenth century, however, to invoke a strict polarity between heroical literature and historical "assessment," as I shall be doing throughout this introductory essay, would still have implied a relatively narrow view of what history is. Theorists like Sidney were certainly aware of Aristotle's distinction between the poet's freedom to make his fable and the historian's duty to record the facts. But a conventional reader such as William Webbe was unprepared even to suggest how an historical work of literature might differ from an ordinary one. The "historicall," in his account, simply comprises "the reste of all such matters, which as indifferent between the other two [comedy and tragedy] doo commonly occupy the pennes of Poets." [14]

The "collaboration" thus proved to be a loose and fruitful one, and nowhere more so than in those stage histories that Heywood so vividly recall. One reason why it became so productive, I shall presently be arguing, is that the dramatist responsible for the largest share of those plays, Shakespeare, recognized that wherever the personal destiny of an heroic man might lie, he also could be understood, and desperately needed to be understood, as a more restrictively "historical" phenomenon. The godlike exemplar aspires to surmount all base impediments to his personal honor; but as that aspiration advances into the more recent past it was inevitable that some tension would arise between the hero's will to individual fulfilment through "lively and well-spirited action" and the pieties that underlay conventional Elizabethan beliefs about politics and war. The history play could still contain these opposed attitudes, however, by reformulating the definitions of human worth received from epic and romance, and the whole notion of heroic aspiration, within the framework of a particular historical ethos. That, I believe, is what very often happens in Shakespeare's histories. The athletic and valiant hero continues to exhibit the highest possibilities of individual fortitude; but at the same time he undergoes a more rigorous appraisal than Sidney's "best" historian was equipped to provide. The original exemplar may, like Hotspur, stand exposed as a moral anachronism and a threat to the state; or, again, he may reappear in such guises as the idealized hero-king or the Machiavellian virtuoso. In one form or another, however, he continues to exercise the playwright's imagination throughout the two tetralogies.

If these are large generalizations, they can be illustrated with some precision by turning to the early histories. That is where Shakespeare first encounters the traditional stage image evoked in Heywood's account; and that is where he first refashions it into characters that bear the evaluation of an historical intelligence even as they strive for a unique personal excellence that continues to resist such interpretation. The argument begins, of course, with the assumption that there actually is a tradition of more purely "heroical" histories standing behind *Henry VI,* and it can hardly be understood at all outside its local contexts. At this point, therefore, it will be useful to consider the problem from that vantage point: Is there an important body of heroical drama that precedes, or is roughly contemporaneous with, *Henry VI?* Did Elizabethan playwrights and their audiences recognize it as such? And is it possible to isolate the stages at which it begins to be more rigorously "historical" in its treatment of heroic aspiration?

A Repertory of Heroical-Historical Drama

To proceed from Heywood's account of the history in its imagined antique purity to its first flowering on the popular stage sometime in the 1580's, one has to enter an area of Elizabethan drama where the chronology is most uneven and uncertain, and the entire question of genre confused in the extreme. In particular, it is helpful to bear in mind one factor that frequently complicates the picture. Heroical history — "worthy and memorable" deeds presented through "lively and well-spirited action" — enters the popular repertory not as a fully developed dramatic form, but rather as an interloper within such familiar genres as the moral interlude, *de casibus* tragedy, chivalric romance, and the Senecan revenge play. Even from Heywood's perspective of 1608, "history" is still more a matter of individual scenes than entire plays. Twenty years earlier, when his "hawty and magnanimous attempts" first gained a real foothold on the London stage, they were almost invariably intermixed with a wide range of character roles and plot situations, and it is rather unusual to find heroic drama pure and simple of Heywood's description (Peele's *Edward I* is one example). Nevertheless, the bulk of the plays presently to be surveyed do fulfil his principal criteria, and they testify to the existence of a sizable repertory that might be appropriately described, in a Polonian phrase, as "heroical-historical"; for their putative "Senecan" or "romance" elements usually amount to little more than a respectable façade for what Othello so aptly recalls as "the big wars/That make ambition virtue" (*Othello,* III.iii.355–356). The easiest way to follow the emergence of the genre is to begin, once again, with some critical observations by contemporary playwrights.

Although their commentary is largely unsympathetic, the flurry of pamphlets occasioned by Stephen Gosson's *School of Abuse* (1578) still provides the best account of the popular stage in a period that is otherwise mainly represented by titles of lost plays. In several of these attacks there are references to a kind of drama, evidently rather fashionable and of recent origin (very few titles are given), that is singled out for its treatment of history:

> And if they write of histories that are knowen, as the life of *Pompeie*; the martial affaires of *Caesar,* and other worthies, they give them a newe face, and turne them out like counterfeites to showe themselves on the stage.[15]

> If a true Historie be taken in hand, it is made like our shadows, longest at the rising and falling of the Sunne, shortest of all at hie noone. For the Poets drive it most commonly unto such pointes, as may best show the majestie of their pen, in Tragicall speaches. . .
> So was the history of *Caesar* and *Pompey*, and the Playe of the *Fabii* at the Theater, both amplified there, where the Drummes might walke, or the pen ruffle.[16]

While these remarks indicate that the dramatic format of a "true historie" (as distinguished from a comedy or romance) is still that of a late medieval *de casibus* tragedy like *Cambises* (1571), it is also apparent that the "gothic" insistence on human failure has receded to make way for "monuments . . . and doting things for men of these latter daies." Thus these plays are amplified at just those moments where the dramatist can employ his most moving rhetorical effects ("there, where the Drummes might walke, or the pen ruffle"); for these occasions, as they are embodied in set speeches of panegyric and lament,[17] commemorate the principal moments of the heroic life ("the rising and falling of the Sunne"), and so create the historical monument that will move an audience to emulation (or to "dotage" if you are of Gosson's persuasion).

The difficulty with such offhand references is that there are no plays to accompany them. One has to rely entirely on an analysis of critical terms. Thomas Nashe's comments in *Pierce Penniless* (1592), besides being more informative and sympathetic, are of particular value here because they are illustrated by reference to a play that is quite well known.

Nay, what if I proove Playes to be no extreame; but a rare exercise of vertue? First, for the subject of them (for the most part) is borrowed out of our English Chronicles, wherein our forefathers valiant acts (that have line long buried in rustie brasse and worme-eaten bookes) are revived, and they themselves raised from the Grave of Oblivion, and brought to pleade their aged Honours in open presence: than which, what can be a sharper reproofe to these degenerate effeminate dayes of ours?

How would it have joyed brave *Talbot* (the terror of the French) to thinke that after he had lyne two hundred yeares in his Tombe, hee should triumphe againe on the Stage, and have his bones newe embalmed with the teares of ten thousand spectators at least (at severall times), who, in the Tragedian that represents his person, imagine they behold him fresh bleeding.[18]

If, as seems likely, Nashe refers to the Talbot who bleeds and triumphs in *1 Henry VI,* his remarks offer a useful lesson in the different perspectives of the Shakespeare critic and the literary historian. What appears in one light as the mere apprentice work to a great career may, in another, look like the highest achievement of a flourishing dramatic tradition. Nashe takes it for granted that Shakespeare set out to recast narrative history into heroic drama, and he clearly finds the result to be a brilliant, if quite representative, success. The criteria involved in that judgment are easy enough to isolate. Like Heywood, Nashe views the chronicles as a repository of "our forefathers' valiant acts," which may be "borrowed," or more precisely "revived," to make historical literature. He would agree, moreover, that this display of "aged honours" properly affects the audience as an incentive to heroic action: the mention of "a reproofe . . . to these degenerate, effeminate days of ours" simply puts the idea a little more strongly. It is also suggested that the perfection of physical courage through valiant action has by now come to be regarded as the distinctive theme of such "histories." The scene that attracted Nashe's attention, and, it is implied, the applause of the ten thousand spectators, is the one wherein the "tragedian's" theme of mortality is eclipsed by that counter-drive towards an immortal purity of action that supports the entire enterprise of heroical literature as it has been so far defined. Nashe does not distinguish between the moment of Talbot's "triumphe" and the moment when he is "fresh bleeding" because those two moments coincide exactly in the hero's dying words, which elevate the physical triumph of "moral energy" into a transcendant "pattern" of ceaseless aspiration.

> *Tal.* Where is my other life? Mine own is gone.
> O, where's young Talbot? Where is valiant John?
>
> .   .   .   .   .
>
> Dizzy-ey'd fury and great rage of heart
> Suddenly made him from my side to start
> Into the clustering battle of the French;
> And in that sea of blood my boy did drench
> His over-mounting spirit; and there died
> My Icarus, my blossom, in his pride.
> > *Enter [Soldiers, bearing the body of]* JOHN TALBOT.
> *Serv.* O my dear lord, lo where your son is borne!
> *Tal.* Thou antic Death, which laugh'st us here to scorn,
> Anon, from thy insulting tyranny,
> Coupled in bonds of perpetuity,
> Two Talbots winged through the lither sky,
> In thy despite shall scape mortality.
> > (*1 Henry VI, IV.vii.1–2; 11–22*)[19]

Applying the criteria for heroical drama that such comments evoke to the popular plays that survive from the period that falls between Gosson's comment and Nashe's (1581–1592), one finds that some fourteen of them present the "worthy and memorable acts" of aspirant conquerors in the fashion that Heywood recommends. These represent what was probably the largest distinguishable body of drama on the eve of Shakespeare's career, and they may be listed as follows:[20] both parts of *Tamburlaine the Great* (1587, 1588), *Alphonsus, King of Aragon* (1587), *The Wars of Cyrus* (1588), *The Wounds of Civil War* (1588), *The Battle of Alcazar* (1589), and *1 Selimus* (1592) among the foreign histories; and *The Famous Victories of Henry V* (1586), *1 The Troublesome Reign of King John* (1588), *Edward III* (1590), *Edmond Ironside* (1590), *1 Henry VI* (1590), *Locrine* (1591), *Edward I* (1591), and *The True Tragedy of Richard III* (1591) among the English chronicle plays. For the most part, these are the plays that Ben Jonson recalled as "the *Tamerlanes,* and *Tamer-Chams* of the late Age, which had nothing in them but the *scenicall* strutting, and furious vociferation, to warrant them to the ignorant gapers." [21] The criticism, which reduces the poetics of heroic drama to parody, is a fair one, for that is what the plays themselves virtually do. Although the publication of such materials soon trickles out, the entries in Henslowe's *Diary* (which frequently correspond to Heywood's references in the *Apology for Actors*) suggest that this kind of drama was still a live theatrical vehicle, at least for Edward Alleyn and the Admiral's Men, throughout the 1590's. [22] The plays that have survived are numerous enough to permit a comprehensive transition from the theory of heroical-historical drama to its practice; but they also are sufficiently varied to ensure that very few generalizations will hold for all of them. It will be easiest therefore to begin by using *Tamburlaine* as a rough paradigm for their "heroical" themes, while drawing on *1 Henry VI* for an example of how those materials were in turn provided with "historical" contexts. A more detailed investigation of the entire *corpus* will appear in chapters 3 and 4.

As Heywood's account suggests, the prototype for a drama of sheer heroic achievement, uncomplicated by any overt social and political implications, would be the twelve labors of Hercules, which arise from a god-given impulse to cleanse the kingdoms of this world by overcoming its base and corrupted elements. Professor Waith's chapter on *Tamburlaine* demonstrates in some detail how Marlowe draws on this conception in such a way as to insulate his hero from conventional moral judgments while still allowing for a complicated range of responses to his violent career. [23] If the play's basic rhetorical cliché is the "outdoing *topos*," its indispensable scenic convention is outlandish exaggeration. Both devices operate to place the emphasis on the effort of a heroic nature to go beyond the accepted limitations of human experience while compelling mere humanity to refashion itself in the lofty heroic mold. In a play where the conquest of the Turkish empire is signified by the stage direction *"Bajazeth flies, and he pursues him. The battell short and they enter, Bajazeth is overcome"* (*1 Tamb.* III. iii.211), [24] it is always evident that the playwright and his audience are preoccupied with whatever links may obtain between the certainty of physical triumph and the possibility of moral superiority.

In its purer forms, Marlovian conqueror-drama is always located somewhere very far away — Scythia, Aragon, Morocco, Turkey, or ancient Britain — where the elemental distinction between natural nobility and inherent baseness can still be imagined to apply. The "base" are the corrupt and ineffectual potentates who oppose the hero's will. They are at once too gross to appreciate his lofty attributes, and too deficient in those attributes themselves to deserve the crowns they wear. Bajazeth, whose "smothering host" hinders the spring, shuts out the sun and rain, and blasts the trees (*1 Tamb*. III.i.50–55), epitomizes the abuse of physical power, and so represents the ideal antagonist for a hero who is himself the perfection of natural virtue. Within this context, "nobility" comes to be associated with a set of rhetorical clichés that are endlessly reiterated by Marlowe's imitators. The hero's physical attributes "Like his desire, lift upwards and divine," and they are visually magnificent, as if he were a god of war, or some reincarnate antique hero (*1 Tamb.*, II.i.7–30). The eloquence of his "high astounding terms" (*1 Tamb.*, Prologue l. 5) is literally overwhelming. Most important, his mind is "dauntless," aspiring beyond the spheres, and its measure cannot be reckoned by the kingdoms in which lesser tyrants place their stock; these are mere "sights of power" to grace his triumphs (*1 Tamb.*, V.ii. 411). His *virtù* can only be understood as an irresistible natural force whose "customs are as peremptory/As wrathful planets, death, or destiny" (*1 Tamb.*, V.ii.64–65). Although his valor expresses itself in a mastery of all the known arts of war, its source can be found only in the "incorporeal spirit" that makes the hero "valiant, proud, ambitious" (*2 Tamb.*, IV.ii.39, 41). This "fiery spirit" is finally too pure even to be contained within Tamburlaine's own body; and its eventual release is described in lines that depend on a striking reformulation of a metaphor often used to explain the psychological "impression" of heroical poetry.

> *Tamb.* But, sons, this subject, not of force enough
>   To hold the fiery spirit it contains,
>   Must part, imparting his impressions
>   By equal portions into both your breasts.
>   (*2 Tamb.*, V.iii.168–171)

Here again the heroical playwright seeks nothing less than to elicit the idealized pattern of physical energy, whose transmission can be accomplished only as it becomes, in Cleopatra's phrase, "fire and air" and gives its "other elements" to "baser life" (*Antony and Cleopatra,* V.iv. 292–293).

It is not to be expected that such a bald summary will do justice to Marlowe's play. Nor would a fuller treatment of the themes set forth here exhaust its possibilities for analysis and interpretation. These were, however, the received materials that Marlowe transmitted into the general domain of the Elizabethan history, and it was through these clichés that the playwrights conceived of a popular heroical drama. At what point, then, can one observe that this prototype has received a historical assessment? To take the example that lies ready at hand, how is it that Nashe's "heroical" Talbot also is Shakespeare's "historical" Talbot? Before answering the question, it will be useful to recall, for a moment, a distinction that was touched upon several pages earlier. When a hero's worthy and memorable acts are taken to signify his virtues, or vices, mainly as they reflect on his personal destiny, and are so arranged as to produce a feeling of universal woe, or admiration, a reader is likely to call the result tragedy, or literary epic, and drop the qualifying "historical." Achilles' decision to lead a noble life rather than a long one springs, as do the choices that face Antony and Coriolanus, from a personal dilemma that eludes the ordinary categories of the Renaissance historian just as surely as it eludes those of his modern counterpart. Similarly, Tamburlaine's "worth" is founded on an ideal of physical bravery and moral purity that cannot be securely identified with, or contained within, any public scheme of values. When, however, the emphasis falls — as Renaissance humanists insisted that it should — on heroic virtue in "the Ethicke and politick consideration," [25] the exemplar's attributes may be assessed in relation to the priorities that are taken to regulate the ethos of a particular civilization; and the result, if it is as highly documented as *Henry VI,* can legitimately be described as history. (I take it as axiomatic that one of the ways in which any system of historical knowledge seeks to know the temporal is by specifying the particulars that create a recognizable ethos or "city." The place of such knowledge within a given history naturally may be large or small.) These loose definitions are not, of course, original with me —

they are virtually implicit in Aristotle's differentiae — and I must stress that they are not intended to demarcate a special area occupied by Shakespeare's histories or anyone else's.[26] They are, however, meant to suggest a framework within which the early trilogy can be seen to evolve a certain distance from its heroical-historical antecedents while remaining, in many ways, closely linked to them. While Shakespeare shared with his predecessors an idea of history that is rooted in the lives of great individuals, he diverged from them, or at least from most of them, in the degree to which he modified certain received definitions of personal greatness. More precisely, working within the current Marlovian conventions, he reshaped Marlowe's heroic values to the point where they could be accommodated within a portrayal of fifteenth-century English history on the Elizabethan stage.

Shakespeare's characterization of Talbot will serve to illustrate the point. The lines already quoted in connection with Nashe's remarks present the core of his heroic identity: the drive towards a godlike transcendence over all that is base and vile, the scorn for death that comes from the assurance of fame (suggested in the implied comparison to Icarus and Daedalus), and the final configuration of a noble life in the timeless "pattern" of personal aspiration. These were the qualities that *Tamburlaine* and its progeny had accustomed Nashe and his contemporaries to prize in historical drama. What happens in *1 Henry VI* is that the "valiant acts" which embody them also take on a specific set of ethical and political implications. Talbot's career still epitomizes "moral energy, triumphing through physical means," and he is largely engaged in fighting a "base" Amazonian monster, but the emphasis on physical power and its purification through action has receded before a systematic attempt to specify the nature of the "means" employed. Thus it is only the French who employ such modern implements of war as artillery and fortified siege walls. The English are carefully restricted to the chivalric "sword and lance" (I.i.122), and they are periodically outraged by the refusal of the French to "take up arms like *gentlemen*" (III.ii.70; my italics). (It is Tamburlaine, incidentally, who teaches his sons how to "undermine a town/And make whole cities caper in the air," erect the most advanced fortifications, and deploy artillery to "Murder the foe, and save the walls from breach" [*2 Tamb.*, III.ii.54–92].)[27] This closer assessment of "lively and well-spirited action" supports an overall reformulation of the heroic life, in which Joan la Pucelle serves as a virtual parody of the Marlovian prototype. It is she who receives the lavish set speeches of physical description in this play. The Countess of Auvergne, who expects Talbot to be

> some Hercules,
> A second Hector, for his grim aspect
> And large proportion of his strong-knit limbs
>
> (II.iii.18–20)

discovers instead that "report is fabulous and false" (II.iii.17). He looks like "a weak and writhled shrimp," but he finds "substance, sinews, arms and strength" in the loyal soldiers who perform his commands (II.iii.23, 62). It is Joan whose victories are celebrated by triumphs that evoke far-flung Eastern landscapes (I.vi.17–31); Talbot is created an Earl in a solemn investiture. It is Joan whose eloquence makes the Dauphin say "Thou hast astonish'd me with thy high terms" (I.ii.93); Talbot's oratory is always chastened by solemn public ceremonies. Most important, where the shepherd's daughter establishes her "natural" nobility of spirit by "single combat" (with a sexual pun) and vague assurances that she is "assign'd" to "be the English scourge" (I.ii.95, 129), Talbot finds the source of his valor in his family "name" and the ancient Order of the Garter. Thus *I Henry VI* is the first heroical-history in which "baseness" generally refers to a character's family origins and social status, even as it continues to connote a style of behavior that is cowardly and ignoble. When Joan is finally burned at the stake, she claims to be pregnant, but the English will "have no bastards live" (V.iv.70). When death comes to Talbot, it is superseded by the "triumph" of "Two Talbots," father and son. And here again, the contrast makes for an implicit judgment on Marlowe's low-born "lord," who kills his eldest son and whose only patrimony for the others is the "incorporeal spirit" that makes him "valiant proud and ambitious" (2 *Tamb.*, IV.ii.39–41).

What is interesting about such reformulations is not that they are negative, but that they are historical. They depend on the specification of an environment in which a mythic figure like Tamburlaine can no longer exist: the hero now defines himself through various limited forms of the noble life. Thus Talbot is at once the last of the great medieval *chevaliers* and a faithful mirror of the Elizabethan aristocracy as it liked to imagine itself in an age that has been aptly described as the Indian Summer of English chivalry.[28] Still disdainful of protective siege walls, horrified by the use of artillery, he epitomizes the feudal *noblesse d'épée,* envisioning every battle as a *beau geste* and a chance to fulfil a vow made on behalf of his fallen peers and his personal honor. Set in contrast to the base pretenders, upstart courtiers, and "tainted" gentry that have infiltrated the French and English courts, his very style of making war serves as a metaphor for an aristocratic mode of life that was finally vanishing while *Henry VI* was being produced. Thus, much of the real poignance that invests his final "triumph" arises from its historical context: henceforth this kind of nobility will be available as an ideal pattern, but never as an attainable reality. It has been isolated in its unique historical form.

The notion of a drama at once "heroical" and "historical," as it has been outlined in these introductory pages, will lead to some new ways of reading the early histories, and some new perspectives on two of the later ones. It has been generally agreed, among such authorities on the subject as E. M. W. Tillyard, Lily B. Campbell, Irving Ribner, and M. M. Reese, that Shakespeare began, like the great professional historians of the Renaissance, with an elaborate theory of history based on the "life of the state," and proceeded forthwith to elicit the plays from the chronicles, while borrowing, from time to time, a few "admired inventions" from the popular playwrights. The processes of development envisioned here are quite different. Shakespeare began, I take it, with the idea of history that was common to most Elizabethan dramatists. It is an idea that had originated in an effort to understand and commemorate the lives of great individuals, and it had shared, ever since antiquity, many of the procedures and preoccupations of heroical literature. The common ground between these two traditions generally lay, as I shall show in the following chapter, in the rhetorical topics and styles used to define and express the attributes of eminent men. Definitions of individual worth based on "deeds" and "parentage," for example, were presented in grammar-school manuals of rhetoric as instruments to be used in the analysis and imitation of set passages from classical history *and* literature; and they were unaccompanied by differentiae between literary and historical personages. Hence it should always be kept in mind that the generation of both "heroical" and "historical" images of human character could proceed from a single act of imagination and could be accommodated within a single literary work. As in Heywood's account, the body of concepts used to determine the "worth" of the semi-mythical Hercules would apply to the historical Alexander as well; and the rhetorical commonplaces that were taken to formulate a Herculean hero might be so reformulated as to define a fifteenth-century English aristocrat, or even an upstart French shepherdess. The differences are mainly matters of emphasis. Sidney's heroical poet locates the *topoi* of courage and magnificence in a milieu where they can be presented as ideal forms of the individual existence. The humanist historian, operating in the intellectual environment of the later sixteenth century, uses them to elicit particular social phenomena from localized stretches of time. As the historical imagination gains precedence, of course, it is to be expected that different kinds of *exempla* will result, and new *topoi* will be introduced. Thus, in the case just examined, the choice of historical materials taken from the English chronicles results in a conception of heroic fortitude that strictly limits the range of exemplary deeds, and a general definition of individual worth that leans heavily on parentage and ancestry, as well as on individual fortitude.

While this way of looking at the problem rules out any hard and fast distinctions, it does provide a scale on which *The Wounds of Civil War,* for example, can be seen as more restrictively "historical" than *Tamburlaine,* while *1 Henry VI* obviously goes further in that direction than either of them. When the principle is applied to all of the plays listed above, moreover, it becomes clear that not only Shakespeare, but a number of other playwrights as well, turned to more closely specified historical environments, and particularly to the English chronicles, in the aftermath of *Tamburlaine.* The rise of the history in its earliest Shakespearian form was, in other words, part of a common effort to understand a familar type of character — the warrior-prince — through contexts that evoked the ethos of a particular civilization.

If one is to deal with the effort in its totality, as these introductory pages venture to do, it finally becomes necessary to inquire into some of the ulterior pressures that set it under way. For there were, as one would expect, a number of voices demanding that the "aspiring mind" be answerable to the official ideology of the Tudor state. It was of course inevitable that any attempt to develop historical contexts for heroic drama would have to draw upon the ethical and political conventions that regulated the life of sixteenth-century England. The whole notion of historical knowledge presupposes that one comes to understand the past by reconstructing it in whatever terms are afforded by the present. It is plain enough that the portrayal of Talbot, for example, depends on an ideal of aristocratic conduct that is indigenous to sixteenth-century England. But it is also not unusual for the ethical preoccupations of any age (and particularly one where the press and pulpit were answerable to the crown) to give rise to an interpretation of history so prescriptive and dogmatic that it is liable to impinge upon but not, one trusts, utterly control the ordinary historical consciousness. It was this "official" view, which has been so well reconstructed by Professors Tillyard and Ribner, that the Tudor ideologues and the Puritan preachers were seeking to superimpose on the fabric of historical literature.[29] The intrinsic merits of that view are not in question here. The problem rather springs from the fact that the Tudor apologists were arguing for a vision of history in which the heroic life, as that concept has so far been defined, would cease to have any real value at all; and the possibility thus arises that the popular history would eventually become unable to support its own leading character.

Tudor Ideology and the Popular History

As anyone who has read the homily *Against Disobedience and Wilful Rebellion* (1571)[30] will know, the hierarchical view of society espoused by the Tudor monarchy was not hospitable to the idea of an aspiring mind that remained innocent of its most solemn ordinances; and it had no place at all for the heroic individual who took his worthy and memorable acts as constituting a legitimate claim to status and power. The playwrights whose commentary I have been using were certainly aware of this problem. Heywood remarks, a little evasively, that the "true use" of histories is "to teach the subjects obedience to their king, to shew the people the untimely ends of such as have moved tumults, commotions and insurrections, to present them with the flourishing estate of such as live in obedience, exhorting them to allegiance, dehorting them from all trayterous and fellonious stratagems." [31] Immediately after his comments on *I Henry VI,* Nashe adds that histories show "the ill successe of treason, the fall of hastie climbers, the wretched end of usurpers, the miserie of civill dissention, and how just God is evermore in punishing of murther." [32] Since neither apologist indicates how it is that histories achieve these pious ends in practice (Nashe has just been defending them against those who fail to respect "what hopes of eternitie are to be proposed to adventrous mindes, to encourage them forward"), it is tempting to dismiss such assurances about their political orthodoxy as being at best irrelevant to the main point. As a rule, certainly, histories did not try to make usurpation, treason, and civil disorder appear as real possibilities within Elizabethan political life. There are very few plays, before Shakespeare's, in which "trayterous and fellonious stratagems" are employed against a divinely appointed sovereign. The subject was too sensitive to be treated in the popular heroic style.

While Heywood and Nashe were doubtless aware of this discrepancy between the homilist's sense of "history," which was wholly preoccupied with the life of the state, and their own, which still was only partially so, they could nevertheless have shown that the gap was not always so great as it might at first appear. As a social ideologue, the homilist was concerned to uphold the sanctity of two ethical postulates: the need to maintain hereditary titles and (what frequently amounted to the same thing) the need to uphold *de jure* sovereignty. If the degree to which these notions impinge on the representation of heroic character can be taken as a rough index to a dramatist's political sensitivity, it will be possible to check very rapidly how far Heywood's and Nashe's claims are borne out by the actual texts that survive. At the lower end of the scale, there are *Tamburlaine* and *I Selimus,* both of which must stand (if they are read in these terms) as violent refutations of everything the homilist held dear. By equipping its romance hero with a nominal title to the first kingdom he conquers, Greene's *Alphonsus, King of Aragon* does make a slight concession to the idea of hereditary rule, and so falls slightly above those two plays. *Locrine* and *Edward I* preserve this distinction between the "legitimate" conqueror and the defeated "usurper," but there is still virtually no attempt to enforce it. *The Wounds of Civil War* and *I The Troublesome Reign of King John* have considerably more to say about the problems of *de jure* sovereignty (in the former play, as it pertains to the elected ruler in Republican Rome) and hereditary right, although these themes are still obscured by a great deal of *"scenicall* strutting and furious vociferation." *Edward III* and *The True Tragedy of Richard III,* on the other hand, attempt full-scale portraits of the legitimate king claiming his natural birthright and the murderous usurper who destroys his own nephews. Finally, one arrives at *Henry VI,* a three-part history in which the legal claim of sovereignty quickly becomes an overriding concern, while any number of pedigrees are investigated in fine detail.

What should be evident from this hasty survey is that the tendency of the popular heroical drama to become more rigorously "historical" in its outlook can easily be viewed as a response to pressures that emanated from the Tudor ideology. The use of rhetorical *differentiae* based on birth and title, for example, doubtless began as a rather casual attempt to legitimize the conqueror-hero, as in the case of Greene's *Alphonsus.* Once they were introduced, however, they could become meaningful only through the discovery of contexts in which they actually counted for something. Hence, even allowing for the uncertain chronology of the plays listed on page 17, the whole repertory shows a noticeable drift towards the historical ambience of fifteenth-century England; for within that environment, all those attributes that the rhetoricians arranged under *genus* — native country, race, ancestors, and parentage — began to assume the status of ethical norms, which is precisely what they were in the Elizabethan polity. By the same token, it then became possible to duplicate such representative sixteenth-century figures as the chivalric aristocrat and the courtly machiavel with some degree of exactitude. Thus, it is in *Edward III* and *The True Tragedy of Richard III* that one finds the first sustained attempts to accommodate the heroic drive to excel within ethical stereotypes that embodied the official Tudor view of politics and war.

The likelihood that the rise of historical assessment in these plays was at least in part impelled by Tudor politics is, once again, hardly surprising in itself; the categories that any age employs as a way of knowing the past necessarily arise out of its own values and preoccupations. Nor is it unusual, really, for historians to use a particular segment of the past to obtain an ethical perspective on the historical myths and literary ideals of their own age. (The efforts of eighteenth-century historians and playwrights to domesticate the history of Augustan Rome would be a case in point.) What may seem rather disturbing in this instance is that the official historiography, with its gallery of miserable rebels and wretched usurpers, should have been ostensibly so ill-equipped to deal with the phenomenon that came its way. Thus the "playwright-historian" with whom we began may now appear in rather a different light. What has thus far been described as a collaboration between heroical poetics and historical assessment can also be viewed as an antagonism between these two habits of mind, one in which the historian, as he relentlessly delimits the acceptable range of individual aspiration until finally it atrophies to nothing, is utterly dedicated to the current political orthodoxy. To a degree this judgment is inescapable. Certainly it is impossible to follow the changing perspectives on heroic ambition between *Tamburlaine* and *Richard III* without taking it into account. The last act of the latter play could hardly be more explicit in its rejection of a discredited theatrical image for "God's Captain," the Earl of Richmond. It was at this point that Shakespeare's sense of history finally did become almost indistinguishable from that of the preface to Hall's *Union of the Two Noble and Illustre Families of Lancaster and York,* or *A Mirror for Magistrates.* His choice of the one epoch that could be fully known by the Elizabethan historian finally limited him to a single way of knowing it.

Political awareness usually is not the same thing as unqualified political orthodoxy, however, and there is no reason to suppose that it necessarily becomes so when it finds expression in historical literature. What is most remarkable about the line of development that leads from *Tamburlaine* to *Richard III* is how rarely the exercise of historical judgment hardens into an uncompromising party line. In general the stage history found its didactic function in mediating between the homilist and the popular hero, rather than in castigating the latter on behalf of the former. Even Talbot, the most conservative of Shakespeare's aristocrats, is "*Created* for his rare success in arms/Great Earl of Washford, Waterford, and Valence" (IV.vii.62–63; my italics). If it is argued that the personal appeal of characters like Suffolk, York, and Richard III is a matter of theatrical convention that does not impinge upon Shakespeare's unwavering commitment to hierarchical social arrangements, one can only reply that a similar ambivalence is frequently apparent in those characters who speak on behalf of the established order. Each of the great spokesmen for the principles of hereditary succession and *de jure* sovereignty, the Archbishop of Canterbury in *Henry V*, Ulysses in *Troilus and Cressida*, and Menenius in *Coriolanus*, is, after all, virtually a professional ideologue, speaking for the view of politics that best secures his own privileged station.

What finally distinguishes the early histories from their antecedents is the fact that only Shakespeare manages to accept the contradictions between individual aspiration and ethical convention in a spirit of conscious irony, rather than wholesale confusion and evasive moralizing. When York determines, in the fifth act of *2 Henry VI*, to claim his right to the throne, he soliloquizes in the accents of Tamburlaine:

> Ah! sancta majestas, who'd not buy thee dear?
> Let them obey that knows not how to rule;
> This hand was made to handle nought but gold:
> I cannot give due action to my words,
> Except a sword or sceptre balance it.
>
> (*2 Henry VI*, V.i.5–9)[33]

As he steps forward, however, he is not in "the stately tent of war" but within an English court, and Clifford's uncomprehending reaction — "To bedlam with him! Is the man grown mad!" (131) — succinctly registers the dramatist's awareness that two honorable but fundamentally incompatible attitudes to sovereignty and war have come into conflict. The heroical and the historical are still in a productive collaboration here; only by this time it has already become clear that their continued association will require a considerable degree of mutual tolerance.

Was There a "Moral History"?

Since all roads lead to Shakespeare, it is not surprising that *Henry VI* has already been furnished with a number of genealogies besides the one that has just been set forth. The most imposing of these is still Tillyard's, which leads through the providentialism of Hall and the Homilies, and the didactic allegory of the Tudor interludes, to the prophetic speeches and teleogical designs that link together the entire tetralogy. One can hardly deny that there are connections between the view of fifteenth-century history cultivated by the professional chroniclers and the total structure of *Henry VI*. It is beyond doubt that Shakespeare was acquainted with the "Tudor myth" whereby the Wars of the Roses were taken to signify a divine judgment upon England in retribution for the deposition and murder of Richard II; and (although that act is mentioned only once in the Yorkist tetralogy) analysis does reveal that a pattern of retributive justice, showing, to borrow Nashe's words again, "the ill successe of treason, the fall of hastie climbers, the wretched end of usurpers, the miserie of civill dissention, and how just God is evermore in punishing of murther" is operative throughout the cycle. What seems to me rather less assured is the degree of success with which the pattern is established, and its status within the plays themselves. For when one looks for the imaginative expression of the Tudor myth there is only a scattered assortment of dreams, prophecies, curses, omens, astrological visitations, and ironic coincidences which, taken together, are sufficiently unrelated to leave some doubt as to how fully the playwright's literary capabilities were engaged in the enterprise. Since the purpose of this study is to introduce new readings, not to question old ones, the point about *Henry VI* is better left to the reader's own judgment. To a considerable extent, however, Tillyard's argument falls back on the notion that there actually was a traditional dramatic form, which may be represented by Bale's *King Johan, Gorboduc,* and *Woodstock,* that was expressly designed to translate Tudor doctrine into homiletic drama, and which found its full flowering in the providential themes of *Henry VI*. As this hypothesis impinges rather severely on the line of development being followed here, it will be useful to look now at some of its ramifications.

It is perfectly clear that there are several interludes, widely separated in date of composition and auspices of production, that combine historical personages and moral stereotypes to produce what is, in effect, a stage homily. A. P. Rossiter has linked these plays together under the designation "moral history" and argued with considerable force that they represent the mainstream of historical drama in Elizabethan literature.[34] His thesis, as it is presented in his introduction to *Woodstock,* demonstrates that there certainly were occasions when dramatists appropriated wholesale the Tudor view of history, and it illuminates several dark corners in the earlier Elizabethan drama; but he does not show conclusively that there was anything like a continuous, traditional dramatic form that effectively erased the gap between Tudor polemic and the conventions of the popular stage. Besides *King Johan* (1538), *Gorboduc* (1562), and *Woodstock* (1592), Rossiter isolates the anonymous *Respublica* (1553) and *2 Henry VI* (1591) as prototypes of the moral history. It will be clear to anyone who has bothered to read them that these plays do not draw upon a common tradition of rhetorical and theatrical practices. On the other hand, it is true that all of them deal explicitly with the moral arguments for political order within the state — as the tradition stemming from *Tamburlaine* usually does not — by organizing characters who stand for fixed moral values into a unified homiletic fable. The problem of whether they represent an assortment of occasional political pieces or a continuous tradition of political and historical drama is not easily resolved. Rossiter, and others who draw the latter inference, would argue that the moral values and the artistic strategies shared by these plays are best explained by a "Law of Primitive Survivals";[35] that is, they are "survivals" from an extensive body of morality drama that recast its old moral abstractions into a *psychomachia* of political vices and virtues. As Rossiter explains, "it was logical for a play type [the morality] dealing with the conflict of externalized qualities to be turned from the services of an established didacticism to the purposes of propaganda." [36] The conclusions that emerge from this reasoning are well summarized by Irving Ribner: "The history play in its highest form emerged from the morality, as we shall see from our study of *Kynge Johan* and *Gorboduc*. The morality play structure was the perfect vehicle for executing the true historical function, for the morality was didactic and symbolic, designed to communicate idea rather than fact, built upon a plot formula in which every event was related to the others so as to create a meaningful whole." [37] Since there are so few "survivals" the argument necessarily hinges on one's assumptions about the nature of the morality play as it evolved throughout the sixteenth century: do the known facts about it encourage the inference that there was at any point a substantial dramatic canon of moral and political allegory?

In general, the available evidence suggests that there was not. First of all, in so far as one can judge from extant texts and titles, the morality tradition never became deeply involved with those polemical questions about the hereditary basis of authority and the nature of rebellion that do emerge in the mature history play. In general, as long as the moral interlude adheres to the allegorical format of the *psychomachia* — from, say, *Mankind* (1475) or *Hick Scorner* (1513) to *New Custom* (1571) — the mankind figure is assailed by a comic medley of virtuous and vicious social types (Tom Tosspot, Nichol Newfangle, Pierce Pickpurse, and so on), and the emphasis falls, for the most part, upon the comic strategies that the vices employ to inveigle the hero into corruption. As the old moral allegory recedes before a secular drama based on narrative materials, these "social" vice-figures do persist, but in a sub-genre of freely satirical morality drama and city comedy.[38] Thus, taking all the extant plays and fragments into account, a detailed genealogy of Rossiter's "morality of state" might run as follows: Bale's *King Johan* (1538), David Lyndsay's *Satire of the Three Estates* (1540), *Impatient Poverty* (1547), *Somebody, Avarice, and Minister* (1550), *Respublica* (1553), *Wealth and Health* (1554), William Wager's *Enough is as Good as a Feast* (1560), *The Pedlar's Prophecy* (1561), Wager's *The Cruel Debtor* (1565), *The Trial of Treasure* (1567), Ulpian Fulwell's *Like Will to Like* (1568), *New Custom* (1571), Thomas Lupton's *All for Money* (1577), Robert Wilson's *The Three Ladies of London* (1581), *The Three Lords and Three Ladies of London* (1588), and *The Cobbler's Prophecy* (1590). These plays represent a continuous tradition of social satire, drawing upon a common pool of character types taken from contemporary English life (rich landlords, religious charlatans, riotous youths, and greedy foreigners), and concerning themselves, to a great extent, with the use and distribution of money in the commonwealth. This tradition has been largely ignored by students of the later Elizabethan drama, perhaps because it does not appear to lead directly towards any of its principal genres. The problem of literary history involved here goes well beyond the scope of this essay, but one tentative conclusion seems in order: although it clearly contributed something to the chronicle history, most notably an emphasis on the *respublica* as a compact social entity, the "morality of state" was not a generic form of historical drama, nor did it offer the playwright anything like a uniform set of strategies for recasting his chronicle sources into drama.

In Bale's *King Johan* and the anonymous *Respublica* this tradition is, to be sure, given a topical variation: the secular magistrate must choose between Catholics and Reformers, who embody the vicious and virtuous social attributes. But the crucial question of authority and "usurpation" arises only in Bale's play, and there only with regard to the specific problem of religious authority. *Respublica* is essentially a comedy of deception cast as moral allegory, and it consists almost exclusively of ecclesiastical satire. Even granting that *Woodstock* and *2 Henry VI,* with their heavy freight of social comment, owe much to this tradition, the place of a topical and satirical allegory of social abuses is surely a subordinate one in the body of Elizabethan history plays. Finally, even if one construes the "law of dramatic survivals" in very broad terms, and simply superimposes the allegory of Bale's *King Johan* upon later chronicle histories, it does not correspond to what is there, except in situations where an evil counsellor misleads a virtuous king. Hence, even though there clearly are cases where it applies, the hypothesis that the old *psychomachia* provided a controlling framework of political allegory for the Elizabethan history finally raises more difficulties than it resolves.

The chapters that follow, then, proceed on the assumption that a humanistic approach to history came intuitively to the Elizabethan dramatists, while the providentialism of the chroniclers, with its tendency to minimize the possibility of individual achievement, was more the exception than the rule. The significant developments in the early histories have instead to do with the gradual qualification and transformation of received humanistic ideals — and especially the ideal of the hero-king — under the auspices of Tudor pieties until, by the end of *Richard III,* the old framework has itself begun to fulfil the didactic tasks of providential history. The chapter that follows will explore the conceptual basis of these developments by isolating, where possible, the rhetorical forms of humanist historiography as they were transmitted from antiquity to the Tudor grammar school, and from thence to the early Elizabethan stage.

2   The Rhetorical Basis

of the Popular History

The pursuit of historical knowledge through literary procedures has fallen into disrepute. If the idea is hardly comprehensible now, it was already beginning to be suspect at the time of Shakespeare's histories. In the "Epistle Dedicatory" to his *Civil Wars* (1595), Samuel Daniel is at some pains to assure his readers that

> I have onely used that poeticall licence, of framing speaches to the persons of men according to their occasions; as *C. Salustius,* and *T. Livius* (though Writers in Prose, yet in that kinde Poets) have, with divers other antient and modern Writers, done before me. Wherein, though they have incroched upon others rights, and usurpt a part that was not properly theirs: yet, seeing they hold so just a proportion, with the nature of men, and the course of affayres; they passe as the partes of the Actor (not the Writer) and are reciv'd with great approbation.[1]

Daniel's distinction between poetical and historical ways of looking at the past reflects, in a general way, the polarity that occupied much of the previous chapter. The interesting thing about his comment is that the old variable scale by which, say, Livy's *Ab urbe condita* would be more "historical" than Tacitus' *Germania,* while Xenophon's *Cyropaedia* would be far more "poetical" than either, has begun to rigidify. While making his apologies as best he can, Daniel feels compelled to acknowledge that some of his readers may wish to observe an inviolable distinction between the license granted to "Poets" and the accuracy expected of "Writers in Prose." He was obliged to put the matter on so strict a basis because he was living in the midst of a revolution in historical thinking, one which has had a profound effect on the way most people think about history today. It is during the later sixteenth century that English historical writing first begins to display the distinctive features of a modern historiography: the formulation of scientific criteria for validating historical evidence; the cultivation of legal and constitutional, and of territorial and local, history; the periodization of ordinary historical chronology; the systematic analysis of political authority and its sources; and the attempt to discover a practical, as opposed to a moral, utility for historical inquiry.[2] As has frequently been observed, the establishment of these premises spelled the dissolution of the traditional humanist synthesis of history and literature.[3] In Sidney's *Apology for Poetry,* as in Aristotle's *Poetics,* the difference between the two forms of discourse is still largely a matter of degree: poetry is *more* concerned with the universal, history *more* concerned with the particular. Daniel, however, has begun to feel uneasy about some of the very rhetorical equipment that had secured the common ground between them. By 1657 Milton could remark that "The offices of a rhetorician and an historian are as different as the arts which they profess." [4]

The contemporary reader, who stands several hundred years on the other side of this remarkable transformation in historical thinking, will have no difficulty grasping Milton's point. What he needs to be reminded of is that Shakespeare and most of his audience would have taken the distinction very loosely, if indeed they gave it any thought at all; for their own education in history, as it was implemented in the Tudor grammar school, still looked to the broad and flexible approach of classical humanism for its purposes and procedures. The point needs emphasizing. If it is not borne in mind that Shakespeare continued to regard "poeticall licence" as the best means of accomplishing what are now taken to be the aims of "Writers in Prose," it becomes all too easy to reduce his histories to mere paraphrases of political concepts. His earlier trilogy is poised at a midpoint in the evolution of Renaissance historiography: the plays everywhere reflect the pressures that were giving rise to a more localized and — politically speaking — systematic approach to the past; but they reflect them in poetical ways, reshaping traditional literary ideals to produce new assessments of human behavior in politics and war.

If the reader is troubled at this point it may be because I have arrived at this appraisal by way of a considerable short-cut. It can hardly be supposed that Shakespeare assimilated the habit of thinking about history in literary terms from Sidney and Puttenham, or from Marlowe, Heywood, and Nashe, however representative those figures may be. The whole enterprise of treating history as a literary form, unfamiliar as it is today, presupposes a thorough grounding in the regular disciplines of classical rhetoric, and an exposure to popular forms of humanist history, that has so far been taken for granted. The present chapter seeks to make amends by exploring in some detail the rhetorical basis of the early popular histories and their common patterns of heroical character. While I hope that this survey will lead to a more comprehensive view of the earlier Elizabethan drama and Shakespeare's place in it, the reader should be forewarned that the discussion will stray far afield from the plays themselves. I have tried to ensure at least a minimal degree of continuity by keeping the center of gravity in the Elizabethan grammar school where Shakespeare received his own instruction in rhetoric, and by concluding with some account of how the transition from rhetorical exercises to historical drama actually came about. If the peculiar conception of heroic character that arises in Marlowe's *Tamburlaine* is now seen to occupy rather a smaller place in the genesis of the early histories, that is at once appropriate and inevitable; for Marlowe's play is only a single manifestation of the larger tradition that includes both it and the plays that come in its wake. *Tamburlaine* remains the efficient cause of the early histories; yet one must look to the manuals of rhetoric for a fuller account of their formal cause.

Rhetorical Figures and Classical Historiography

The great historians of Greece and Rome, as R. G. Collingwood explains, began with a philosophical commitment to the final reality of metaphysical categories. Consequently, as they organized the rough data of the past into written history, they sought to isolate the operation of those unchanging entities that must lie behind the mere surface of events.[5] They were writing, in Thucydides' words, for "whoever shall wish to have a clear view both of the events which have happened and of those which will some day, in all human probability, happen again in the same or a similar way." [6] The consequences of this doctrine are best illustrated in Tacitus and the later Roman historians, where the preoccupation with the "real" categories of philosophy has the effect of reducing the received facts of history to the status of illustrative footnotes in what is essentially a literary exercise.[7] Collingwood, using the language of a professional philosopher, succinctly describes the kind of "history" written under these auspices: "A 'character' is an agent, not an action; actions come and go but the 'characters' (as we call them), the agents from whom they proceed, are substances, and therefore eternal and unchanging." [8] Thus history finds its surest field of inquiry in the lives of individuals, or of national types; and those lives are meaningful only when they can be transposed into the received abstractions that delimit the areas of philosophical truth and humanistic value. So Tacitus' "professed purpose in writing," as his editor Furneaux explains, "is to hold up signal examples of political vice and virtue for posterity to execrate and admire." [9] Furthermore, since historical figures are of interest primarily in so far as they are concrete instances of permanent categories, it follows that their essential nature never changes: "When Tacitus describes the way in which the character of a man like Tiberius broke down beneath the strain of empire, he represents the process not as a change in the structure or conformation of a personality but as the revelation of features in it which had hitherto been hypocritically concealed. . . . A good man cannot become bad. . . . Power does not alter a man's character; it only shows what kind of man he already was." [10]

Working on these premises, the historian naturally relies on the set procedures of the rhetorician, which are in turn derived from the categories of formal philosophy. (Aristotle's *Rhetoric* takes its categories from his logic and adapts them to the purposes of discursive writing.)[11] Not only do these specify precisely what attributes of character are of permanent interest (notably in the "topics" of demonstrative oratory), but they also explain what devices of style are most effective in bringing those attributes before a reader's attention. The most conspicuous form of rhetorical embellishment, for example, is the interpolated speech, a device which presupposes a preference for the "perfect patterns" of formal rhetoric and a considerable disregard for the evidentiary criteria that are vital to any scientific historiography. Erich Auerbach, in his discussion of Tacitus, describes the function of such speeches as "graphic dramatization (*illustratio*) of a given occurrence, or at times the presentation of great political or moral ideas," adding that they are "products of a specific stylistic tradition cultivated in the schools for rhetors." [12] In general, to quote Auerbach again, this "combination of ethical and rhetorical preoccupations" is what gives antique historiography its "high degree of order, clarity, and dramatic impact." [13] At the same time, it is what gives antique historiography certain limitations: the historian can explain why certain men are makers of history; and he can use his rhetorical categories to produce ethical judgments on such men; but he cannot conceive of history as a process, extending through time, that develops according to its own knowable laws.[14] Mere events, as they "happen" to succeed one another, are unreliable data. They are useful in that they can be manipulated to express permanent truths about the kinds of men who generate them; but they will not display any meaningful pattern in themselves.

History written on this basis is always in danger of permitting its "ethical and rhetorical preoccupations" to pre-empt even the most minimal concern with the local characteristics of a particular chronological era. And whenever this occurs, antique historiography will naturally tend towards purely rhetorical structures. Xenophon's *Cyropaedia,* despite its loosely chronological format, is entirely dependent on the "topics" of the rhetor. As O. B. Hardison's analysis of that influential fourth-century panegyric biography shows, "the techniques by which he sketched out the education of his ideal leader are those of the epideictic orator, tailored to the requirements of a long work intended for reading rather than public delivery." [15] In effect the author has abandoned any pretence of writing "history" as such. Hence Sidney describes the work as "an absolute heroicall poem":[16] "absolute" because the mere facts of Cyrus' life have been completely subsumed under the set topics of the rhetorician and thus transformed into that "loftie image" which Sidney regards as the common denominator of all heroical poetry.

While the notion of writing straightforward narrative history had been questioned at least since the time of Isocrates, it is around the second century AD that the rhetorical instruments for composing pseudo-history such as the *Cyropaedia* begin to acquire something like a monopoly in the classical schools. In the *Lives of the Twelve Caesars* Suetonius deliberately presents his materials, as he explains, by categorical topics rather than in chronological order (*neque per tempora, sed per species*).[17] During this period both poetry and history are reappraised on the basis of their fidelity to prescribe rhetorical categories, and, as a result, the Aristotelian distinction between the poet's freedom to improve upon nature and the historian's bondage to literal fact becomes virtually unenforceable. In an important chapter of *European Literature and the Latin Middle Ages,* Ernst Robert Curtius has succinctly described the extraordinary transformations that were set under way when antique rhetorical theory undertook to classify all the materials of humane discourse within a comprehensive system of topics: "Rhetoric lost its original meaning and purpose. Hence it penetrated into all literary genres. Its elaborately developed system became the common denominator of literature in general. This is the most influential development in the history of antique rhetoric. By it the *topoi* too acquire a new function. They become clichés, which can be used in any form of literature, they spread to all spheres of life with which literature deals and to which it gives form." [18]

If these remarks seem to open up an impossibly large expanse of post-classical literary theory and practice, I must stress that our interest is limited to certain practical consequences of the developments that Curtius describes. The point in question can be summarized quite briefly: the extensive training in rhetoric included in the Elizabethan grammar school curriculum presented history in much the same light as do the late classical rhetoricians; that is, the student was taught to analyze the materials of history (as well as those of narrative poetry) in terms of set topics and styles. There is, to be sure, considerable evidence that the same claim could be made for the ordinary student in the Middle Ages as well. I am not concerned with a "rediscovery" of classical historiography, but rather with one small corner of an unbroken tradition of humanistic learning.[19]

The implications of this carryover for the Elizabethan history play are vast, but difficult to specify, because they have as much to do with the structure of the plays as with their themes. Through the subterranean channels of his grammar-school education in rhetoric, every Elizabethan playwright, and much — perhaps most — of his audience, was systematically trained in the outlook and procedures of humanist historiography. "History," as it was filtered through the pedagogical disciplines of the grammar school, was untouched alike by the medieval effort to construct a theodicy and the Italian school of political analysis. It was still primarily a matter of discovering an "exact knowledge of the past" by adjusting bare facts to a set of predetermined rhetorical patterns. As he read a narrative account, the student was taught how to isolate its "agents"; reconstructing it in his commonplace book, he learned how to fashion the exemplary acts of those agents into brief lives, each organized around its apposite "topic." In the case of the playwright, the exemplary biography becomes a "history": a loose, episodic structure, organized around set oratorical themes, which aims to produce an "eloquent" or "moving" rendition of its central character in action. It follows that such structures will ordinarily share the peculiar features of all humanist history: a high degree of "clarity, order, and impact" in the delineation of the hero, and an indifference to the temporal shape of events, which is represented only through omens, prophecies, ironic coincidences, and the erratic movements of fortune. Stylistically, such "histories" can be expected to lean heavily on the set speeches and rhetorical commonplaces that were used to celebrate the worthies of antiquity. Further, the "action" will ordinarily depict a central character in the process of realizing his own identity through a series of exemplary deeds. The characters themselves do not change, however; rather the audience's sense of who they are moves toward that lofty, "categorical" moment in which "Antony is himself" once and for all.

School Exercises in Rhetoric and History

The most convenient starting point for a brief account of these developments is provided by Aphthonius' *Progymnasmata,* which was written in the fifth century AD and survived to become the most popular manual of rhetoric in Renaissance grammar schools.[20] The *Progymnasmata* consists of sample exercises in fourteen elementary rhetorical strategies. In the standard sixteenth-century editions, each exercise is supplemented with extensive *scholia* by Rheinhardus Lorich, a fifteenth-century grammarian. Five of these exercises (all of which are classified under the *genus demonstrativum*) set forth the basic rhetorical equipment used in writing humanist history: *laus, vituperatio, comparatio, ethopoeia* ("impersonation"), and *ecphrasis* ("close description").

Laus is a brief exercise in panegyric designed to introduce a student to the topics of demonstrative oratory. These "topics" are simply the received categories of "what to say" about a noteworthy individual; they are the "places" (Cicero's *sedes argumentorum*) from which meaningful statements about character can be drawn. Aphthonius, following Quintilian and the *Rhetorica ad C. Herrenium,* classifies them as follows: first, under *genus,* race, native country, ancestors, and parentage; secondly, and without any heading, manner of education; and finally, under *res gestae,* physical attributes (*bona corporis*), spiritual attributes (*bona animi,* notably courage, wisdom, justice, temperance), and gifts of fortune (*bona fortunis*).[21] These topics define, in effect, the point of departure for a theory of humanist historiography or heroical literature. They comprise the *a priori* categories through which the writer isolates "substantial" images of character from the rough data given in his source. Traditionally, the most important of these were the *bona animi,* or cardinal virtues. They originate in the fourth book of Plato's *Republic,* receive an extensive reformulation in Cicero's *De officiis* and *De inventione,* and persist through medieval catalogues of vices and virtues and the *Speculum principiis* tradition, into the courtesy literature of the sixteenth century.[22] It is only rarely, of course, that one encounters a fully developed topical portrait of a character in a stage history (York's set *vituperatio* of Margaret in *3 Henry VI* is one example). But their importance as residual clichés will, I hope, be sufficiently apparent from the previous chapter, and from the analysis of the second scene of *1 Tamburlaine* that concludes this one.

Proceeding to more purely stylistic devices, after praising (or blaming) someone from the topics, the student would compare him to some other figure "in order to infer a greater position for that which is being praised, through the procedure of placing it next to something else." [23] This maneuver corresponds to what Curtius describes as the "outdoing" topic:[24] the hero's deeds "outdo" analogy. Aphthonius' exercise in *comparatio* calls for an extended comparison of one historical or literary character to another in terms of the topics. As a structural procedure, this device enables the historian to work outwards from a single life

towards a more inclusive kind of historical portraiture. The figure underlies, for example, the format of Plutarch's "Parallel Lives" as well as
Fluellen's rage to compare Harry of Monmouth to the great princes of
antiquity. Its real importance for practicing playwrights, however, lay
not in such incidental habits of speech, but in the conceptual framework
that it provided for reshaping chronicle into drama. Here one thinks
not only of the extended comparisons of English to French nobility, but
also of such "parallel lives" as Hal and Hotspur, or Antony and Caesar.

   Ethopoeia (frequently called *prosopopoeia* in classical rhetorics)[25]
is the figure of "impersonation." It is a stylized reconstruction of what
some person, or some person's ghost (*eidolopoeia*) or some thing would
have said on a particular occasion. This figure provides a formal basis
for the interpolated speech in classical history and for such "set" speech
forms as the lament, which recur constantly in early Elizabethan tragedies and histories.[26] *Ecphrasis,* or *descriptio,* is the figure used to
"amplify" topical statements through close detailed description of some
person, place, or action (I use "action" as a rough equivalent to Lorich's
"*Res, ut navales pedestresque pugnae, quemadmodum Historicus
fecit*").[27] Extended descriptions of military encounters, such as those
which are found in *Tamburlaine* and *Henry V,* were of the greatest
importance in "moving" the spectator, and they are the staple of all
those "messenger scenes" in which the word is to be taken for the deed.

   The point here is not simply that the rhetorical system underlying
classical historiography survived into the Renaissance, but, more importantly, that it continued to be regarded as a way of treating historical
data. In every one of these exercises the *scholia* refer the student to
passages from the classical historians for "study and practice." The
commentary on *laus,* for example, is illustrated by brief citations of
several Greek and Roman historians, and by extensive quotation from
Livy.[28] The laments of Cornelia and Cleopatra in Plutarch's *Lives* are
offered as examples of *ethopoeia.*[29] Livy's comparison of Pyrrhus to
Philip of Macedonia is a model for *comparitio;*[30] and his description
of a great naval battle in the second Punic War illustrates *res descriptionis.*[31] These references represent only a handful of Lorich's citations
of classical historians; and still more, presumably, would be added in
the classroom itself.

   What no mere list of citations can convey, moreover, is the thoroughness with which these passages were broken down into their bare rhetorical schemes; for the point of such exercises was nothing less than to isolate the conceptual basis of history itself. Simply to observe that Marlowe and Shakespeare learned the figures that underlay classical historiography, and to cite parallels from the plays, would be to over-simplify and understate the thrust of their education in rhetoric. In practice they were indoctrinated in the entire discipline of humanist historiography. The best way to illustrate how thoroughly that discipline shaped their imagination of history will be to reconstruct, for a moment, the actual processes by which it was instilled.

Within the classroom the set passages of history were closely studied to discern precisely how rhetorical topics and styles can be used to transpose bare fact (*narratio nuda*) into meaningful statement. The section given from Livy to illustrate *laus,* for example, is introduced by the rubric "An example, from the history of Titus Livius, of how to enlarge upon a circumstantial narrative from the 'places,' with a brief explication of the same [passage]." [32] The passage itself then begins with Livy's description of Hannibal. Lorich's prefatory "explication" comments, "So that one may understand directly just what sort of man this was, who put the name of Rome in such peril, he [Livy] first of all depicts the leader himself from the place of description [that is, from the places, or topics, of praise and blame] with these words," [33] after which the grammarian proceeds to quote verbatim Livy's lengthy encomium of Hannibal's courage and temperance.[34] The collaboration between rhetoric and historiography in the passage from Livy is made utterly explicit in Lorich's commentary. The grammarian registers Livy's discernment of the authentic "agents" in the Punic Wars (*"qualis is esset . . . Romanum nomen"*) precisely in terms of the encomiastic topics (*"ex descriptionis loco"*). And he extends this little "commentary on Livy" through several pages of the historian's account of Hannibal's early exploits. Each paragraph of Livy's text is heavily interlarded with Lorich's pedagogical citations of spots where arguments from the *loci* draw permanent truths out of *narratio nuda*. His attention to the minutest details indicates something of the thoroughness with which such passages were analyzed. For example: Livy mentions in passing that Arbacala, through the manliness and number of its inhabitants, was able to make a long defense against Hannibal; and Lorich notes that this remark, through its use of the "adjuncts" *virtus* and *multitudo,* heightens a passage that is otherwise bare and unadorned. The collaboration between rhetoric and historiography that was noted above occurs here on the minutest scale: the inhabitants of Arbacala become, for a moment, recognizable "agents" in a welter of shapeless historical fact. Livy discerns them in the flux of time and recasts them into a rhetorical statement; the student discerns them in Livy, and continues the process of refinement by preserving them in his commonplace book as *exempla* classified under *"virtus."*

The goal of this training was the formation of a systematic approach that would apply to any body of historical source materials;[35] and the "historian" who emerged from this process may be fairly represented by the playwright-historian present in Heywood's account of the way in which stage histories came to be written. It should now be clear that the procedures by which those "worthy" examples were to be selected and arranged are the very strategies by which any history was, in the rhetorician's jargon, "invented."

It was also suggested, in connection with Heywood's account, that to consider the maker of histories as a poet one has only to emphasize how those worthy exemplars might be made to move an audience to an active emulation of their highest attributes. Here again, one finds that the theory set forth by Elizabethan critics was simply the discursive expression of a discipline that was originally instilled through textbooks in rhetoric. The transition from rhetorical selectivity to rhetorical embellishment — that is, from studying history to writing it — occurred as the student began to fashion his own *exempla.* To convert a "categorical" item of historical information (such as the behavior of the Arbacalans in the text just cited) into an exemplum, the student would recast the original passage so as to heighten and emphasize its significant meaning. Susenbrotus' *Epitome troporum ac schematum,*[36] the first primer in rhetoric, introduces *exemplum* by remarking that the deeds and sayings of great men have a special efficacy both for persuasion and for moving the spirit to the emulation of virtue (*et ad persuadendum et ad inflamandos animos aemulatione virtutis*).[37] The key terms in this definition, "moving" and "persuading," are virtually identical to those that were observed in the discussions of heroical literature cited from the writings of Sidney, Heywood, and Nashe in the previous chapter; they recur in similar contexts when Italian critics discuss the function of *admiratio*.[38] Here again the student was not merely being made acquainted with a particular verbal device. An *exemplum* was a "figure of thought" in the most inclusive sense of that phrase, and it was supported by the entire notion of *eloquentia* as the Tudor humanists conceived of it.

Indeed, as R. R. Bolgar has shown, the collection of commonplace *exempla* was the only form through which many Renaissance readers were exposed to the literature of antiquity.[39] In *Utraque rerum ac verborum copia,* which was studied after the *Epitome,* Erasmus provides the student with extensive instructions for heightening and collating the *exempla* that he would be extracting from his reading. Just as the individual example is identified by its topical basis ("For example, if one should use a Spartan deed or saying, he could say by way of preface that this race had far excelled others in wisdom, and military and civil discipline"),[40] so whole groups of *exempla* were to be assembled and classified under "commonplace" attributes of character, such as *"pietas."* [41] Behind such exercises there stood both the classical tradition of fame and the whole Erasmian effort to use the lives of great men as an instrument of moral education in "the Ethicke and politick consideration." [42] If, finally, these connections between literature, historiography, and rhetoric appear to presuppose a rather forbidding degree of ingenuity on the part of teacher and student, two contemporary definitions of history, the first from Sir Thomas Elyot's *Book Named the Governor,* the second from Puttenham's *Art of English Poetry,* will at least suggest how easily they were assimilated in practice:

> [History] nat onely reporteth the gestes or actes of princes or capitaynes, their counsayles, and attemptates, entreprises, affaires, maners in lyvinge good and bad, descriptions of regions and cities, with their inhabitauntes, but also it bringeth to our knowlege the fourmes of sondry publike weales with augumentations and decayes and occasion thereof; more over preceptes, exhortations, counsayles, and good persuasions, comprehended in quick sentences and eloquent orations.[43]

> Right so no kinde of argument in all the Oratorie craft, doth better perswade and more universally satisfie then example, which

is but the representation of old memories, and like successes hap-pened in times past. . . . No one thing in the world with more delectation reviving our spirits then to behold as it were in a glasse the lively image of our deare forefathers, their noble and vertuous maner of life . . . [There] was nothing committed to historie, but matters of great and excellent persons and things that the same by irritation of good courages (such as emulation causeth) might worke more effectually, which occasioned the story writer to chuse an higher stile fit for his subiect, the Prosaicke in prose, the Poet in meetre.[44]

A phrase like "moral example" can, of course, cover a multitude of virtues that fall outside the special domain of epic. From Tacitus through Sir Thomas More, humanistic history had been the willing servant of all "the king-becoming graces,"

> As justice, verity, temp'rance, stableness,
> Bounty, perseverance, mercy, lowliness,
> Devotion, patience, courage, fortitude.
>
> (*Macbeth,* IV.iii.91–94)

Educators were agreed that the study of history should lead to an understanding of the ideal ruler, who was the highest type of man in society. But it could certainly be argued that they were more concerned with the philosopher-king than with the warrior-prince who came to dominate the earlier Elizabethan drama. In general, though, the two concepts necessarily stood in an intimate relationship to one another, the goal being, in the classroom as in imaginative literature, to unite the manly virtues with an aristocratic consciousness of courtesy and civility. The subsequent prominence of the martial hero on the London stage can moreover, be explained by reference to social pressures that have already been touched upon and will presently be considered in greater detail.

Whatever his political beliefs may have been, the Elizabethan play-wright was equipped with a comprehensive rhetorical apparatus for eliciting from his chronicle sources the kind of heroical-historical play that I began by describing; and he would probably have taken either of the passages just quoted as a fair summary of the purposes that his own histories were meant to fulfil. As purely didactic vehicles, the plays may be viewed as part of the "mirror for princes" tradition, which included both manuals of courtesy and ethical treatises such as Bryskett's *Discourse of Civil Life*. The governing conceptions of charactor in most of them can be deduced from the set topics of demonstrative rhetoric. Courage and wisdom, strength and beauty, eloquence, and (especially in the English histories) the incentive of a great ancestral tradition are the attributes that will explain why certain men are the makers of history. The predominance of such set-speech forms as the vaunt, pane-gyric, and lament naturally accentuated the gravitational pull towards prescribed oratorical themes. As Wolfgang Clemen has shown, such set speeches were at once the common coin of earlier Elizabethan drama and the standard vehicles for all the "topics" that had come down from antiquity through the Latin middle ages.[45] And these formal devices, in their various permutations and combinations, produce in turn those larger configurations — battle and funeral scenes, "parallel lives" pre-sented as wars of conquest — which comprise the rhetorical scenarios of heroical-historical drama.

At the same time it should be pointed out — if only in passing — that these very strategies would tend to impede the playwright's ability to recreate the temporal structure of Christian historiography. Towards the end of the previous chapter I suggested that the citations of Provi-dence in popular histories are often flat, dull, and perfunctory; they cannot compete imaginatively with the celebration of human capabilities that establishes our main angle of vision on the events being presented. Now this will necessarily be the case as long as every event in a character's life — except his death — is referred to the categorical at-tributes of his character; for if the reader is to credit explicit assertions of providential intervention, he must be persuaded that the final con-figuration of events is beyond the capabilities of any human "agent" and yet meaningful in itself. The classic discussion of this problem, which may clarify the point in question here, occurs in *2 Henry IV*. Midway in the play, the aging Henry Bolingbroke recalls Richard II's prophecy of the civil chaos that would ensue upon his deposition; and the recollection prompts Warwick's great afterword on the theme "There

is a history in all men's lives/Figuring the nature of the times deceased"
(III.i.80–81). This "history," which is the "hatch and brood of time"
(85) can be foretold, and it can be seen in retrospect. The playwright,
moreover, can reveal its "figure" through his power of artifice, even
though its working out is beyond the control of Bolingbroke or Northumberland, just as it was beyond the reach of Richard himself.

Such intimations that historical events assume a distinctive and meaningful configuration in time are at once a culmination of the providential
tradition in Elizabethan historiography and a peculiar achievement of
Macbeth and the mature histories. In the earlier tetralogy the workings
of Providence are at least faintly implied wherever dreams, prophecies,
curses, omens, astrology, ironic coincidence, and similar devices are
used to show part of the truth about history. But these usually convey
nothing more than a dim apprehension of retributive justice working
through individual malefactors. Even in *Richard III*, where such references proliferate, they do not seem to me to carry the poetic conviction
that arises whenever the characters actually confront their own con-
sciences. In the later histories, especially *Richard II* and *2 Henry IV*,
the speeches of prophecy and retrospect take on genuine significance
because they are embedded in those metaphors (the garden of state, the
body politic) by which Shakespeare assimilated political obligation to
the "hatch and brood of time." In other words (to put the problem in
overly simple terms) they depend on an analogy between the political
and the natural order, each of which gravitates inexorably from disorder
through a period of cleansing and expiation to a final stability. This is
providential history to be sure. It is rooted, however, not in the facile
moralizing of Holinshed and Hall, but in a complex symbolism that had
centuries of Biblical exegesis behind it. And it depends, to a great extent,
on Shakespeare's peculiar ability to represent the interior life of an
individual soul and its private sufferings.

A formal explanation of why, conversely, the early Shakespeare, and
all of the other playwrights treated here, found it difficult to discern a
providential pattern beneath the rises and falls of heroic drama can be
deduced from what has already been said: their approach to the past
left them without any sense of history as a coherent process. In his discussion of Tacitus, Auerbach reduces the problem to its bare epistemological outlines. Any reconstruction of history that follows "an unchange-

able system of categories" necessarily "cannot produce synthetic dynamic concepts" even though it may proceed "in strict chronological order." [46] Shakespeare's predecessors tried to get around this problem by endowing their "categorical" heroes with a preferred set of ethical and political credentials, and assuring Puritan critics that the result was providential history. In the long run, Shakespeare's thoroughly remarkable achievement was to discover for himself a set of "synthetic-dynamic concepts," a sacramental conception of history and politics, that could be played off against the partial vision of men like Henry Bolingbroke and Harry Hotspur. In the short run, however, a more limited intellectual range, coupled with a no less stringent artistic conscience, obliged him to give the logic and categories of humanist history something like a free hand. The result was *Henry VI*.

From Rhetoric to Drama

The connections that bind the stage history to its basis in literary theory have so far been treated only on a rather theoretical plane. With the benefit of hindsight, one can describe the rhetorical procedures that underlie a sizable body of Elizabethan history plays. The problem can hardly have been so straightforward for the playwrights who had to discover these connections for themselves. When Marlowe began *1 Tamburlaine* he did not, of course, simply invent the form out of popular chronicles and manuals of rhetoric. He had, among other things, an assortment of sophisticated commonplace books on humanistic themes and a native tradition of secular interludes to draw upon; and both sets of materials — the commonplace books and the interludes — can legitimately be treated as popular forms of humanist history. They represent, in effect, an evolutionary link between the assumptions about historiography and rhetoric that I have been developing in this chapter and the actual body of drama to be treated in the next one. The commonplace books indicate how those assumptions could give rise to a type of exemplary biography that served as an authoritative model of "history" for many Elizabethan readers, and which appears to have influenced the popular playwrights; several of the later interludes show how the leaven of rhetorical *exempla* could transform traditional morality drama into germinal histories."

The student's commonplace book served to prepare him for further reading in a wide range of didactic literature.[47] The classical and medieval *speculum principis,* for example, treated the topics as "regnative virtues," while the Renaissance courtesy book showed how they went to fashion a gentleman who was fit for all aspects of public life. Such manuals can scarcely be called histories, however, because the encyclopaedic framework usually precludes any attention to the whole life of even a single individual. These were rather the "forests" from which the "timber" of reasoned discourse could be taken, with each item stored in one of the common rhetorical "places." More immediately suited to the demands of narrative drama were such collections as Erasmus' *Apophtegmata,* where the exemplary "timber" actually gets fashioned into brief lives of noteworthy individuals. The attraction that such anthologies held for the early Elizabethan playwrights, who were just learning how to fashion a popular drama out of secular narrative, is easily understood. All the important "deeds and sayings" of each character had been preselected and interpreted by the compiler. Their moral utility was assured. The playwright had only to elaborate on the most stageworthy episodes, following the set topics and styles, without any regard for the controlled, sequential plot that one normally expects to find in narrative drama. The perfect case in point is provided, as it happens, by a play that was lifted whole from Richard Taverner's redaction of the *Apophtegmata:* Thomas Preston's *Cambises.* It is impossible to say how many playwrights followed Preston's example (Marlowe was one), but it is not unlikely that such collections were the seedbed for many of the favorite worthies of the later Elizabethan drama.[48]

Erasmus' own collection of "deeds and sayings" was translated by Nicholas Udall and circulated widely in Tudor grammar schools.[49] It treats hundreds of worthies, from Diogenes to Julius Caesar, with each "life" organized around the cardinal virtue of its subject — Diogenes the shrewd, imperturbable sceptic, Philip of Macedonia the just, temperate magistrate, and so on. The section on Alexander the Great, for example, proceeds through Alexander's childhood, his notable conquests, and his death, in a random sequence of episodes that exemplify his "singular courage, stomake, and towardness." [50] These topical attributes are expressly cited in the glosses that follow each anecdote. Thus in the first entry the youthful Alexander shows a precocious discomfiture at his father's triumphs, and complains "my father will leave nothing at all for me. . . . I shall have none affaires whereabout to bee dooyng and to be sette on werke." [51] The compiler duly comments, "even at that age might a bodye right well espye and knowe in hym a spark of an ambicious and actif or stiering nature towarde." [52] The other incidents of Alexander's life selected for presentation elaborate these attributes of character so as to provide a brief, episodic chronicle of the heroic life: as a boy Alexander will play only with the offspring of monarchs; as a man he distributes kingdoms to his lieutenants; he is more concerned with fame and glory than with earthly conquests; he may even be a son of the gods.[53]

In his preface, which is also a set of instructions on how to compile *exempla,* Erasmus makes it clear that such collections represent "history" in its ideal form. The episodes are arranged "so that the reader by the saiynges of a fewe persones may familiarly knowe the ordre of the whole historie," thereby avoiding the formless prolixity of the chronicles.[54] The entire collection is characterized as "golde alreadie fyned and made in fagottes or plate." [55] Thus the discrete events in this Erasmian history are related to one another as if they were the individual parts of a finely-wrought artifact made from "precious stones that are chosen pieces and well poolyshed alreadie sette in golde or upon cuppes of precious metalle." [56] The historian's goal, in other words, is to achieve the highest level of rhetorical "polish" and thematic cohesion, and he is free to disregard the temporal priorities that control the movement of ordinary narrative history.

Elsewhere in the preface to the *Apophtegmata,* Erasmus suggests that the "speeches of the partes" in plays comprise collections of exemplary "sayings" that are roughly comparable to his own:

> But in the speeches of the partes, in comedies (that is merie entreludes) and in tragedies (that is, sadde entreludes which wee call staige plaies) there is some more life and pith [than in philosophical dialogue], and a greate grace thei have beeyng sette in an apte and fitte place, albeeit the name of apophthegmes, no saiynges can have except the speaker out of whose mouth thei dooen procede bee a persone of greate name and the woordes purposely applyed to some mater beeyng even at that presente

houre in communicacion, yea and muche the better to bee liked, if thei bee a little difframed to an other sense, or a ferther meanyng then the veraye woordes dooe purporte.[57]

The implicit premise here is that the playwright shares the purposes and strategies of the rhetorician-biographer. Each works in a form that is concerned with displaying some noteworthy character in a series of representative episodes; and for both dramatic sayings and apothegms the overall aim is to render distinctive attributes of character aptly and persuasively. Erasmus naturally sees these purposes as problems of rhetoric: like the maker of *exempla,* the dramatist is concerned with using expressive speech to create effective portraits. The only difference is that, strictly speaking, the individual must be "of greate name" for the label "apophthegmes" to apply. In both cases, the central problem lies in striking a balance between dramatic immediacy ("the woordes purposely applyed to some mater beeyng even at that presente houre in communicacion") and generalized statement (the "other sense" or "ferther meanyng" to which the words should point). Once speeches with this kind of "life and pith" are devised for a particular character, they are even more effective for being set in context with one another, and with comparable speeches by other characters ("and a greate grace thei have beeyng sette in apte and fitte place").

Erasmus' suggestion that the episodes in a play may be treated as staged *exempla* coincides precisely with what one finds in several of the earliest English plays to be based on historical materials. An anonymous and obscure interlude entitled *King Darius* (1565) will serve to illustrate the point. For the most part the play is a secularized *psychomachia,* as are most moral interludes. Constancy, Charity, and Equity contend with Partiality, Inequity, and Importunity somewhere in the precincts of King Darius' court. Abruptly interspersed with these allegorical figures, however, are two exemplary deeds from the life of King Darius. I quote from David Bevington's summary:

In the first Biblical incident (scene two of the play) [Darius] entertains the monarchs of Ethiopia, Persia, Judah, and Media. He is hospitable and bounteous to his guests, and allows them to return amicably to their own lands. In the second Biblical incident (scene four) Darius judges a debate by three courtiers on the subject of the strongest force in the world. The two flattering courtiers (labeled only as Stipator Primus and Secundus) urge the power of wine and regal authority. The honest courtier, Zorobabell, praises the power of love both earthly and divine. Darius rewards Zorobabell generously for his virtuous answer. The King thus demonstrates the impartiality of a true prince, and Zorobabell the sincerity of a loyal courtier.[58]

The two historical *exempla* have been brought into the piece to illustrate the "topics" represented by the Virtues: Zorobabell, the faithful courtier, exemplifies Constancy, while Darius exemplifies Charity (when he is hospitable to the visiting monarchs) and Equity (when he rewards Zorobabell rather than the flattering courtiers). Here, then, there is "history" but not even a minimal sense of plot or chronology; the episodes are like entries in a commonplace book (where they were doubtless found), disposed under the topical categories that are supplied by the morality format. As part of this process, moreover, a secular, humanistic scale of values has begun to encroach on the old homiletic framework: the Pauline virtue, Charity, is exemplified as if it were the classical good, Hospitality.

In other hybrid moralities the germinal fable of the character-example expands and takes over the body of the play, while the personified "topics" disappear from view. The exemplary purposes of John Phillips' *Play of Patient Grissel* (1559), R. B.'s *Appius and Virginia* (1564), and Richard Edwards' *Damon and Pythias* (1565) are virtually declared by their titles; and the common complaint that such plays as these are "plotless, fragmented, and strereotyped" is, accordingly, quite beside the point.[59] For they are expressly meant to present idealized qualities of character: not through the old morality types, but through significant *exempla* of the categorical virtues that those types had represented. Hence they do not even attempt to furnish a plotted sequential action involving a change of fortune. Instead they culminate in "moving" statements about "patience," "chastity," and "friendship." In each case the climax consists of an exemplary demonstration of the particular virtue being dramatized and an enactment of the proper response. *Damon and Pythias* is a staged debate on the efficacy of true friendship, in which two worldly parasites contend with the titular heroes. The familiar conclusion finds each of the celebrated pair urging the tyrant Dionysus to execute him and spare the other; and the reply of Dionysus, who is more an ideal spectator than a character, makes it clear that their "rare example" in action has carried the day by both "persuading" and "moving" him:

> O noble friendship, I must yield! At thy force I wonder.
> My heart this rare friendship hath pierc'd to the root,
> And quenched all my fury: this sight hath brought this about,
> Which thy grave counsell, Eubulus, and learned persuasion could
>   never do.[60]

The Play of Patient Grissel embodies still another exemplary demonstration, and a similar act of recognition on the part of the obstinate Marquis:

> O Grissill, thy Vertues I must commend,
> Even thou onely, deservest perpetuall prayse:
> What tounge sufficiently, can thy laude ostend,
> I have not seen thy lyke in all my dayes,
> For faithfull love, thou doest far excead,
> *Dido, Penellope,* or anie sutch in dead.[61]

In much the same fashion, *Appius and Virginia* presents its martyred heroine (she chooses death before dishonor) in such a way as to make the rhetorical dimension utterly explicit: "*Doctrina* and *Memorie* and *Virginius* bring a tome," reads the stage direction; and Memorie proceeds to enter the *exemplum* in the registers of fame:

> I *Memorie* will minde hir life, hir death shall ever raine
> Within the mouth and minde of man, from age to age again.[62]

Preston's *Cambises* (1561) more surely adumbrates the exemplary format that the "heroical-historical" drama was to take three decades later. As Willard Farnham remarks, the playwright has simply "let Taverner's arrangement of anecdotes take on dramatic meaning and be sufficient in themselves for the main business of the action." [63] Each incident has its own little "plot" culminating in some meaningful statement about tyranny. When, for example, Cambises slays his counsellor Praxaspes' son with a bow and arrow to prove that wine does not affect his marksmanship, the point of the incident (as Falstaff recalls it a generation later) can be traced back to Taverner's gloss: "so barbarouse, so savage, and so tyrannicall maners, doeth dronkennes brynge upon the myndes of men." [64] This exemplary lesson is duly amplified in the formal commentary provided by little "set" speeches: Cambises' vaunt beginning "Behold Praxaspes, thy son's own heart" (563–566) demonstrates his cruelty, while the mother's lament (579–601) emphasizes the pathos of the episode.[65]

Since the incidents that Preston selects are framed by a fall from prosperity to death, the play has the rough outline of *de casibus* tragedy; but there is no attempt to forge the incidents into a sequential plot culminating in a punitive denouement. The murder of Praxaspes' son is not, for example, accompanied by the curses, prophecies, or other premonitions of divine vengeance that would foretell the miscreant's eventual destruction. Hence Cambises' last words, "A just reward for my misdeeds my death doth plain declare" (1166) are meant to move the spectator, but not to give a cause for Cambises' death: the very form of the exemplary biography acts to inhibit any attempt to show that events move through time in a meaningful pattern. Cambises' first outcry, "Wounded I am by sudden chance" (1153), provides a fully plausible explanation for the cause of his death, even though his demise also is the "just reward" for his misdeeds.

Eugene Waith has said of the structure of *Tamburlaine* that "there is a forward movement . . . in unfolding not only the narrative but the full picture of the hero"; and, further, that within this movement "each successive episode contributes something to the dominant idea . . . the definition of a hero." [66] Whatever Marlowe may have thought of the rhyming mother wits who devised the interludes that I have been surveying, he too constructs his play around a selection of exemplary episodes; and in doing so he is, like Preston, only following the lead provided by his sources.[67] Pierre de la Primaudaye's *French Academy* is a commonplace book in the form of a "school" for nobility in which

Tamburlaine is an example entered under the headings "Glory" and "Fortune." [68] Pedro Mexia's *Forest; or Collection of Histories* is, as its title suggests, a "forest" of commonplace material arranged as brief exemplary histories. Tamburlaine is offered there as the great example of modern "chivalrie, who in no point was inferiour to that prince of the world, Alexander." [69] The French historiographer Louis Le Roy elaborates this conception at great length. In his wide-ranging survey of history entitled *The Variety of Things,* Tamburlaine emerges as the forerunner of Renaissance achievements in arms, one who "desired nothing more, finding himself strong and fortunate in war, then to undertake great, and difficult things." [70] Like Marlowe, Mexia and Le Roy endeavor to establish Tamburlaine's character through a few exemplary "sayings and deeds": the acknowledgment of his natural pre-eminence by his Scythian companions; the circumspect discipline with which he manages his camp; his custom of hanging out the ensigns of red, white, and black; his slaughter of the virgins of Damascus; and his humiliation of Bajazeth. When Marlowe staged these episodes, he created a theatrical experience that is aptly characterized by the Prologue as a "progress" of pageants: that is, the successive episodes, like the great royal pageants sponsored by the Tudor nobility, mirror the hero's panoply of regnative virtues.[71] The "action" chiefly consists of pairing Tamburlaine with antagonists who provide a test for his special attributes of character. His conquests punctuate these encounters and so provide the rudimentary "plot" required for theatrical production. But the sequence of events takes its interest from what it gradually reveals of the hero's character, rather than from a plot depicting historical development and change;[72] the processes of history, such as they are, depend on an erratic, and potentially tragic, interplay of fortune and the human will.

For Marlowe's contemporaries, as Howard Baker's genealogy of the "mighty line" suggests,[73] the immediate importance of the play lay in the amplitude and polish of its rhetorical designs. Like *The Shepherd's Calendar* and *Astrophel and Stella, Tamburlaine* showed an entire generation of writers how the set procedures of formal rhetoric could be used to fashion imaginative literature. It is the first play that draws upon all the important resources of humanist theory to produce a "history" that is fully organized around its central figure. Each episode is a germinal *exemplum,* copiously elaborated from the set topics and figures. The topics furnish the themes for the great speeches that "amplify" local episodes into resonant statements about heroic character. Early in act two of *1 Tamburlaine,* for example, Menaphon delivers the set-piece of description[74] beginning "Of stature tall and straightly fashioned" (II.i.7–30) that establishes the hero's physical identity. Subsequently Tamburlaine's apostrophe to "Nature, that framed us of four elements" (II.vii.12–29) demonstrates the aspirant fortitude of his spirit, while his first great vaunt before battle re-emphasizes his personal superiority to fortune with the formula "I hold the fates fast-bound in iron chains" (I.ii.165–208). The "outdoing topos," to borrow once again Curtius' phrase for the invidious comparison, recurs continuously throughout the play; it reaches a crescendo of sorts towards the end of part two, when Tamburlaine "triumphs" over the "pampered jades" and pictures the monuments of his own magnificence to be erected in Samarcanda (IV.iv.97–133). The note of formal invective also reaches a climax in *2 Tamburlaine,* when Jerusalem, Orcanes, Trebizond, and Soria denounce Tamburlaine for the murder of his son Calyphas (IV.ii. 94–106). And, in the aftermath of battle, the dramatic lament comments on the departed glories of the defeated: "Behold the turk and his great emperess" (*1 Tamb.,* V.ii.284–308).

But no inventory of set speeches can account for the ways in which the strategies of formal rhetoric enable Marlowe to draw out the latent significance of particular dramatic situations. Here the second scene of *1 Tamburlaine* will offer an especially useful example for purposes of analysis. Zenocrate's second line, "If, as thou seem'st thou art so mean a man — " (8) poses the central question of this episode and, one might add, of the entire play: by what criteria does one distinguish between a "Scythian shepherd" and a "mighty monarch"? How is Tamburlaine's identity to be known? The putative hero responds by referring the question to the customary topics:

> I am a lord, for so my deeds shall prove,
> And yet a shepherd by my parentage.

> (I.ii.34–35)

The distinction is of considerably more importance than it may at first appear to be. "Deeds" corresponds to the rhetorical classification "achievements," or *res gestae* (see page 41 above), from which Tamburlaine can cite, for example, his nobility of spirit, his physical strength and beauty, and his gift of eloquence, to "prove" that he is a "lord." "Parentage" can be taken to represent all of those things to be considered "before a mannes life," [75] which are listed under *genus:* race, native country, ancestors, parentage. Derived from the Tartar race, a native of Scythia, with shepherds for his ancestors, and, it is later suggested, "some infernal hag" (*2 Tamb.,* V.i.110) for a mother, Tamburlaine does not, to put it mildly, exhibit the generic attributes of a "lord," at least by Elizabethan standards. If, indeed, Tamburlaine had been of gentle birth, there would have been no problem of definition and small occasion for formal rhetoric of this sort. By the conventions of heroical romance, which the audience must have had in mind, the handsome shepherd should have thrown off his lowly weeds and identified himself as Zenocrate's betrothed-in-disguise, the long-lost prince of Arabia. Instead he throws them off to show that

> This complete armor and this curtle-axe
> Are adjuncts more beseeming Tamburlaine.
>
> (*1 Tamb.,* I.ii.42–43)

The rhetorical term "adjuncts" is not entirely fortuitous here, for the matter of Tamburlaine's nobility — at least in its literary dimension — has now to be resolved through rhetorical elaboration of his "deeds." Along with the "jigging veins of rhyming mother wits" (Prologue, l. 1), Marlowe has evidently resolved to banish all the miraculous tokens of heroical romance, in which the "amorous knight . . . can not be knowne but by some posie in his tablet, or by a broken ring, or a handkircher, or a piece of a cockle shell." [76] Marlowe's hero cannot be "known" in this way because he lacks noble parents, and, what is more to the point here, because the dramatist is writing history — not romance — and trying to identify one of those "agents" that stand behind it. Hence, subsequent passages testify to Tamburlaine's strength and beauty, his affecting eloquence, and his distinctive quality of mind, *fortitudo.* It is the last of these topics, in particular, that supplies Marlowe with the image of the "aspiring mind" that shuns whatever is base and earthly, the extravagant self-confidence, and the "magnificent" distribution of rewards to his followers ("Thyself and them shall never part from me/ Before I crown you kings in Asia" [244–245]).[77]

Within the drama of this scene, these attributes are cited for the express purpose of "moving and persuading" Zenocrate and Theridamas. That is how the shepherd finally "proves" that he is a lord, by convincing the one to live with him and the other to emulate him. Theridamas' responses — beginning with his contemptuous "Where is this Scythian, Tamburlaine?" — register the desired range of rhetorical effects almost as explicitly as do those cited a few pages earlier from the Tudor interludes:

Where is this Scythian, Tamburlaine?

(152)

Tamburlaine! A Scythian shepherd so embellished
With nature's pride and richest furniture!

(154–155)

Not Hermes, prolocutor to the gods,
Could use persuasions more pathetical.

(209–210)

Ah, these resolvèd noble Scythians!

(224)

Won with thy words and conquered with thy looks,
I yield myself, my men, and horse to thee. . . .

(227–228)

Extending the strategy of this local episode over an entire play, one arrives at a scenario that will hold, to a greater or lesser degree, for all of the plays that I have provisionally designated as heroical-historical in kind. Each hero "earns his place in the story" by exhibiting those categorical virtues that set him apart from the common run of men. Specifically, he disproves a putative "baseness" through military encounters, and his special abilities are ordinarily displayed in those scenes "where the drummes might walke or the pen ruffle" — scenes of challenge, battle, triumph, and funeral. Although he wins power and titles by his victories, the hero does not fight to acquire kingdoms as such, but rather to exhibit and satisfy his innate nobility of nature. This nobility is defined through a set of residual clichés that mainly recur in set speeches of praise and triumph, and in vaunts delivered before battle. The hero's mind is "dauntless"; his physical attributes and his entire entourage are visually magnificent, as if he were some "god of war" or a reincarnate antique hero; his deeds are notable, if not because of any particular virtues they embody then just because they "outdo" analogy. Although the plays are about war, there is surprisingly little in the way of overt political moralizing. *Alphonsus, King of Aragon, The Wounds of Civil War, The Battle of Alcazar,* and *1 Selimus* are foreign histories which freely mingle wars of conquest and civil dissension. The English histories are necessarily more cautious, politically speaking, and in these the demand for heroic display is usually met by portraying a national hero conquering foreign armies. *The Famous Victories of Henry V* (which of course precedes *Tamburlaine*), *1 The Troublesome Reign of King John, Locrine, Edward III,* and *Edmond Ironside* all center upon such figures. As in the foreign histories, the antagonists exist primarily to elicit and test the hero's special virtues. The wrongness of their cause is simply a *donnée,* a means of releasing the hero from any political odium. Nevertheless, it was still important that the victor should not merely be engaged in acquiring titles and kingdoms. Whenever the English foray into France, the battle is made into a test of nobility by having the French aristocracy question the English leader's claim to heroic worth. Hence Henry V's riotous youth, Edward III's unmanly lust, and the Black Prince's callowness all receive considerable attention.

It would be easy enough to produce rhetorical critiques, roughly similar to the one just given, for individual scenes from any of these plays. Most readers would doubtless agree, however, that such purely formal analyses possess a limited critical value, if only because they are so liable to circumvent the sources of that mimetic vitality that usually attracts one to Elizabethan drama in the first place. No amount of rhetorical analysis will explain why Marlowe chose to fashion a hero whose greatness arises from his deeds rather than his parentage. Nor will it explain why his successors, Shakespeare among them, were so fascinated by Marlowe's image of heroic greatness, and yet so eager to reformulate it. Seeking answers to such questions, criticism necessarily radiates out from the language of the plays into broader reaches of Elizabethan culture — its political and social attitudes, and its literary resources — in order to discover how the form and pressure of the times supplied the heroical history with its distinctive array of themes, characters, and ethical dilemmas.

3 "Parentage" and "Deeds":

The Heroic Example from

Tamburlaine to *Richard III*

You know in great matters and adventures in wars the true
provocation is glory: and who so for lucres sake or for any
other consideration taketh it in hande (beside that hee never
doth any thing worthie prayse) deserveth not the name of a
gentleman, but is a most vile marchant.

(Baldassare Castiglione, *The Book of the Courtier,* trans.
Sir Thomas Hoby, 1561)

The developments that ensued in the wake of *Tamburlaine* have been
tentatively described as the assessment of a literary ideal in historical settings. Elizabethan playwrights and their audiences placed a premium on
athletic displays of "lively and well-spirited action" which were felt to
realize their implicit didactic values in performance. The preference
naturally found expression in a drama of heroic exploits and martial
fortitude. Further, once the enterprise was under way, it was seen to
pose a peculiar challenge to the controlling pieties of Elizabethan politics and society, and thus its continued popularity was in part determined
by the unanswered questions that Marlowe bequeathed to his successors.
A full account of the history play as it evolved under these conditions
would require collating a variety of independent developments: the re-
currence of topics drawn from *genus* and *res gestae* in set speeches of
praise and description, the recasting of execration and lament into
choric speeches invoking political judgments, the increasing use of *exempla* taken from the English chronicles, the reformulation of materials

borrowed from the literature of chivalry and from the Senecan revenge drama, and finally the complex of social attitudes represented by the popular audience itself. Each area of development contributed something to the gradual transformation of the history into a vehicle for a more "modern" — that is, more closely documented and more politically sensitive — view of the past than was immediately available from the traditions described in the previous chapter. My survey will deal in detail only with the last two items that appear in this inventory. There simply are not enough texts available to permit a thorough investigation of the entire process, and the possibilities for error on the score of textual corruption, authorship, and chronology are virtually endless. It seems the better part of valor, therefore, to lay emphasis on those aspects of the problem that allow for a more speculative treatment.

Accordingly, most of this chapter will be concerned with the evolution of the "Herculean hero" into ethical stereotypes that permitted the formation of a more complicated kind of historical example than Marlowe's heroic drama could ever have contained. I begin with a brief excursion into the puzzling relationship that obtains between Marlowe's hero and the social attitudes of his audience, in the hope of isolating some of the extrinsic forces that set the process under way and determined the direction that it was to follow. When a "literary" or rhetorical ideal elicits this kind of response, and exhibits this degree of resilience, one gathers that it has managed to involve itself with cultural ideals as well. It will be evident from much of the analysis that follows, for example, that "baseness" frequently appears to be a codeword for low social status, just as "loftiness" often refers to social eminence. Further, the action whereby a hero achieves his "magnificent" situation in life will usually involve the acquisition of titles, property, and possessions. In other words, the representation of a modern "worthy" aspiring to heroic fortitude generally resembles the most important social phenomenon of the later sixteenth century: a rapid rise in social status by an individual who looks to his personal abilities rather than his gentle birth to justify his high worldly station.[1] The reason the phenomenon would have to be insulated within a "literary" format is obvious enough: there was no place for it in the presiding ideology, which looked to an entrenched monarchy that was highly conservative on the whole question of social mobility.[2] It would have been impossible for a Tudor historian to have written about Tamburlaine in the manner of Louis Le Roy; no set of concepts was available whereby the jump from "Scythian shepherd" to "mighty monarch" could be seen as a typical, or at least a potentially typical, kind of event. But once the phenomenon was located within the fabric of an heroic play, there was a large audience fully prepared to see a set of social meanings latent in the most commonplace *topoi* of the popular history.

I do not offer the hypothesis as a way of explaining the popularity of *Tamburlaine* — there are many reasons for that — but more particularly (to resume the line of reasoning begun in chapter 1) as a way of explaining the subsequent mutations of Tamburlaine. For it is precisely as the social implications of his career come to light that the Herculean hero begins to acquire an historical identity, and to undergo the series of transformations that lead to *Henry VI*.

1 Tamburlaine: Literary and Social Conventions

1 Tamburlaine begins, it will be recalled, just at the point where the romance plot, with its highly conservative social implications, is exploded.

> [*Tamb.*] But tell me, madam, is your grace betrothed?
> *Zeno.* I am, my lord, for so you do import.
> *Tamb.* I am a lord, for so my deeds shall prove,
>   And yet a shepherd by my parentage.
>
> (I.ii.32–35)

In place of some miraculous proof of noble birth, Tamburlaine offers his "deeds," or personal attributes. The *topoi* that he draws upon are familiar enough: fortitude, "magnificence," strength and beauty, eloquence. Now these are sufficient, perhaps, to make Tamburlaine a "lord" according to certain humanistic theories; but in order for theory to be translated into social fact, the ideal attributes have to be accompanied by the actual hallmarks of status and power. Tamburlaine's identity poses an acute problem in this scene because he declines simply to be a noble shepherd. He wants it both ways. In effect, his topics have to be enlarged to accommodate the acquisition of material rewards, even at the risk of falling into "Scythian bathos." Hence, interfused with his loftiest rhetorical appeals, there are references to the actual possessions and power that he means to gain. For example: La Primaudaye's description of fortitude as a state of mind that "desiring the greatest and best things, despiseth those that are base and abject, aspiring to celestiall and eternall things" [3] might serve as a model for Tamburlaine's appeal to Theridamas,

> Thus shall my heart be still combined with thine,
> Until our bodies turn to elements,
> And both our souls aspire celestial thrones

(234–236)

were it not for that ambiguous word "thrones," with its connotations of a tangible reward for Theridamas, an eternity of power and authority. (The context makes it clear, by the way, that these are not the "Thrones" of Christian cosmography, although the association may add an extra hint of blasphemy.) This interplay of lofty ideals and material realities is no less evident in Tamburlaine's boast that he and his followers "in conceit bear empires on our spears/Affecting thoughts co-equal with the clouds" (64–65), or in his assurances that when he and Theridamas "walk upon the lofty clifts" they will be saluted by "Christian merchants" ploughing the sea below (192–195). If these touches seem too slight to embody any real qualification of Tamburlaine's ideal, his two lieutenants are considerably more direct about the matter. When Techelles has completed his set piece on their general's physical splendor, it is Usumcasane who bluntly draws the moral: "And making thee and me Techelles, kings" (58). And after Tamburlaine's great "pathetical persuasions," it is they who reckon up the dukedoms and kingdoms that are to be had. Tamburlaine only supplies the cue in this case, reminding Theridamas that he will "find my vaunts substantial" (212).

By transferring familiar rhetorical ideals into these new contexts, Marlowe keeps open the question of whether or not Tamburlaine's "deeds shall prove" that he is a "lord," while moving it directly into the area of social tension and conflict. Here the issue is not simply parentage versus achievements, but whether the very act of acquiring power and wealth identifies the protagonist as a "lawless thief" or, as he would have it, a "greater man" than Zenocrate's father. For Tamburlaine, as for many an Elizabethan *parvenu,* the crux of the matter lay in one's attitude towards his newly acquired wealth. Thus all of the discrepancies just noted help to focus one crucial question: are the actual prizes that objectify Tamburlaine's "deeds" a visible proof of his nobility, or are they just so many stolen goods? In this case, again, the apposite topic is "magnificence, which is a vertue concerning riches also [i.e., like liberality]; which the magnificall man useth in great things, and such as are to have long continuance, and are done in respect of vertue, as sumptuous buildings, rich furnitures, and the like." [4] Now "magnificence" is the first attribute of fortitude, and it stipulates that the mind which is not fastened upon earthly things will nonetheless use them, but only in such a way as to display its own greatness. When Meander subsequently commands his "noble" soldiers to strew the battlefield with gold in order that

> . . . while the base-born Tartars take it up,
> You, fighting more for honor than for gold,
> Shall massacre those greedy-minded slaves . . .

> (II.ii.65–67)

he is acting on the assumption that Tamburlaine and his followers are not "magnificall men." In a society where the arts of conspicuous consumption were of primary importance in determining social status, "magnificence" was the virtue that best characterized the true aristocrat. His opposite, the hoarder, was generally stigmatized as the base fellow whose acquisitive drive expressed itself in ceaseless accumulation, unrelieved by either munificence or style. But what finally constitutes the proper "style"? And who is to say when someone has achieved it? Living in a period when money — but not titles — was changing hands with unprecedented celerity, the audience must have seen in the "golden wedges," the resolute shepherd, and the wavering princess a configuration that promised a direct assault on those most unsettling questions.

Here again Marlowe contrives a fine tension between the claims of pure virtue and the ambivalent requisites of social status. It is, after all, necessary to get riches before you can be magnificent with them. The implicit ironies of the situation are most finely conveyed in those passages where Tamburlaine speaks of his burgeoning "state."

> Come, lady, let not this appall your thoughts;
> The jewels and the treasure we have ta'en
> Shall be reserved, and you in better state
> Than if you were arrived in Syria . . .
>
> (I.ii.1–4)
>
> But since I love to live at liberty,
> As easily may you get the Soldan's crown
> As any prizes out of my precinct.
> For they are friends that help to wean my state,
> Till men and kingdoms help to strengthen it . . .
>
> (26–30)

In the first of these, where the word carries its idiomatic Elizabethan sense of "stately," it nicely registers the shepherd's open, aristocratic generosity towards his captive princess. In the second, it is far closer to "estate," or even the modern "state," as one thinks of it in the phrase *raison d'état*. As usual, Techelles and Usumcasane provide a referent at the lower end of the scale:

> *Tech.* We are his friends, and if the Persian king
> Should offer present dukedoms to our state,
> We think it loss to make exchange for that
> We are assured of by our friend's success.
> *Usum.* And kingdoms at the least we all expect,
> Besides the honor in assured conquests . . .
>
> (213–218)

Tamburlaine himself, although he is no less entrapped in these contradictory attitudes, manages to see beyond them to the heart of the problem; for the acquisition of those prizes that "wean my state" is linked, in his case, to gestures that indicate how little meaning the treasure *per se* has for him. It is Zenocrate and her escorts, he perceives, who are uniquely able to confer aristocratic status. Their treasure is only a means to that end.

> Disdains Zenocrate to live with me?
> Or you, my lords, to be my followers?
> Think you I weigh this treasure more than you?
>
> (82–84)

So, when Theridamas approaches, Tamburlaine for once chooses not to attack, but instead gives the command, "Lay out our golden wedges to the view" (139). He has arrived at the classic dilemma of the *nouveau riche:* he would prove himself a lord by his deeds, but he must prove himself to those who are lords by birth as well. Whether Tamburlaine's "state" is truly "magnificent," the emblem of his noble nature, or merely a martial joint stock company, is a question that can finally be answered only by Zenocrate and Theridamas. They must decide whether or not to join it.

Thus the rhetorical drama of "moving and persuading" here becomes a matter of the social relationships between Tamburlaine and the Persian nobility. The "*sure* and *grounded* argument" that Tamburlaine offers to Theridamas is the "Soldan's daughter, rich and brave" who will be his "queen and portly emperess" (183–186; my italics). Moreover, he treats the "valiant man of Persia" almost as an equal in this scene, a status that is never enjoyed by the two Scythian shepherd-lieutenants:

> Both will we walk upon the lofty clifts
>
> (192)
>
> Both will we reign as consuls of the earth
>
> (196)
>
> Then shalt thou be competitor with me
> And sit with Tamburlaine in all his majesty
>
> (207–208)
>
> Thus shall my heart be still combined with thine.
>
> (234)

Together they represent an aristocratic perfection that neither the uncultivated plains of Scythia nor the decadent court of Persia could ever produce alone. Tamburlaine will of course remain pre-eminent in this partnership, but it is already clear that his triumphs will not be complete unless they are graced by Theridamas and, ultimately, Zenocrate. Thus, if Theridamas' capitulation marks the climax of this scene, Zenocrate's, which Tamburlaine can now anticipate, will put a close to the success story that is the play itself: "For you then, madam, I am out of doubt" (257).

   To approach *Tamburlaine* with an eye to its immediate social implications is a highly uncertain undertaking, nor would further analysis along these lines result in anything like a full interpretation of Marlowe's play. The question at hand, once again, is rather the nature of the response that Marlowe's prototype evoked among his contemporaries; and specifically, the point at which a literary type such as Marlowe's Herculean hero begins to elicit an exhaustive scrutiny of its ethical and political implications. If it can be assumed that the original audience of the scene that was just examined responded to its rhetorical differentiae in the same way that I have, the answer is readily apparent: the literary ideal had begun to embody the real, but highly suspect, aspirations of a large part of Elizabethan society; and its further development therefore took place in an ambience in which implicit social meanings were bound to become more explicit as they touched upon the immediate preoccupations and anxieties of the popular audience. Although the question can scarcely be resolved in the space of a few pages, there are good reasons for supposing that an Elizabethan theatergoer would have registered instinctively the social overtones that I have been trying to detect.
   As the extensive researches of Ruth Kelso, J. E. Mason, and others have shown,[5] the relative importance of gentle birth and achieved virtue as criteria for an elite aristocracy was endlessly debated in the courtesy literature of the sixteenth century. Moreover, the debate was conducted, as one might expect, in terms of the set topics of personal worth, and especially, the four cardinal virtues of classical and Christian humanism. In this case the genealogy runs from the *Republic* and the *Nichomachean Ethics,* through Cicero's *De officiis,* down to Elyot's *Book Named the Governor;*[6] and it persists through much of the middle class courtesy literature that Louis B. Wright gathers under the heading "Handbooks to Improvement." [7] In other words, before a typical spectator went to the Fortune to see *Tamburlaine,* he was likely to have been conning such a work as William Baldwin's *A Treatise of Moral Philosophy, Containing the Sayings of the Wise* to learn how the achievement of fortitude and magnificence might help *him* to emulate an aristocratic style of life: for

the theatrical venture and the editorial one (which would include most of the commonplace books mentioned in the previous chapter) were addressed to the same audience, dealt with the same subjects, and relied on the same conceptual framework. The economic events that help to explain these literary enterprises do not lend themselves to casual summary. Most Tudor historians would agree that the flow of gold from the new world opened up the Elizabethan money market, while the sale of Church holdings opened up the land market; and few would dispute that the perennial problem of converting wealth into social status took on a peculiar urgency in the later sixteenth century. Lawrence Stone estimates that the holdings of those who were members of the peerage at the time of Elizabeth's coronation declined by about one-fourth during the latter half of the sixteenth century.[8] Without entering into the vexed question of exactly where that wealth was going — the debate over the "rise of the gentry" — one can understand why commonplace books of aristocratic behavior such as *The French Academy* and the *Discourse of Civil Life* proved so fascinating to the reading public. They provided a respectable literary framework in which to raise one of the most troublesome questions about Elizabethan society: What are the deeds that prove a man to be a lord? If an ordinary member of Marlowe's audience actually attired himself in "nature's richest furniture" he was liable to fines and imprisonment for violating sumptuary laws that had been enacted to keep him in his "place." In a courtesy book or a play, the relation of "magnificence" to gentle birth could at least be openly debated.

Lest I seem to be requiring an untoward degree of mental agility from the typical paying customer, it should be remembered that the Elizabethan playhouse was a place where social tensions were liable to rise to the fore of their own accord. First of all, it was the only place in sixteenth-century England where members of all social classes regularly gathered under one roof, a peculiarity that did not go unnoticed by contemporaries. As Alfred Harbage's study makes clear, it was precisely because the playhouse was a uniquely "democratic" institution that it aroused so much antagonism among the municipal authorities.[9] And the evidence that he has collected suggests to me that such brawls and mutinies as did occur there usually were the product of class antagonisms. In 1580 there was "a certaine fraye betwene the servauntes of th'erle of Oxforde

and the gentlemen of the Innes of Courtes." In 1581 it was the gentlemen of Gray's Inn and some of Lord Berkeley's servants. In 1584 "nere
the Theatre or Curten at the tyme of the Playes," a group whom the
recorder of London described as "litell better than roogs that took upon
them the name of gentilmen" found occasion to declare that "prentizes
were but the skomme of the worlde"; during the melée that ensued "my
lo ffitzgerold with a nosmber of gentilmen" struck a "tall yong fellowe
being a pretize . . . upon the face with his hatt" and was "glad to take
howse" in the aftermath. In 1592 it was the fellmongers of Southwark
who assembled near the playhouse to escalate their quarrel with the
officers of the Knight Marshall. While such incidents cannot have been
frequent, they do bear witness to tensions which must have been continuously present among Shakespeare's audience, and which are faith-
fully reproduced in, for example, the servants' quarrels of *1 Henry VI,*
or the uprising of Jack Cade and the murder of Suffolk in *2 Henry VI.*

In the face of such evidence, it is hard to preserve the image of an
audience whose capacities for reflection on historical themes could be
aroused only by solemn homilies on the miseries of civil dissension and
the splendors of hierarchical order. No one doubts that the apprentices
of London had a proper fear of civil war; but that is, in a sense, precisely what they were engaged in when they chased "my lo ffitzgerold"
(who had himself struck the first blow) into the nearest shelter. The
artisan who could afford a penny for a play was probably doing well
enough to have a genuine interest in preserving the social order; but by
the very act of taking the afternoon off and going to a play he was mo-
mentarily repudiating his own place in the received hierarchy. And the
municipal authorities and preachers never let him forget it.

No amount of commentary on the social preoccupations of the audience can, to be sure, supply the plays with meanings that are not realized
in the texts themselves; and it must be conceded that the connections
between heroic aspirations and social ones are usually too oblique to
permit the kind of analysis that was attempted a few pages earlier. Indeed, the economic distinction between the "base" soldier of fortune,
who treats war as a crude business venture, and the true prince, who
welcomes the opportunity to exhibit his aristocratic mettle, is not fully
developed until Shakespeare comes to write *1 Henry IV* (see chapter 5
below). Nevertheless, the link between the two processes offers an im-

portant clue to the gradual transformation of heroical character types between *Tamburlaine* and *Richard III*. It seems likely that from the very outset the "aspiring mind" became a focus for the acute conflict between self-esteem and a fixed social hierarchy that pervaded Elizabethan London. As a result, its artistic future, at least in the short run, lay in the direction of closer social definitions and sharper ethical portraiture: for it was only in this way that the original tensions could be brought to consciousness and adjudicated.

So long as the *topoi* of personal nobility merely constituted a license to make glorious war, heroical-historical drama could be counted on for moral evasiveness and mild entertainment, but little else. What had to occur, if that drama was to remain alive in its local contexts, was a thoroughgoing reappraisal of the heroic life, a clearer view of the relationship between personal aspirations and social convention. The immediate problem, very simply, was how to find a hero whose aspiring mind defined itself in deeds that were morally edifying — for good or for ill — so that the phenomenon could at least begin to be understood in the ethical dimension. More particularly, the Marlovian conqueror had to be made to answer to the conventions of the Elizabethan "state," rather than one of his own making. It was for precisely these reasons that playwrights gradually turned to a more restrictively ethical and eventually "historical" delineation of heroic character. In essence, the problem of characterization continued to hinge on the crucial distinction between parentage and deeds, *genus* and *res gestae*. Not that parentage, by itself, was difficult to establish: genealogies could be falsified in Elizabethan drama, just as they were falsified in Elizabethan society. The real demand, however, was for the figure whose deeds would affirm the value of his family name even as they promoted his material glory — or, conversely, would expose the futility of violating "primogeniture of birth" even as they assured his own ignominy.

Forms of Ethical Assessment: The Chivalric Knight and the Senecan Villain

In describing the ways in which Shakespeare and his contemporaries responded to these problems, one might begin with two forms of ethical assessment that are common to many of the progeny of *Tamburlaine:* the hero as chivalric knight, and the hero as Senecan villain. In *Henry VI* these types appear respectively as Sir John Talbot and Richard, the murderous Earl of Gloucester; in the popular repertory they are best represented by the titular heroes of *Edward III* and *The True Tragedy of Richard III*. Now as regards the genesis of these character roles, there is at least some basis for supposing that each of them arose as part of a common effort to isolate the ethical possibilities of Marlowe's prototype and to represent those possibilities in literary terms. In *Henry VI* the rudimentary commonplaces of heroic virtue, parentage and deeds, are given a "public" interpretation, so that Talbot's regard for his family name is, for example, virtually identical with his sense of feudal proprieties, just as Richard's violation of family pieties is of a piece with his unfitness for aristocratic life in all its phases. In *Edward III* and *The True Tragedy,* by contrast, these images of character are invoked, but since they are not so securely rooted in a full historical context of social and political conventions, those plays are proportionally closer to Marlowe. Both include appeals to hereditary honor and family pieties, but these tend to be voiced from the sidelines or in choric speeches that are given to the central figure without much regard for dramatic consistency. For the most part the hero simply continues to intone an idiom that is altogether brave and admirable. This way of looking at the problem is helpful not only in distinguishing Shakespeare from his contemporaries, but also in discriminating between the more coherent of the popular histories, such as *Edward III* and *The True Tragedy of Richard III,* and the less coherent ones, such as *Alphonsus King of Aragon* and *The Battle of Alcazar*. It is in the latter two plays, and others like them, that the principle of due succession, and the conceptions of character that would support the principle, are almost entirely obfuscated by the "*scenicall* strutting and furious vociferation" of unimproved conqueror-drama.

There is, in other words, an "ideal development," in the Crocean sense, within the heroical-historical repertory, one which proceeds from a post-Marlovian intoxication with heroic clichés to a fuller portrayal of aristocratic values realized in historical settings. It leads to the early Shakespeare. On the lowest rung of the ladder stand those heroes who utterly refuse to submit to any form of ethical judgment. Surrounded by urgent questions about hereditary right, the morality of civil dissension, and the claims that might justify foreign wars, they take refuge behind a vague Marlovian idiom that will not suffer detraction. Just above them (sometimes these are the same characters in a pious mood) there are the "legitimate" victors and the nominal "usurpers." Here one finds some deference to the principle of "parentage," but the distinction remains, by and large, *pro forma*. The characters themselves will not relinquish their commitment to the language of pure *virtù*. Where more complicated species of heroic life do arise, they generally take either of the two forms just noted. For those who wished to draw upon it, the sixteenth-century revival of medieval chivalry offered the image of a martial hero who was also a gentleman possessed of a punctilious code of family honor. Conversely, Senecan tragedy charted out the path that led downward, from personal honor and family pride to cunning, deceit, and domestic murder. Here one can begin to look for traces of an heroic drama that is "historical" in the Shakespearian sense, but there are still large differences in the degree to which the ethical and political potentialities of the literary image are exploited.

This scheme of development plays fast and loose with chronology, and it is not meant to provide even a rough anatomy of the popular history in all its various forms. I offer it only as an account of some of the final stages on the road that leads from the broad traditions of Renaissance humanism to the peculiar achievement of Shakespeare's earliest histories. To begin with, there is the raw idiom of *Tamburlaine*.

> *Alphon.* And nought is left for me but *Aragon?*
> Yes surely yes, my Fates have so decreed,
> That *Aragon* should be too base a thing,
> For to obtaine Alphonsus for her King.
>
> (*Alphonsus King of Aragon*, 816–819)[10]

> *Scilla.* You Romaine souldiers, fellow mates in Armes,
> The blindfold Mistris of incertaine chaunce,
> Hath turnd these traiterous climers from the top,
> And seated Scilla in the chiefest place.
> The place beseeming Scilla and his minde.
> For were the throne where matchles glorie sits,
> Empald with furies threatning blood and death,

Begirt with famine and those fatall feares
That dwell below amidst the dreadfull vast:
Tut Scillaes sparkling eyes should dim with cleere
The burning brands of their consuming light,
And master fancie with a forward minde,
And maske repining feare with awfull power.
For men of baser mettall and conceipt
Cannot conceive the beautie of my thought.
I crowned with a wreath of warlike state,
Imagine thoughts more greater than a crowne,
And yet befitting well a Roman minde.
                 (*The Wounds of Civil War,* 371–392)[11]

[*Stuk.*]   There shall no action passe my hand or sword,
That cannot make a step to gaine a crowne,
No word shall passe the office of my tong,
That sounds not of affection to a crowne,
No thought have being in my lordly brest,
That workes not everie waie to win a crowne,
Deeds, wordes and thoughts shall all be as a kings,
My chiefest companie shall be with kings,
And my deserts shall counterpoise a kings,
Why should not I then looke to be a king?
                 (*The Battle of Alcazar,* 494–503)[12]

Hubba.   Let come what wil, I meane to beare it out,
And either live with glorious victorie,
Or die with fame renowmed for chivalrie,
He is not worthie of the honie combe
That shuns the hives because the bees have stings,
That likes me best that is not got with ease,
Which thousand daungers do accompany,
For nothing can dismay our regall minde,
Which aimes at nothing but a golden crowne,
The only upshot of mine enterprises,
Were they inchanted in grimme *Plutos* court.
And kept for treasure mongst his hellish crue,

> I would either quell the triple *Cerberus*
> And all the armie of his hatefull hags,
> Or roll the stone with wretched *Sisiphon*.
>
> (*Locrine,* 1113–1127)[13]

Instead of responding to Marlowe's heterodoxy, the writers of these plays have simply neutralized it. In every instance the speaker asserts some connection between an aspiring mind that scorns the base respects of fortune and the title to rise and rule. But the assertions invariably rest on the vaguest appeals to personal glamor. The disjunction between the topics and the claims that are made on their behalf is most pronounced in the awkwardness of the first and third passages, which blatantly force the connection:

> Yes surely yes, my Fates have so decreed,
> That *Aragon* should be too base a thing . . .

> Deeds, wordes and thoughts shall all be as a kings
>
>   .   .   .   .   .
>
> Why should not I then looke to be a king?

Why indeed? So long as "Deeds, wordes and thoughts" remain the frailest of verbal gestures, the question can only be referred to the fates. Those who wish for a more closely documented portrayal of the martial spirit must content themselves with Scilla's boast that "men of baser metall and conceipt/Cannot conceive the beautie of my thought." The only picture of the aspiring mind in action is carefully insulated within a literary formula ("Even if the crown were in the midst of the most dreadful landscape, I would seek it out") which goes back to Tamburlaine's advice to his sons (*2 Tamb.*, I.iv.79–84) and reappears in the second and fourth passages quoted above. In *Tamburlaine,* just as later in *3 Henry VI,* when Richard proposes to hew his way to the crown "with a bloody axe" (III.iii.181),[14] the dreadful landscape is still familiar enough to convey a sharp sense of civil outrage; here the mythological apparatus only serves to distance the picture in such a way as to suspend social and political judgments while the hero proceeds with his hollow attempt to "move" the onlookers.

The effort to legitimize and redefine these crude materials ordinarily begins with a nominal distinction that appears to reverse Marlowe's original conception: the fate that fortune bestows on the man of arms, be it for good or ill, must follow the principle of hereditary succession. Greene's *Alphonsus,* which was produced immediately after the appearance of *1 Tamburlaine,* will serve to illustrate just how flimsy this convention could prove in practice. After the fashion of heroical romance, Greene's aspirant conqueror is designated the long-lost heir to the kingdom that he sets out to subdue, and so duly rises from the "baseness" of his station in act one to a position of sovereignty that suits his natural attributes. Thus, by an easy transition, Marlowe's glorification of "natural" worth has been given a new and conservative interpretation. The difficulty here is that the distinction between Alphonsus' legitimate aspirations and his sheer heroic ambition remains merely nominal. The hero still acts to display a "vertue" that is perceptible only in battle scenes.

The dependence of Greene's play on *1 Tamburlaine* will be evident from the barest outline of the plot.[15] The lowly Alphonsus (Tamburlaine) wins Albinius (Theridamas) to his side and then supports Belinus, King of Naples (Cosroe), in his unjust attack on Flaminius, King of Aragon (Mycetes); after the victory Alphonsus turns on Belinus, who flees to the Sultan Amurak (Bajazeth); Alphonsus defeats Amurak, falls in love with Amurak's daughter Iphigenia (Zenocrate), and spares the Sultan's life at her entreaties. Greene's innovation lay in designating Alphonsus "the sonne and heire to olde *Carinus*" (416), and, more generally, in recasting him as the disguised prince of the prose romance and romantic comedy that were his stock in trade. In itself, this conception is perfectly consistent with Elizabethan notions of heroic poetry. Puttenham, for example, conflates metrical romance with classical epic as kinds of "historicall poesie," and he offers *Bevys of Hampton* and *Guy of Warwick* as examples of early English epic.[16] But if this deference to the decorum of heroic romance gentles his condition, it hardly makes Alphonsus into a paragon of political rectitude. As he appropriates Tamburlaine's more sensational speeches, Alphonsus does not express the outlook of a prince regaining his hereditary birthright, but rather that of a martial superman in pursuit of limitless conquest. At the moment of decision, Greene rather awkwardly preserves his hero's virtue by having the Sultan strike first, but it is clear from Alphonsus' speech on this occasion that the playwright and his audience were scarcely enthusiastic about such a strategy. One can almost hear the reluctance with which Alphonsus proceeds from his lofty vaunt

> And nought is left for me but *Aragon?*
> Yes surely yes, my Fates have so decreed,
> That *Aragon* should be too base a thing,
> For to obtaine Alphonsus for her King,

to its contorted sequel:

> What heare you not how that our scattered foes,
> *Belinus, Fabius,* and the Millaine Duke,
> Are fled for succour to the Turkish Court?
> And thinke you not that *Amurack* their King,
> Will with the mightiest power of all his land,
> Seeke to revenge *Belinus* overthrow?

(816–825)

Other playwrights at least found less tortuous ways to indicate the importance of parentage. In *The Famous Victories of Henry V* and *Edward III,* the act of conquest is prefaced by "historical" genealogies which establish the right of the English king to the French crown. Absence of the right pedigree, on the other hand, accompanies the downfall of Humber in *Locrine,* Muly Mahammet and his followers in *The Battle of Alcazar,* Lluellen and Balliol in *Edward I,* Richard III in *The True Tragedy of Richard III,* and Canutus in *Edmond Ironsides.* Except for *The Wars of Cyrus* and *The Wounds of Civil War,* which are set in classical times, and *I Selimus,* which promises a sequel, all of these playwrights are careful to equate military superiority and titular legitimacy. But in spite of this superficial orthodoxy, most of them were hardly more successful than Greene at locating Marlowe's heroic prototype within a social medium where the pursuit of glory could receive firm ethical evaluations. Despite his new gentility, the successful conqueror still explains his triumphs by reference to an heroic temperament that regards social conventions as the servant, rather than the master, of the individual aspirant. His politics have shifted — ever so slightly — in the direction of Elizabethan orthodoxy, but the language and the landscape are still Marlowe's. Hence, whatever his genealogical rights may be, he will ordinarily insulate his "deeds" from the claims of patrimony and due succession. In *The Famous Victories,* Henry V conquers France because "nothing wil serve him but the Crowne" (985)[17] and flippantly explains to his defeated rival, "Why my good brother of France,/You have had it long inough" (1332–1333). Edward I admonishes the Welsh pretender Lluellen, not with quotations from the homilies, but with the injunction "knowest thou what I am,/How great, how famous, and how fortunate" (*Edward I,* 910–11).[18] It is not because he is the hereditary ruler that Locrine foresees victory for his army, but because he is "like the mightie god of warre/When armed with his coat of Adament," and he asks only that "Sweet fortune favour *Locrine* with a smile" (*Locrine,* 1225–1226; 1246). Although these are "legitimate" sovereigns chastising nominal "usurpers," everyone seems to share the premise that the relevant factors have to do with individual "worth"; or, failing that, with the inconstant ways of fortune.

It is certainly not Providence that oversees these ventures. The defeated do not even avail themselves of the customary opportunity to accept defeat as Heaven's will and sue for mercy.[19] For them, these plays are tragedies of ambition in a world where fortune inevitably betrays the aspirant conqueror in favor of a new pretender. Their cardinal sin is to permit themselves, by asserting their individual claims to worldly eminence, to become her fools. "Heere endeth Fortune, rule, and bitter rage," muses the dying Tom Stukeley, echoing the Presenter's sad reflection, "Ay me, that kingdomes may not stable stand" (*The Battle of Alcazar, 1503; 1287*). Lluellen reads his defeat not in the ways of Providence or the dictates of social order, but in the "soror aspects" of "the dreadful Planets" (*Edward I,* 2351). The hero of *The True Tragedy of Richard III* (who comes to see that more than chance is involved in his own downfall) succinctly expresses their common point of view: "Yet faint not man, for this day if Fortune will, shall make thee King possest with quiet Crown, if Fates deny, this ground must be my grave, yet golden thoughts that reached for a Crowne, danted before by Fortunes cruell spight, are come as comforts to my drooping heart, and bids me keepe my Crowne and die a King" (1993–1998).[20] These "usurpers" rarely discern a moral lesson in fortune's cooperation with the claims of parentage. They only perceive that fortune will always desert aspirant *virtù* in the end. And the conquerors, despite their preferred hereditary status, have no larger vision of order with which to oppose this anarchic interpretation of the heroic life — for they exist in a world that is still largely innocent of politics and history. Essentially, their personal ideals continue to revolve around the assertion of sheer *virtù*. Thus the dramatist's conception of heroic worth is usually irrelevant — or, indeed, opposed — to the hierarchical legal formula which furnishes the initial basis for political judgments.

In general, the playwright who sought to place his hero's right to conquest on a more concrete ethical basis could look to two broad traditions which are generally — though not always — distinguishable from one another. One might be represented by Caxton's translation of the *Order of Chivalry,* the other by Elyot's *Book Named the Governor.* The first of these choices was more immediately accessible, because it had roots in the heroical romance, and because it reflected Marlowe's emphasis on the splendor of martial achievement. Moreover, such prototypes of humanist biography as Tito Livio's *Vita Henrici Quinti* and Hall's *Union* are themselves saturated with chivalric idealism. (Even Chapman's Homer has its knights and squires and "surcuidrie." [21]) *The Wars of Cyrus,* performed at the Blackfriars playhouse, is the only history play outside of the academic stage that evaluates its hero from Ciceronian notions of "good government." Such peaceable virtues as compassion, continence, and prudence are, it is true, occasionally used to civilize the heroes of popular histories. Exchanges with women, for example, will exemplify the propriety of tempering valor with compassion (Alphonsus and Iphigenia), the necessity of bridling unmanly lust (Cyrus and Panthea, Edward III and the Countess of Salisbury), and the prudence needed to counteract feminine treachery (Edward I and Eleanor of Castile, Talbot and the Countess of Auvergne). But none of these characters — not even Cyrus — exhibits much interest in the governance of an orderly political hierarchy.

The redefinition of heroic greatness in terms of chivalric honor represents the more conspicuous line of development. The almost automatic association of the English past with chivalric virtues came naturally enough with the Tudor revival of the Arthurian genealogies and legends.[22] It appears as an undernourished cliché in *The Famous Victories of Henry V, Edward I,* and *Edmond Ironside,* where the hero is conceived as a chivalric example, but only in a loose, incidental way. *Edmond Ironside,* which takes place in the early days of "new Troy," pictures "how the English Lords Contend/Whoe should exell in feates of Chivaldry" (941–942);[23] and in *The Famous Victories* Henry V proudly asserts that "the French king shall never surpasse me in/Curtesie, whiles I am *Harry* King of England" (1272–1273). But neither of these plays has much to say about the ethical attributes of "Chivaldry" or "Curtesie." A more peculiar instance is found in *Edward I,* where the Welsh rebel Lluellen asserts his own local heroic tradition in a few loose allusions: "Follow Lluellen . . . /Sprong from the loines of great *Cadwallader,*/Discended from the loines of *Troian Brute*" (299–301). Here the playwright's chivalric romanticism is so indiscriminate as actually to blur his elementary distinction between sovereign and rebel.

Edward III represents a far more sophisticated attempt to project a version of heroic honor based on feudal custom and medieval chivalry. Like *I Henry VI* and *Henry V,* the play is largely occupied with an exposition of two approaches to the conduct of war. The French king hires powerful allies (III.i.49–50), offers a bribe to his foe (III.iii.63–71), urges his son to break his oath (IV.v.80–91), and regards the English with shallow contempt (III.iii.46–65) and slanderous innuendo (III.iii.155–57).[24] The English observe a solemn chivalric ideal that is rooted in "ancient custom" (III.iii.174) and dedicated to the glory of God, the service of "the fatherles and poore," and the "benefite of Englands peace" (III.iii.212–215). Before death, the participants display an unshakable *contemptus mundi,* secure in their belief that "to live is but to seeke to die,/And dying but beginning of new life" (IV.iv.158–59). As a result, Edward's ambition is placed in a recognizable framework of "English" values. In the first two acts he must overcome the sway of his personal affections, so as to join in the "Marshall harmonie" (II.ii.211) of the last three. His participation in a traditional fellowship of arms is fully articulated through the recurrent public ceremonies of the play, most notably in the investiture of his son, the

Black Prince (III.iii.179–218). And in the aftermath of battle, the public rituals of chivalric courtesy enable its votaries to look beyond the accidents of fortune into the realm of a noble memory. Audley's last request is typical:

> Good friends, convey me to the princely Edward,
> That in the crimson braverie of my bloud
> I may become him with saluting him.
> Ile smile, and tell him, that this open scarre
> Doth end the harvest of his Audleys warre.
>
> (IV.viii.6–10)

In *Edward III*, then, the requisites of chivalric worth are enlarged beyond the narrow confines of current patriotism to include the hero's responsibility to a public tradition of spiritual values. Nevertheless, the relevance of this heroic ideal to the central action of the play remains unclear. What is the nature of Edward's "right" to France? One often gets the impression that Edward's aggression is warranted by his austere code of arms instead of the hereditary claims of his family name. The implicit fallacy here is succinctly, and unwittingly, formulated in *Edmond Ironside* when Edmond accuses Canutus of seeking to suborn his kingdom "by treason not by force of valliant arms" (1825), as if "valliant arms" would somehow preclude the possibility of "treason." The refrain of Edward's investiture ceremony, "Fight and be valiant, conquere where thou comst!" (III.iii.184) evokes the same priorities. Deeds of renown are still admired without much regard to their underlying political implications. Prince Edward's description of his victory as "An argument that heaven aides the right" (IV.ix.11) is, therefore, still a facile homiletic postscript to an artful heroic play, since by "right" he presumably means "legitimate heir": for this idea of political "right" remains little more than a genealogical legalism. Nowhere in the play is it seen as vitally connected with Edward's responsibility to chivalric tradition. Even when the playwright has Edward assert that he is fighting to "approve faire Issabells discent" (I.i.47), the connection between the family name and the national one sounds clumsy and forced:

> *King.* This counsayle, Artoyes, like to fruictfull shewers,
> Hath added growth unto my dignitye;
> And, by the fiery vigor of thy words,
> Hot courage is engendred in my brest,
> Which heretofore was rakt in ignorance,
> But nowe doth mount with golden winges of fame,
> And will approve faire Issabells discent,
> Able to yoak their stubburne necks with steele,
> That spurne against my sovereignety in France.
>
> (I.i.42–50)

Edward's chivalry is still too purely a matter of personal "dignitye" to be seen as part of a thoroughgoing commitment to a concrete vision of social and political order.

While the order of composition remains uncertain, the artistic sequel to *Edward III* is *1 Henry VI*, the first four acts of which hinge on an extended *comparatio* between English chivalry, as it is represented by Talbot, Bedford, and Salisbury, and the mock-heroic pretensions of Joan la Pucelle and the French peers. Shakespeare enlarges the central political issue beyond the narrow problem of hereditary legitimacy, and he sees more in heroic worth than a personal fidelity to knightly ideals, although that is included. The right of the English in France is given an historical basis rather than an exclusively genealogical one (now it is the French who revolt against the status quo), and the emphasis is placed on those attributes that reveal why the English have traditionally been rulers of the French. Although Talbot does fight to maintain his personal honor, that honor is systematically contrasted to the wholesale disregard for feudal convention that characterizes the French "revolt."

The revolt is framed, at the outset of the play, within the cosmic disorders occasioned by the "bad revolting stars,/That have consented unto Henry's death" (I.i.4–5). Within this context, French infamy goes far beyond the chivalric bad manners of *Edward III*. Their campaign depends upon an unnatural alliance with a "base" pretender to nobility, and all of their victories are won through treachery and deceit (the treachery of York and Somerset in the final instance). Joan la Pucelle poses as a patriot, but she is essentially a spokesman for the anarchic tergiversations of social "revolt" in all its forms. She congratulates her new ally Burgundy with the encomium, "Done like a Frenchman! [*Aside*] — turn and turn again" (III.iii.85), when he returns to the fold; so Charles congratulates her, "Thy promises are like Adonis' gardens,/That one day bloom'd, and fruitful were the next" (I.vi.6–7). She is the appropriate "saint" for a cause where princes "buckle" with a shepherd's daughter, and nobility has to contend with casual snipers. Appropriately, her fall does not come about as the caprice of fortune, but rather as the grave consequence of the public trial scene that leads to her execution. "Prick'd on by public wrongs sustain'd in France" (III.ii.78), Talbot opposes his heroic worth to her treacherous stratagems at Orleans and Rouen. In these two battles he makes redress for the shameful deaths of Salisbury and Bedford, the other two representatives of Henry V's vanished order, and recovers for chivalry what was lost to treachery. His general commitment to a public ideal of aristocratic service is exemplified by his act of fealty "with submissive loyalty of heart" (III.iv. 10) before King Henry at Paris. If he fights, like Edward III, for the honor of his family name, there is now a considerable attempt to portray the entire complex of aristocratic values which support that idea. The most important scenes here are those which lead to the death of Old and Young Talbot. It is in those debates about whether the son should flee and continue the family line, or stay and perpetuate their name by dying for it, that the high priority placed on a noble lineage at last emerges into full literary consciousness. His death, finally, is portrayed not as the triumph of fortune over mere humanity, but rather as the achievement of fame within a celestial order.

Shakespeare's initial achievement in the *Henry VI* plays, then, lay in preserving the theatrically viable stage business and rhetoric of heroical-historical drama while placing it in a richer context of ethical and political values. Nashe's remarks about Talbot's theatrical popularity indicate clearly enough that he was the admirable English warrior *par excellence*. At the same time, Talbot justifies Nashe's remarks about the didactic value of this kind of drama by demonstrating how the attributes of martial greatness define themselves in acts of ethical and political rectitude. Moreover, Shakespeare effectively sets off Talbot's special virtues by contrasting him to characters who indicate how the heroic nature becomes corrupted from within. For the miscreants of this play are not simply the morality abstractions that criticism so frequently takes them to be. Joan la Pucelle and the Dauphin, Richard Duke of York and Suffolk, are endowed with all the theatrical and rhetorical resources of heroical-historical drama to indicate what is glamorous about them. Yet the very language in which they express themselves is so distorted and exaggerated as to indicate what is fatally limited about their brave postures. The bawdy *doubles entendres* of "holy Joan," the Dauphin's uncontrolled paganism, and Suffolk's courtly effeminacy all suggest how such distortions of heroic language furnish an initial basis for ethical judgments. The "ill successe" of these characters is not a facile homiletic postscript to a glittering career; it is the predictable outcome of their limited view of life. In sum, *1 Henry VI* succeeds in doing what other imitations of *Tamburlaine* had tentatively essayed. It presents a complex image of personal worth that continuously recalls the social meaning of heroic greatness.

The format of the revenge play provided an opportunity to explore the waste of ambition unchecked by family pieties. As heroic violence — again taking its cue from *Tamburlaine* — wears the face of intemperate greed and wanton murder, the conqueror becomes a negative ethical example; and he is fittingly destroyed by the aggrieved kin of his victims. Playwrights who cultivated this image of domestic violence were following a course that was roughly opposite to the one set forth by *Edward III*: they emphasized the hero's systematic violation of social custom and value. The one act which completely identified public and personal impiety was the murder committed to secure an inheritance; for the purely social functions of the Tudor family were hardly less important than its potentialities for sustaining ties of love and affection. As a recent historian has observed, it was "an institution for the passing on of life, name, and property" that was supported by "law, custom, and convenience." [25] Contemporaries must have found Tamburlaine's repudiation of primogeniture, made final by the murder of his eldest son, among the most shocking of his outrages. In the later plays, it is just such violations of familial bonds that most often identify the protagonist as an outlaw. The worst villains are those who, like Edmund, will "if not by birth, have lands by wit," and so initiate an action wherein "the base/Shall top th' legitimate" (*King Lear,* I.ii. 199; 20–21).

The logic by which these premises were set within the contexts of heroic drama is succinctly conveyed by Gentillet's refutation of Machiavelli's maxim that a prince ought "to imitate Caesar Borgia the sonne of Pope Alexander the sixt": where personal power is unchastened by ethical reason it will ultimately be destroyed in a fury of public revenge and civil wars.[26] Gentillet's anthology of miscreants (such as "Alphonsus, a bastard of the house of *Arragon,* who was marvellous cruell") generally adheres to this pattern. Almost invariably he recurs to the commonplace notion that the tyrant dies, having "by his crueltie . . . procured the hatred of his subjects, the wrath of God, and the enmitie of all the world." [27] The revenger, linking personal sentiment to public demands, is the dramatic figure who can represent all of these outraged parties, and his own family's honor besides, by destroying the offender. The "public" dimension of this conception is epitomized in the last act of *Richard III,* where the souls of all Richard's victims visit Richmond's tent and assure him of success. In most cases, however, the apparatus of the revenge play simply provides a rather superficial camouflage for a substratum of alarms and excursions. As Fredson Bowers remarks of *The Battle of Alcazar,* the primary interest still lies in "bickerings, consultations, plan, and battles." [28] The most unnatural villains continue to solicit admiration for their courage and resolve; and the revenger continues to act on behalf of his private code of honor.

This reduction of martial violence to unnatural and luridly glamorous displays of domestic violence is given unmistakable emphasis in several of the plays that were cited in the introductory chapter. The protagonist of *1 Selimus,* as the title page explains, "most unnaturally raised warres against his owne father *Bajazet,* and prevailing therein, in the end caused him to be poysoned. Also with the murthering of his two brethren, *Corcut* and *Acomat.*" [29] *The Battle of Alcazar* begins with the atrocities prescribed in this stage direction: "Enter the Moore and two murdrers bringing in his unkle Abdelmunen, then they draw the curtains and smoother the yong princes in the bed. Which done, in sight of the unkle they strangle him in his chaire, and then goe forth" (36–39). The uxorious Locrine degenerates to "filthie crime" (*Locrine, 1928*), violates his promise to his father Brutus, banishes his wife, and brings about his uncle's death. The murder of the princes in *The True Tragedy of Richard III* and the ambiguous death of Arthur in *The Troublesome Reign of King John* carry this theme of unnatural cruelty into the English chronicle play.

Allowing for the element of sheer sensationalism involved, it seems clear that these distortions of heroic violence were meant to set an absolute limit to the reach of personal ambition. But in most of these plays the judgment is left rather vague. Rarely does the playwright's emphasis on the protagonist's personal cruelty become part of any steady criticism of personal ambition in social or political terms. As in *The Famous Victories, Edmond Ironside,* and *Edward I,* there is no soil where the new character role can take root and grow into full ethical consciousness: the settings are still too fabulous and remote. The retribution exacted by the revenger may suggest that a kind of rough justice has been done; but the familiar cry of "O fickle fortune, O unstable world" (*Locrine*, V.iv.116) frequently tends to undercut such an inference. In *Selimus* and *The Wounds of Civil War* the playwright's manifest admiration of heroic *virtù* sits uneasily with his repudiation of excessive violence. This ambivalence is even more exposed in *The Battle of Alcazar,* where one must distinguish between the "honorable" misadventures of Don Sebastian and Captain Stukeley, and the "criminal" revolt of their ally Muly Mahammet.

The True Tragedy of Richard III is more consistently organized around the idea of heroic worth perverted into domestic violence. The central figure is immediately recognizable as a variation on the Marlovian prototype. He begins by asserting, "To be baser than a king I disdain" (364), and at the last his page describes him as "worthie Richard that did never flie, but followed honour to the gates of death" (2026–2027). As we might expect, he is also the "bloodie murderer" (1748) of his innocent nephews, and the anonymous playwright gives an extensive, lurid emphasis to this aspect of his character. The title page advertises "the smothering of the two yoong Princes in the Tower," and shortly we hear Richard asking, "Why what are the babes but a puffe of Gun-pouder?" (376–377). His last project has a vividness of detail that is hardly matched by Seneca at his most grotesque: "and this, I this verie day, I hope with this lame hand of mine, to rake out that hatefull heart of Richmond, and when I have it, to eate it panting hote with salt, and drinke his blood luke warme" (1977–1980). This documentation of the hero's cruelty is, however, effectively complemented by an account, at once Senecan[30] and Christian, of the inner torment he is undergoing. His page pictures him as "Hidious to behold" (1774) in his anxiety, and Richard himself gives an elaborate account of "The hell of life that hangs upon the Crowne" (1874–1914). Richard's soliloquy beginning at line 1398 places this anguish securely within the traditional framework of Christian eschatology:

> The goale is got, and golden Crowne is wonne,
> And well deservest thou to weare the same,
> That ventured hast thy bodie and thy soule,
> But what bootes Richard, now the Diademe
> Or kingdome got, by murther of his friends,
> My fearefull shadow that still followes me,
> Hath sommond me before the severe judge,
> My conscience witnesse of the blood I spilt,
> Accuseth me as guiltie of the fact,
> The fact, a damned judgement craves,
> Whereas impartiall justice hath condemned.
> Meethinkes the Crowne which I before did weare,
> Inchast with Pearle and costly Diamonds,
> Is turned now into a fatall wreathe,
> Of fiery flames and ever burning starres . . .
>
> .   .   .   .   .
>
> Appeale for mercy to thy righteous God,
> Ha repent, not I, crave mercy they that list.
>
> (1398–1412; 1418–1419)

This picture of a sinner confronting his own afterlife introduces a stringency of moral judgment that is unexampled in the plays so far discussed. As Willard Farnham remarks, *The True Tragedy* "combines the cruel aspiring force of a Tamburlaine or a Machiavellian villain with the capacity of a Dr. Faustus for conscience-stricken introspection." [31] At its best, in other words, the play moves outside the ordinary conventions of the history, and into those which govern the morality drama and the final soliloquies of Faustus, Shakespeare's Richard III, and Macbeth. If only for a moment, the hero sees beyond human history into eternity and discovers that he must measure the sweet fruition of an earthly crown against the Christian absolutes of sin and damnation. "The fact," as Richard says, "a damned judgement craves."

In the present line of analysis, however, it craves an earthly judgment as well, one that arrives at some appraisal of Richard's action in "the ethicke and politick consideration." By this light the anonymous playwright comes off rather less well. The ethical crux in *The True Tragedy* is essentially that of *Edward III*, and, however remotely, of almost all the popular histories. Richard formulates it in his first soliloquy, when he asks "Shall law bridle nature, or authority hinder inheritance?" (353). The author of *Edward III* deals with the problem by connecting the superior "nature" of his hero with the "law" of chivalric tradition, and then permitting him to claim what genealogy shows to be his birthright. Conversely, *The True Tragedy* emphasizes the intrinsic futility of a "natural" valor that does not observe the divine law against domestic murder; and since Richard's violations of that law are shown to be his only means of rising in the world, his fall embodies a genuine criticism of individual prowess that prospers without regard for moral rectitude. Nevertheless, divine law operates here only as a special prohibition, one that is hardly ever connected with ordinary social and political beliefs (as it is in, say, *Macbeth*). As a result, the dramatist seems often to accept uncritically Richard's equation of personal ambition with the pursuit of honor.[32] If Richard falls at last, it is because in his backstairs violence he makes too many enemies and falls into sin, thereby arousing the conventional retributions of revenge tragedy and Christian damnation. But there is virtually no attempt to link his personal ambition with a recognizable set of political attitudes. Certainly his heroic stance remains too idealistic for him to be a confirmed Machiavel; and there is no character who can give us a mature view of the ways in which personal honor and political ambition are inconsistent with each other. What does obtrude, in occasional flashes, is the tragic dilemma of a confirmed criminal wrestling with his remorseful conscience. Outside of such moments, Richard's motto is: "Valor brings fame, and fame conqueres death" (398); and at the last, instead of recognizing his sin, he rails on "Fortunes cruell spight" (1996). His atrocities are a by-product of his heroic ambition; but they remain, in the end, too incidental, alongside the admirable quest for personal honor, to be seen as a real aggression on the ethical conventions of a recognizable society.

Shakespeare's Richard III, throughout the last two plays of the trilogy, best demonstrates how the idea of unnatural violence and cruelty could be organized to control the materials of heroic drama. From the outset "Dicky . . . that/Was wont to cheer his dad in mutinies" (3 Henry VI, I.iv.76–77) takes an undue relish in deeds of violence. "Priests pray for enemies, but soldiers kill" (2 Henry VI, V.ii.71) he tells his father at the close of the second play, and in the first act of the third he remarks of himself:

> I cannot rest
> Until the white rose that I wear be dy'd
> Even in the lukewarm blood of Henry's heart.
>
> (I.ii.32–34)

From these beginnings, Shakespeare's conception of the Elizabethan tyrant *par excellence* gradually emerges. Sir Thomas More, whose account is reprinted by Hall and Holinshed, characterizes Richard as "dispitious and cruell, not for evill will alway, but ofter for ambicion." [33] In Shakespeare's characterization, his "evill will" becomes the very source of his highest ambitions, as Richard himself makes clear in the three expositions of his "deformity" respecting normal human relationships (3 Henry VI, III.ii.124–95 and V.vi.67–93; Richard III, I.i.1–27). He presents himself as the very pattern of anarchy:

> Then, since this earth affords no joy to me
> But to command, to check, to o'erbear such
> As are of *better person than myself,*
> I'll make my heaven to dream upon the crown . . .
>
> (3 Henry VI, II.ii.165–168; my italics)

The sentiment is familar from *Tamburlaine,* but the motive — envy — is new. There is no admixture of heroic honor in Richard's ambition. His aspirations express his natural deformity rather than his natural

virtue, and his final self-characterization dispenses entirely with the flippant, Marlovian veneer:

> I that have neither pity, love, nor fear.
> Indeed 'tis true that Henry told me of:
> For I have often heard my mother say
> I came into the world with my legs forward.
> Had I not reason, think ye, to make haste
> And seek their ruin that usurp'd our right?
> The midwife wonder'd, and the women cried
> 'O Jesu bless us, he is born with teeth!'
> And so I was, which plainly signified
> That I should snarl, and bite, and play the dog.
> Then, since the heavens have shap'd my body so,
> Let hell make crook'd my mind to answer it.
> I have no brother, I am like no brother;
> And this word 'love,' which greybeards call divine,
> Be resident in men like one another,
> And not in me: I am myself alone.
>
> (*3 Henry VI,* V.vi.68–83)

If the speech still portrays the familiar bogeyman of stage and legend,
the strategy of the entire play is to place the figure in a landscape that
fully illuminates his destructive potentiality. Through the scenes that
lead up to the murder of York and young Rutland, it becomes clear
that politics have been reduced to a ruthless logic of outrage and
revenge: the very concepts of king and prince and peer have ceased to
matter. By the same token, in the aftermath of those ritual slaughters,
the surviving Yorkists discover that "brother" has ceased to matter also.
Hence, the total collapse into that anarchy where the son kills his own
father, the father his own son, becomes, as it were, Shakespeare's
metaphor for civil war in all its manifestations. Richard appears, finally,
less as a quirk of "dissembling nature" and more as a choric spokesman
for the loss of those communal pieties that make social and political life
possible at all.

To describe the character in these terms is, of course, to insist that
3 Henry VI not only completes but also moves well beyond the local

dramatic tradition from which it arises. Like his father York and Sir John Talbot, Richard is in part the result of Shakespeare's continuing allusion to Marlowe, and in part the unique product of the vast historical trilogy that the next chapter will proceed to consider.

If Talbot and Richard represent two extremes of heroical characterization within *Henry VI,* the achievement of the entire cycle is to delineate the gradations by which one side of the polarity, the epitome of true chivalry, devolves into its opposite, the "rag of honor" (*Richard III,* I.iii.132).[34] Here again, of course, the total process of development points towards a more historical kind of drama. Within the expanded contexts afforded by the three-part cycle, Shakespeare places each variation in its appropriate social medium: the fields of France with their last vestiges of medieval chivalry; the English court, with its peculiar blend of gentility and intrigue; and finally the open arenas of civil war, Towton and Wakefield, presided over by the revenger and the Machiavel.

4   The Hero in History:
A Reading of *Henry VI*

"What at present I have chiefly in view is, to account for the visible *inequality* in these pieces." [1] Such is the problem that Edmund Malone, one of the first and most perceptive critics of *Henry VI*, bequeathed to later students of the trilogy. Malone was especially struck by a manifest unevenness in "the diction, the figures, or rather the allusions, and the versification" of *1 Henry VI*,[2] which seemed to vacillate aimlessly among the rhetorical clichés of Kyd, Marlowe, Peele, and Greene. Relying for the most part on stylistic criteria, he argued that all three plays were originally the work of Shakespeare's immediate predecessors, slightly revised by him in the case of *2* and *3 Henry VI* as part of his "apprenticeship" to the university playwrights. If Malone's theory proved persuasive it was because, as he perceived, the "visible inequalities" in these plays extend well beyond considerations of rhetoric and versification. The playwright frequently seems concerned merely to translate those chronicle materials that had become crystallized in popular legend into rough theatrical equivalents, without attending to continuities of plot or theme. The *de casibus* tragedies of Talbot, Humphrey, Duke of Gloucester, Richard, Duke of York, and King Henry VI do suggest a didactic chain of events linking the entire trilogy; but within the individual plays these events are encased in a diversity of materials drawn from popular comedy, Senecan tragedy, and Marlovian conqueror drama that hardly seem relevant to the lessons of tragedy in the tradition of *A Mirror for Magistrates*. Hence, it was only natural for those who shared Malone's critical standards to grow sceptical about the authorship of the "extraneous" episodes, while occasionally detecting the hand of Shakespeare at a culminating moment in each "tragedy" — notably the remorseful end of Humphrey's murderer, Winchester (2 *Henry VI, III.iii*), and the ghastly revenge of Margaret and Young Clifford upon York (*3 Henry VI, I.iv*).

The modern effort to contravene Malone's reasoning and establish Shakespeare's full responsibility for the trilogy has proceeded on two fronts. First of all, Peter Alexander's classic study of the text, along with Madeleine Doran's, overturned Malone's hypothesis that 2 and 3 *Henry VI* represent Shakespeare's selective revision of *The Contention between the Two Famous Houses of York and Lancaster* and *The True Tragedy of Richard Duke of York*. It is now generally agreed that these are memorial reconstructions of 2 and 3 *Henry VI*.[3] Alexander's theory does not, to be sure, rule out the possibility that *Henry VI,* or some part of it, is itself the product of several playwrights working in collaboration. But it does put the burden of proof back on those who would deny the attribution of Heminge and Condell. There can be no doubt that all three plays are derivative in style and fragmented in structure to a degree that is unparalleled even in such very early works as *The Two Gentlemen of Verona* and *Titus Andronicus.* On the other hand, it is not unusual for a major poet at an early age to be relatively expert in one form and the merest apprentice in another. What is unusual is for his earliest attempts at one of the more demanding genres to be preserved for the scrutiny of later readers. No one would imagine that Keats, and not Leigh Hunt, had written *Endymion* if there were only the mature works of each poet to judge by; and yet that most uneven and derivative of poems was published within a year of Keats' most fertile period. Such an analogy may not throw any light on the authorship of *Henry VI,* but it may cast some doubt on the dubious Coleridgean practice of setting the most baldly imitative verse in the trilogy before the judicious "ear" and concluding that Shakespeare could not possibly have been responsible for such stuff. He could have.

Malone's more telling point that the "visible inequalities" of *Henry VI* suggest mutiple authorship — has been met by a redefinition of its genre. When they are read as "histories" rather than as overgrown tragedies, these plays may be said to fulfil a set of formal requirements that Malone never envisioned: each episode is didactically purposeful, enacting its own particular "lesson" about politics and ethics; and the sequence of episodes provides us not with a conventional plot based on historical materials, but rather with a continuous commentary on an irreducible set of historical facts. Where nineteenth-century critics, following A. W. Schlegel, tended to beg the question of genre by describing all ten histories as a national epic,[4] recent studies have persuasively argued that they are exemplary and episodic in their design, didactic in their intentions, and far more concerned with achieving an effective unity of statement than with approximating the format of tragedy, comedy, or epic.[5] It would be pointless to quarrel with the rightness of such an approach to Shakespeare's histories. The earlier parts of this book have rather endeavored to supplement it by surveying the theatrical and rhetorical traditions from which Shakespeare's notions of exemplary history would have been derived. As a result of that survey, however, certain limitations in the approach to *Henry VI* taken by most recent studies will perhaps suggest themselves. Most importantly, the modern reinterpretation of the histories, as represented by Tillyard's study, has tended to limit its access to the plays by focusing its attention on the official ideology of the Tudor state, while largely ignoring those materials that do not translate readily into homiletic patterns of sin and retribution.

The difficulty with such an orientation becomes apparent as soon as one recurs to the problem of style: for it is still impossible to account for the diverse rhetorical and theatrical gestures that presumably support whatever lessons the dramatist intended to convey. To take only the most conspicuous examples, consider the encounter of Talbot and the Countess of Auvergne (*1 Henry VI*, II.iii) or Suffolk's farewell to Margaret (*2 Henry VI*, III.ii). Can one confidently agree with Tillyard that both scenes are "pieces of sensation that pleased the people but could be spared from the play"?[6] (Professor Sprague notes that they still please the people.)[7] Or, worse yet, must they be construed in some deviously abstract sense that seems in keeping with the "theme of general disorder and chaos"?[8] Even leaving such isolated scenes out of the account, can the formalism and allusiveness of Shakespeare's rhetoric, and the pageantry of his staging, continue to be regarded as if they were, in the main, ornamental, and in any event essentially irrelevant to his primary intentions?[9] Any conception of genre that is formulated at the expense of so many particulars must surely be open to some qualification. The traditions of exemplary history and heroic drama dealt with in the preceding chapters will, I hope, furnish a basis for supplementing the rather doctrinaire conception of the Shakespearian history play that is still fashionable. For within the homiletic contexts provided by the choric pronouncements and the political moralizing, there are the oratorical forms of praise, lament, and self-assertion, and the set *topoi* of personal worth that were the common currency of heroical-historical drama. To attend to this rhetoric is to acknowledge that the succession of characters so defined act from a sense of personal or family honor which loses much of its meaning when it is reduced to a lowest common denominator of rebellion or loyalty. Even when Shakespeare deals in ethical stereotypes, they are liable to carry meanings that cannot be easily paraphrased. This is not to say that the ethical values exemplified and debated by his heroic aristocrats are in any final sense more important than those invoked by such choric figures as Exeter, Alexander Iden, or the nameless Father and Son; but it is to insist that they are central to Shakespeare's reconstruction of history, and must be included in any conception of the history play that would come to terms with Malone's observations on the language of *Henry VI.*

The question of style is crucial because it is through allusion that Shakespeare recreates, and revalues, the conceptions of character that had come down from *Tamburlaine* and its progeny. The working assumption here is that when Shakespeare alludes to Marlowe he usually does so for a specific reason, and not simply to fill out the page. In examining his recreation of the character roles surveyed in the first and third chapters, I shall endeavor to see where those roles fit into his continuous reconstruction of Henry's reign, and why he so often found it appropriate to make those little adjustments that suggest parody or deliberate exaggeration. Shakespeare's extraordinary freedom in manipulating these styles and the roles that they support follows from his grounding in the tradition of humanist history described in chapter 2; and I shall, for the most part, be more concerned with what he made of that tradition than with his occasional deference to the workings of Providence.

Henry VI is designed to disclose a set of exemplary truths drawn from the playwright's reading of fifteenth-century English history. There is little basis, however, for supposing that these truths will always conform to orthodox Tudor doctrine, and still less to indicate that they point to a stable, didactic allegory of "moral history" underwritten by a providential guidance.[10] One may begin simply by postulating that the trilogy encompasses Shakespeare's presentation of the "agents" that gave the reign of Henry VI its distinctive contours. Like any good humanist historian, he is concerned to produce moral judgments, but these will involve a wide spectrum of ethical standards. As a humanist discipline, exemplary history was an extremely broad and flexible instrument for interpreting the past. The working assumption is that any historical narrative will yield "lessons" of all sorts. And any rhetorical recension of history — such as the *Apophtegmata, Cambises,* or *The Troublesome Reign of King John* — may include a good deal of edifying material that is only obliquely relevant to the "lives" of its central characters. In reading this kind of literature, then, one must be modest in his demands for continuity and plot while remaining attentive to those small constellations of exemplary episodes that emerge in every play. More particularly, it should be stressed at the outset that in no one of these plays — to say nothing of the entire trilogy — is there some unifying idea that will enable the reader to place every episode (except the "extraneous" ones) in its proper context.

With this caveat in mind, I shall pursue through all three plays Shakespeare's treatment of one very general theme: the gradual deterioration of heroic idealism between the Hundred Years' War and the Yorkist accession. Not that this interpretation of his chronicle sources was necessarily in Shakespeare's mind from the start; but it does provide the most thorough account of his historical judgments about the reign of Henry VI. The problem is introduced in the funeral oration that begins the trilogy, with its simple and unequivocal claims for Henry V's personal stature:

> [*Bed.*] Henry the Fifth, too famous to live long!
>   England ne'er lost a king of so much worth.
> *Glou.* England ne'er had a king until his time.

> Virtue he had, deserving to command:
>
> .   .   .   .   .
>
> What should I say? His deeds exceed all speech:
> He ne'er lift up his hand but conquered.
>
> (*1 Henry VI,* I.i.6–9; 15–16)

This choric address is, of course, merely a tissue of rhetorical clichés, but that is entirely suitable, given its function. It asks the audience to recall a "pattern" of heroic perfection so pure as to excite the enmity of the "bad revolting stars" and the "dishonorable" aggressions of Death. If the idea, as well as the pageantry, the astrology, and the verbal sonorities in which it is draped, all suggest the ambience of *2 Tamburlaine,* the resemblance is not entirely fortuitous. For Shakespeare's plays embody a kind of sequel to Marlowe's, an assessment of the chaos that ensues when the weakling son succeeds the all-conquering father. That earlier ideal is glimpsed only through its disintegration, a process that begins with the demise of Henry's great lieutenants, Bedford, Salisbury, and Talbot. These three chevaliers must encounter obstacles unthought of in Marlowe's stately tent of war: a master-gunner's boy adept in the art of secret ambush, a shrewd "witch" who conquers "by fear, not force, like Hannibal" (*1 Henry VI,* I.v.21), and a critical "want of men and money" (I.i.69) that is aggravated by domestic factions. Like their illustrious forebear, they are "too famous to live long," and Talbot's last words, "commendable prov'd, let's die in pride" (IV. vi.57), acknowledge that their aspirations too can be realized only in an eternity of heroic fame. The first generation of Lancastrians and Yorkists provides the invidious contrast to their idealism. Motivated by a far more narrow and courtly sense of ancestral honor and rank, they are unsympathetic to Talbot's vision of the heroic life, but their shortcomings are nevertheless measured against that ideal. In *2 Henry VI* aristocratic *hauteur* generates the unseemly contention for the ensigns of courtly status and privilege that is epitomized by York's Machiavellian plotting and Suffolk's effort, through his covert attachment to Margaret, to manipulate Henry. At the conclusion of *2 Henry VI* and in the opening acts of *3 Henry VI* Young Clifford and York's son Richard finally reduce the incentives of personal and family honor to the naked and uncontrolled lust for blood revenge that is symbolized by the slaughter of the helpless infants Rutland and Prince Henry. Beyond these barbarities lies the remainder of *3 Henry VI,* in which even the network of loyalties sustained by family ties is so fragmented and exploited as to leave the last word with the Machiavellian Duke of Gloucester: "I am myself alone" (*3 Henry VI,* V.vi.83).

These aspects of the trilogy are isolated for study primarily because they suggest an extended rhetorical and dramatic focus for the playwright's episodic reconstruction of Hall. We shall, in other words, be able to deal with a significant number of episodes, from all three plays, that illuminate a problem central to the playwright's imagination of history; and we shall be able to deal with them in specific terms, asking specific questions about the function of their rhetoric and staging. Much of the comedy in these plays can, for example, be treated as a series of experiments in mock-heroic, and more narrowly, as parodies of the special poetic idiom of *Tamburlaine.* Conversely, the moments of high achievement often depend on less obtrusive imitations of the "mighty line." The special meanings that such echoes will carry usually depends on the historical contexts that contain them. Hence the discussions of each play begin with an account of its social and political bearings and then proceed to consider its important literary designs. The recurring "lesson" here is simple enough in its bare outlines, but rather devious and complicated in its implications. In effect these plays keep saying that the received ideals of heroic greatness may be admirable in themselves, but they invariably decay, engender destructive violence and deadly rivalries, and, in the process, make chaos out of history. They lead to anarchy because the notions of "honor" that regulate the heroic life can never be securely realized within any stable, historical form of national life. The problem disappears only in some mythical past, when the feudal subordination of the noble to his king is united with the martial subordination of the lieutenant to his commander. This situation can be imagined of the French wars conducted by Edward III and Henry V, or of the Crusades of still an earlier generation; but it can never be realized in the present.

The trilogy is at once an embodiment and a criticism of the literary traditions that I have been describing. If one simply considers the rhetorical strategies through which the plays restructure their chronicle sources, all three of them can be shown to rely on the procedures outlined in the second chapter. The audience is carefully instructed, through the conventional *topoi* and oratorical forms, about whom to admire and whom to execrate. The objects of the most elaborate praise and blame, Talbot and Richard, are, moreover, historical reconstructions in a still more restrictive sense as well. They are portrayed with reference to the social and political conventions that Shakespeare's contemporaries used to understand their own recent past: the one is a great feudal aristocrat, the other an unscrupulous younger son, intent on rising in the world. This kind of historical documentation is unexampled in English drama previous to *Henry VI,* and its immediate effect is to disclose a wealth of connections between the literary conventions and the social ones. As soon as one considers the direction which the entire trilogy pursues, however, as it moves from Talbot to Richard, a further layer of meaning comes into view. In the ideal Erasmian scheme, history is made glorious by a succession of great men, each of whom educates and inspires his successors. As Heywood explains, the pattern of heroic virtue is transmitted from Hercules to Achilles to Alexander to "the Princes of our times" in undiminished brilliance. Look at the process in its historical setting, Shakespeare implies, and you will find that the pattern loses some of its antique luster with every transfer. The special accomplishment of *Henry VI,* within its dramatic tradition, was to establish the social and political ramifications of Marlowe's prototype, *Tamburlaine,* by providing the fullest available historical contexts. But the import of the entire cycle is that the original drive towards a godlike pre-eminence cannot, finally, be contained within any human society that would be recognizable to an Elizabethan audience.

I Henry VI

The first part of *Henry VI* recasts the latter part of the Hundred Years' War as an exercise in "parallel lives." The opening funeral oration indicates that the emphasis will be upon an ideal of heroic conduct, and the ensuing sequence of two council scenes (one English, the other French), three battle scenes, a "triumph," and a second funeral confirms this impression while introducing us to the two principal antagonists, Talbot and Joan la Pucelle. It is clear from *Edward III* and *The Wounds of Civil War* that Shakespeare would have regarded an extended rhetorical *comparatio* between two such figures as a legitimate dramatic form, but in this case the terms of comparison are rather difficult to isolate, and criticism has been inclined to write the play off as an uncontrolled exercise in rhetorical imitation. Malone could see nothing but pedantry in Shakespeare's attempts to define character through simile and allusion, and his judgments have generally been accepted:

> It is very observable that in *The* First *Part of King Henry VI.* there are more allusions to mythology, to classical authors, and to ancient and modern history, than, I believe, can be found in any one piece of our author's written on an English story; and that these allusions are introduced very much in the same manner as they are introduced in the plays of Greene, Peele, Lodge, and other dramatists who preceded Shakespeare; that is, they do not naturally arise out of the subject, but seem to be inserted merely to shew the writer's learning.[11]

It must be granted at the outset that the poetic texture of *1 Henry VI* does not encourage one to expect anything very subtle or even clearly defined in the way of characterization, and my own efforts to show Talbot and Joan as two sides of a complex statement about aristocratic values will rely more on an analysis of the rhetorical structure of the play. But even in the transparently bookish similes cited by Malone there may be some basis for a comparison between the two characters in ethical terms. When Shakespeare compares Talbot to Hercules, Hector, and the "desperate sire of Crete" who sought his fame in "the lither sky" (IV.vi.54; IV.vii.21), on the one hand, and Joan to Hannibal, the greatest of military strategists, and Mahomet, a "pagan" hero who is recalled as a magician and a religious charlatan (I.ii.140), on the other, it need not be supposed that the allusions are inserted "merely to shew the writer's learning." In order to appreciate their specific meanings, however, they must be seen within a narrow range of conventions and a special system of values — one that is perhaps most easily introduced by some further reference to the profession of arms as it is practiced in *1 Henry VI*.

The historical basis for all of the distinctions that I wish to emphasize is treated in such works as Sidney Painter's *French Chivalry* and Arthur

Ferguson's *The Indian Summer of English Chivalry*,[12] but the contrasts within *I Henry VI* will be clear enough without any special commentary. A few specific details, taken from the battle scenes, will serve to indicate where Shakespeare's interests lie. While the English, on the one hand, seem scarcely aware that gunpowder has been invented, the French do use artillery, and with devastating effectiveness, on the only occasions when they kill English peers. The master-gunner's boy ambushes Salisbury in the first act, and in his final battle at Bordeaux Talbot finds that "Ten thousand French have ta'en the sacrament/To rive their dangerous artillery/Upon no Christian soul but English Talbot" (IV.ii.28–30). By contrast, the English limit themselves to feats of sheer personal strength. It is reported in the first act, for example, that Talbot has "Enacted wonders with his sword and lance" (I.i.122), and that his French captors held him with a "guard of chosen shot" because they surmised that he could "rend bars of steel/And spurn in pieces posts of adamant" (I.iv.50–53) with his arms, not to mention his "bare fists' (I.iv.35) and "horses' heels" (107).

With regard to military strategy, the French generally seek the security of siege walls, and in two different scenes (III.ii; IV.ii) they taunt the English from the upper gallery of the stage. The English never adopt this posture, and Talbot is quite explicit in his opinion of it: "Dare ye come forth and meet us in the field?" he asks; "Will ye, like soldiers, come and fight it out?" (III.ii.61; 66).

> Base muleteers of France!
> Like peasant foot-boys do they keep the walls,
> And dare not take up arms like gentlemen.
>
> (III.ii.68–70)

The "muleteers" refuse to behave like *chevaliers,* however, and they never do "take up arms like gentlemen." Talbot's capture, as reported in the opening scene, occurs when "A base Walloon, to win the Dauphin's grace,/Thrust Talbot with a spear into the back" (I.i.137–138), while the "treacherous manner" of Salisbury's death has already been noted. Thereafter the Dauphin relies on Joan's "stratagems" and "policy," a mixture of deception and diplomacy by which he "wrongs his fame" (II.i.16) — but gets results.

By contrast, the English are so much concerned with fighting by the book as to appear, at times, almost oblivious to any ulterior objectives. When Talbot first speaks, he is complaining that the French had offered to exchange him for a "baser man of arms" than "the brave Lord Ponton de Santrailles" (I.iv.29; 27). Not only was this offer refused, but Talbot "craved death" in preference to being "so vile esteem'd" (31–32). Whenever the British do battle, it is specifically in revenge for some breach of martial decorum: the "torments" Talbot endured as a French prisoner, the treacherous ambush of Salisbury and Gargrave, the "hellish mischief" used to capture Rouen, and the "false dissembling guile" of Burgundy. For them, every battle represents the fulfilment of a vow to right some violation of chivalric ideals. Their ostensible cause for fighting, Henry's "right," is mentioned only once in all of those battle scenes, and then in a decidedly offhand manner ("Now, Salisbury, for thee and for the right/Of English Henry" [II.i. 35–36]).

These specific contrasts between two different ways of making war form one basis for Shakespeare's general effort to reformulate Marlowe's heroic ideal in a framework of aristocratic values. In the sixteenth century, as in the fifteenth, the right to bear arms was still an operative definition of a gentleman. And the source of that right continued of course to be gentle birth (technically speaking, armigerous parents). Accordingly, the play includes a parallel set of contrasts juxtaposing characters of base and gentle birth, and these comprise the other important factor in the ideal of aristocratic conduct that emerges. A brief exchange between Talbot and his son, who is being urged to flee from the fatal battle of Bordeaux, will help to illustrate how the Talbots unite both requisites:

> *Tal.* Thou never hadst renown, nor canst not lose it.
> *John.* Yes, your renowned name: shall flight abuse it?
>
> (IV.v.40–41)

Talbot's "renown," or fame, is the permanent record of his honorable deeds, and it is symbolized by his "name," which recalls those deeds. The soldier who finds that "The cry of 'Talbot' serves me as a sword" (II.ii.79) is simply putting this premise to practical use. The basis of

Talbot's readiness to face death and his circumspect valor is the understanding that his "name" is a timeless family possession, to be transmitted to his son, who will in turn be incited to meet that standard.
The Talbots construe this doctrine so literally that valor becomes, in
effect, a test of legitimacy: "Surely, by all the glory you have won,/And
if I fly, I am not Talbot's son" (IV.vi.50–51), argues Young Talbot.
By the same token, the stain of illegitimacy is presumptive evidence of
someone's unworthiness to bear arms, as Talbot reminds the Bastard of
Orleans:

> I quickly shed
> Some of his bastard blood, and in disgrace
> Bespoke him thus: 'Contaminated, base,
> And misbegotten blood I spill of thine,
> Mean and right poor, for that pure blood of mine
> Which thou didst force from Talbot, my brave boy.'
>
> (IV.vi.19–24)

If the "Bastard" is a special case here, Joan's career embodies an
extended parody of this ideal, in which her unorthodox tactics on the
battlefield only serve to expose the baseness of her origins. When she is
introduced to the Dauphin's court (appropriately, by the Bastard of
Orleans), the French peers are told that she is a "shepherd's daughter"
who has been inspired to forsake her "base vocation" and "be the
English scourge" (I.ii.72, 80, 129). She seeks to establish her claims
to nobility by "high terms" and "single combat"; but both her sex and
her parentage would disqualify her from bearing arms at all. If her
martial career amounts to a shameful assortment of policies and stratagems, her death scene, which can be taken as an ironic counterstatement to those of the Talbots, only brings to light the fact that she lacks
any family name to augment and transmit. In a desperate effort to
escape death she denies her father (an inoffensive old rustic who ma-
terializes to make the fact of her base origins perfectly clear) and claims
to be issued from the "progeny of kings" (V.iv.38). As this transparent
hoax fails to win any mercy from her captors, she claims to be with
child herself; but the English will "have no bastards live" (70) and
duly proceed to burn her as a witch.

The larger network of comparisons of course extends beyond the special case of Talbot and Joan. If she epitomizes the external forces that threaten the aristocratic ideal of military service and gentle blood, there are signs of internal erosion as well. The most ominous of these come from the professional civil servant Winchester, who is a "bastard" by birth (III.i.42), and from the contentious, quarrelsome gentlemen of the Inns of Court, one of whom, York, also bears a dishonored family name. "Stand'st thou not attainted,/Corrupted, and exempt from ancient gentry?" (II.iv.92–93).

The literary expression of these social distinctions is still largely contained within the idiom of *Tamburlaine,* and focused in the portrayal of Talbot and Joan. The Talbots stand as a refutation of Tamburlaine's dictum "That vertue solely is the sum of glorie/And fashions men with true nobility" (*1 Tamb.,* III.ii.115), because they insist that heroic virtue be distinguished from mere *virtù,* and construed rather as a set of ethical imperatives, nurtured and transmitted by a select group of "peers"; at the same time, *virtù,* sheer "capability," is redefined by its limiting concern with tangible victories, its consequent reliance on base policy and stratagems, and its sham nobility. On this level, Joan becomes the vehicle for a broad parody of Marlowe's heroic prototype, and, more specifically, for a parody of the recognition scenes from *1 Tamburlaine.* The outlines of the parody are clear enough from the first scene in the French camp. The offspring of an ungentle shepherd finds herself "assign'd" to leave her "base vocation" so that she may become a famous warrior and the scourge of God. She proceeds to declare her personal superiority through Marlowe's familiar gestures of challenge and vaunt, and she elicits the usual response:

> [*Joan.*]   My courage try by combat, if thou dar'st,
>   And thou shalt find that I exceed my sex.
>   Resolve on this; thou shalt be fortunate
>   If thou receive me for thy warlike mate.
> Char.   Thou hast astonish'd me with thy high terms.
>
>   .   .   .   .   .
>
>   Was Mahomet inspired with a dove?
>   Thou with an eagle art inspired then.

> Helen, the mother of great Constantine,
> Nor yet Saint Philip's daughters, were like thee.
> Bright star of Venus, fall'n down on the earth,
> How may I reverent worship thee enough?
>
> (I.ii.89–93; 140–145)

Shakespeare has here collapsed the germinal clichés of *1 Tamburlaine* into a space of about one hundred lines, and has encased them in miniature set speeches of description, vaunt, and praise. Like the second scene of *1 Tamburlaine,* this is a miniature drama of social recognition, one in which the *topoi* of aristocratic status are used to move and persuade a prince of the blood royal. It is converted to comedy by using this very rhetorical apparatus to expose the comic underside of Joan's character: her base origins. The strain of bawdy *double entendre* is inaugurated by Reignier's admiring "She takes upon her bravely at first dash" (71). It is formulated more explicitly when Joan tells Charles that if he tries her in "combat" he will find that she exceeds her sex (89–90; see also 92, 95, 103); and it is even given a touch of sublimity in Charles' "Bright star of Venus fall'n down on the earth" (144). The effect of this bawdy punning is to reverse completely the ostensible show of physical energy elevated to moral purity. At best this squeaking boy actor is a figure from a comedy, or perhaps a comic subplot, pretending to belong in an heroic play. A later parody of Marlovian "magnificence," delivered by Charles after Joan has led the French to victory at Rouen, preserves this emphasis while extending the range of implied judgments:

> . . . all the priests and friars in my realm
> Shall in procession sing her endless praise.
> A statelier pyramis to her I'll rear
> Than Rhodope's of Memphis ever was;
> In memory of her, when she is dead,
> Her ashes, in an urn more precious
> Than the rich jewel-coffer of Darius,
> Transported shall be at high festivals
> Before the kings and queens of France.
> No longer on Saint Denis will we cry,
> But Joan de Pucelle shall be France's saint.
>
> (I.vi.19–29)

Here Marlovian paganism becomes confused with Romish Catholicism in a speech calculated to remind the Elizabethan audience that heroism without ethical sanctions merely becomes another corrupt secular religion. As the representative of that religion, Joan herself would suggest not only divine Zenocrate, but also the charlatans and impostors who peddled "masses and marries" in the popular interludes.[13]

Beneath these postures, Joan is generically an impostor, created only to exhibit the ornate theatrical façade, as well as the policy and "stratagems," by which aspirant baseness masquerades as nobility. Hence the scenes in which she is exposed and burnt as a witch, like the stripping of Duessa in *The Faerie Queene,* serve a formal expository purpose that supersedes any need for a controlled, sequacious plot. A consort of "familiar spirits" (V.iii.10) arrives to make unmistakably plain the truth that lies behind her claim to be the chosen agent of God. These are followed by the shepherd who underscores the real baseness of her origins with his unvarnished testimony that "She was the first fruit of my bachelorship" (V.iv.13). Finally, the reiterated innuendo of sexual misconduct is made utterly explicit in her confession that Charles (or Alençon or Reignier) has left her with the child whom the English will not allow to be born.

Where the rhetoric surrounding Joan uses the conventions of praise to project an image of spurious glamor, the deeds of Talbot and his son, and of Salisbury, Bedford, and their great predecessor Henry V, are for the most part treated through forms of the funeral oration. More than a third of Talbot's three hundred lines would fall into this oratorical genre, and most of what remains either grows directly out of it (as the vow to revenge is a kind of *hortatio*) or is distinctly elegiac in tone (for example, the speech in rebuke of Falstaffe at IV.i.33–44 beginning "When first this Order was ordain'd, my lords,/Knights of the Garter were of noble birth"). Indeed, Talbot's main function in this play is to solemnize the fall of the great English peers, of whom he is the last representative. While his antagonist defines what is ephemeral and merely glamorous about heroic "bravery," Talbot finds a context in which to define true heroic virtue and the permanent compensation that it offers in the face of death: the immortality conferred by earthly fame. Fame is introduced as the set topic of *consolatio* in the extended funeral oration for Henry V that opens the play.

[*Bed.*] A far more glorious star thy soul will make
Than Julius Caesar or bright —

Enter a Messenger.
(I.i.55–56)

Introduced, but never formulated: the elegy is broken off by the messenger's "sad tidings" from France. The unresolved problem of fame and the consolation that it provides remains, however, the signal problem posed by the life of Talbot. Does an "honorable" death justify a life that has proved futile in the unforeseeable calculus of human history? Or does the final word remain with Joan as she insults over Talbot's body: "Him that thou magnifiest with all these titles,/Stinking and fly-blown lies here at our feet" (IV.vii.75–76)?

Surveying Talbot's own reflections on this question, as they are formulated in his orations on the deaths of Salisbury, Bedford, Young Talbot, and himself, one finds that there are significant variations in the answers that he provides. The death of Salisbury is first lamented as a "tragedy" that might have been inspired by *A Mirror for Magistrates*:

Accursed tower! accursed fatal hand
That hath contriv'd this woeful tragedy!
In thirteen battles Salisbury o'ercame;
Henry the Fifth he first train'd to the wars;
Whilst any trump did sound, or drum struck up,
His sword did ne'er leave striking in the field.

(I.iv.75–80)

But subsequently Talbot placates the shade of Salisbury by conquering Orleans, and he commemorates this achievement in a formal elegy over the tomb erected there:

Now have I paid my vow unto his soul;
For every drop of blood was drawn from him
There hath at least five Frenchmen died to-night.
And that hereafter ages may behold
What ruin happen'd in revenge of him,

Within their chiefest temple I'll erect
A tomb, wherein his corpse shall be interr'd;
Upon the which, that every one may read,
Shall be engrav'd the sack of Orleans,
The treacherous manner of his mournful death,
And what a terror he had been to France.

(II.ii.7–17)

By introducing topics that lie outside the *Mirror* tradition, with its essentially medieval insistence on the futility of earthly aspiration, Talbot is able to offer Salisbury's death as an argument for the imperishable value of the heroic life. Every drop of his blood was worth the lives of five treacherous Frenchmen, and his tomb will remain in the "middle center" of Orleans as a permanent testimonial to that "worth." His epitaph for Bedford (III.ii.131–137) is less assertive ("But kings and mightiest potentates must die,/For that's the end of human misery"), but its very tranquillity depends upon a parallel situation. Bedford's own faith in English valor has been justified by a visible English victory at the very moment of death; and his exequies can be "fulfill'd *in* Rouen" (III.ii.133; my italics) with due gravity.

At Talbot's last battle, however, the problem of consolation arises in quite a different context. Talbot and his son must die, and Bordeaux will never be retaken. For Shakespeare, this is to be the last battle of the Hundred Years' War and the last stand of English chivalry. Whatever "victory" Talbot and his son might achieve there will not be commemorated in the actualities of human history. Talbot unwittingly formulates their problem when he commands his son, "Fly, to revenge my death if I be slain" (IV.v.18–21). Young Talbot's answer — "He that flies so will ne'er return again" (19) — serves to expose the insolubility of their dilemma. If Young Talbot flees this battle, he will, as it were, cease to be Talbot's son:

Is my name Talbot? and am I your son?
And shall I fly? O, if you love my mother,
Dishonour not her honourable name,
To make a bastard and a slave of me!

(12–15)

But if he remains, as the father reminds the son, their "name" will be extinct in another sense: "In thee thy mother dies, our household's name,/My death's revenge, thy youth, and England's fame" (IV.vi.38–39). Like Antony and Coriolanus, the Talbots discover that the ideal figured by their heroic "name" is too pure for sublunary existence. It can be ratified only in the very act of death. Talbot's final words, spoken over the body of his dead son, accept and transcend this dilemma by returning to the classical consolation of fame and formulating it in an enlarged context:

> Thou antic Death, which laugh'st us here to scorn,
> Anon, from thy insulting tyranny,
> Coupled in bonds of perpetuity,
> Two Talbots winged through the lither sky,
> In thy despite shall scape mortality.
>
> (IV.vii.18–22)

Here the humanistic reward of earthly fame (suggested by Icarus and Daedalus) is combined, at least implicitly, with the Christian consolation of resurrection after death. Their "name," and the aspirant quest for fame that motivates the noble life, is not cut off by death, but translated into the permanence of rhetorical *exemplum*. From this last oration Talbot moves surely to the clear-eyed acceptance of his fate that concludes the speech, even as it foreshadows the final lucidity of Shakespeare's later tragic heroes.

> Soldiers, adieu! I have what I would have,
> Now my old arms are young John Talbot's grave.
>
> (IV.vii.31–32)

The funeral oration that began the play and was interrupted by the "sad tidings" from France here finds its *consolatio:* the "bright star" of Henry's fame has been set within a larger constellation.

The subplot involving Somerset, York, and the quarrel of the roses provides a third set of contrasts: the fields of France shrink to the Inns of Court, the epic warrior gives way to the fashionable courtier, the incentives of ancestral fame are replaced by a contentious aristocratic disdain, and the rites of war are but faintly recalled by adversaries who are careful, as Touchstone would say, to "quarrel in print, by the book, as you have books for good manners" (*As You Like It*, V.iv.94–95). Unlike Joan, the young men who quarrel in the Temple Garden have every reason to behave like aristocrats. They stand as Shakespeare's example of natural nobility diverted to trivial ends. If their modish and courtly wit is something of an anachronism in Talbot's world, the anachronism nevertheless helps us to see just where that world was heading.

The ironic relevance of their quarrel to Talbot's heroic ideals becomes most apparent in their appeals to family honor. York entreats "him that is a true-born gentleman/And stands upon the honour of his birth" (II.iv.27–28) to pluck the white rose, while Somerset taunts the "yeoman" Plantagenet for being "attainted" by his father's ill fame:

Was not thy father, Richard Earl of Cambridge,
For treason headed in our late king's days?
And by his treason stand'st thou not attainted,
Corrupted, and exempt from ancient gentry?
His trespass yet lives guilty in thy blood;
And, till thou be restor'd, thou art a yeoman.

(II.iv.90–95)

The faint parallel to the Talbots' ancestral values is intended, of course, to point up the larger contrasts. Where Talbot's "name" is fully identified with the cause for which he fights, Somerset and York are divided by "nice sharp quillets of the law" (17) too slight even to be mentioned, and immediately forgotten by both sides. The crowning irony of *1 Henry VI* is that this essentially trivial sense of honor should prove a greater threat to Talbot's ideals, and indeed to his very existence, than all the base stratagems devised by the French. In the climactic scenes of act four, while Talbot is "ring'd about with bold adversity" (IV.iv.14), York and Somerset are characteristically quarreling about which of them is to be held responsible for his plight. "York lies," Somerset insists,

he might have sent and had the horse:
I owe him little duty, and less love,
And take foul scorn to fawn on him by sending.

(IV.iv.33–35)

Talbot is thus sacrificed to a point of courtly etiquette. When this happens, Somerset and York stand judged as "seditious" peers, and in a context that would have seemed especially appropriate to the Elizabethan audience. The courtier has failed to accept his real responsibilities as a social and military leader; and this decay of the aristocracy, which is assailed from without by "upstarts" of ungentle birth like Winchester and Joan, portends a more general decline in national greatness.

Hence the final act can be taken as further commentary on the failure of a courtly aristocracy to provide an adequate image of feudal service and chivalry. Criticism of *1 Henry VI* has understandably tended to treat Margaret and Suffolk as an end-link to the next play in the trilogy, but they also serve to bring the general declension from heroic action to courtly posturing to its appropriate conclusion: the pseudo-Petrarchan lover. Suffolk appears as a mannered Elizabethan amorist from his earliest exchanges with Margaret:

> Be not offended, nature's miracle,
> Thou art allotted to be ta'en by me:
> So doth the swan her downy cygnets save,
> Keeping them prisoner underneath her wings.
> Yet, if this servile usage once offend,
> Go and be free again as Suffolk's friend.

(V.iii.54–59)

What is at stake here is the power of these romantic clichés to corrupt still further the integrity of the English court. Suffolk's success in installing his "friend" as the English queen effectively violates Henry's contract with the Earl of Armagnac's daughter, which was to have been the basis for an honorable peace. And the reason for that success is fully apparent in Henry's transparent intoxication with such Petrarchan rhetoric as this:

> Your wondrous rare description, noble Earl,
> Of beauteous Margaret hath astonish'd me:
> Her virtues graced with external gifts
> Do breed love's settled passions in my heart:
> And like as rigour of tempestuous gusts

Provokes the mightiest hulk against the tide,
So am I driven by breath of her renown
Either to suffer shipwreck, or arrive
Where I may have fruition of her love.

(V.v.1–9)

Still later, as if the very triteness of these clichés were not sufficient to make the point, Suffolk concludes the play by acknowledging his own cynical motives, and foreshadowing, in a final portentous allusion to the Trojan *débacle,* the havoc of *2 Henry VI*:

Thus Suffolk hath prevail'd; and thus he goes,
As did the youthful Paris once to Greece;
With hope to find the like event in love,
But prosper better than the Trojan did.
Margaret shall now be Queen, and rule the King;
But I will rule both her, the King, and realm.

(V.v.103–108)

Here the tradition of fame serves as an ironic backdrop, a final testimony to the ethical and political confusions of the present. What began as a viable aristocratic ideal of conduct, rooted in social customs and familial bonds, has become a mere precedent for aristocratic misadventure. The Talbots' fame, as it was earned at Bordeaux, embodies the high ethical ideals of the play; and their death effectively removes those ideals from the world of the play. From the moment of their apotheosis in the "lither sky" their name forfeits its slender hold on the actualities of history and achieves the perfection of heroic *exemplum* — a tale to be told in an increasingly harsh world.

2 Henry VI

The opening acts of *2 Henry VI* transport a reader of the trilogy from the siege walls and battlefields of France to the public halls and inmost recesses of the English court. For a popular history belonging to the early 1590's, the setting is still relatively novel, especially when it is recalled that this play probably preceded *Woodstock* and *Edward II*.[14]

The stage directions that the New Arden editor supplies for its first eleven scenes will immediately suggest how foreign its dramatic environment is to the tradition of *Tamburlaine:* London, the palace, the Duke of Gloucester's house, Gloucester's garden, Saint Alban's, the Duke of York's garden, a hall of justice, the abbey at Bury St. Edmunds, a room of state, a bedchamber. By introducing a set of Elizabethan courtiers into *1 Henry VI,* Shakespeare had begun to engage the political crises of sixteenth-century England within the conventions of popular heroic drama. In *2 Henry VI* the nobility become recognizable as precisely what they were for Shakespeare's audience: "brave halfe paces between a throne and a people," [15] in Fulke Greville's phrase, centered at the court in London. Scenes such as the one where Suffolk discovers some villagers with a petition "Against the Duke of Suffolk, for enclosing the commons of Long Melford" (I.iii.20–22) dramatize the social status of that nobility in terms that could hardly be more explicit. Nor is this episode at all unusual. Comparable transactions bring the court aristocracy into conjunction with a disloyal household servant (I.ii), a pair of coney-catching vagabonds (II.i), a treasonous armorer and his loyal apprentice (II.iii), an outraged House of Commons (III.ii), a crew of discontented seaman (IV.i), the rebellious tradesmen of Kent (IV.ii–x), and a representative of the squirearchy named Alexander Iden (V.i). As if to emphasize and complicate the social and political implications of these encounters, Shakespeare makes Henry's court into what is virtually a cross section of sixteenth-century aristocracy: there is the judicious administrator and friend of the commons, "Good Duke Humphrey" of Gloucester; the proud, ambitious, and unscrupulous prelate Winchester; the loyal members of the country aristocracy, Salisbury and his son Warwick, who is commended for his "plainness" and "housekeeping" (I.i.190); the courtier Suffolk, an "Image of Pride" (I.iii.176) who has exchanged "two dukedoms for a duke's fair daughter" (I.i.220) in France; and the glamorous conqueror-intriguer York, who is already maneuvering for the "golden mark" of Henry's crown.

Those who agree with Johnson that the principal defect of the early histories "is that they have not sufficient variety of action, for the incidents are too often of the same kind" will welcome this elaboration of social details, and concur in his judgment that the second is the best play of the trilogy.[16] Certainly all that is known of the Elizabethan repertory between 1587 and 1595 indicates that *2 Henry VI* occupies a crucial place in the development of historical drama. Its portrayal of a weak king, flanked by a loyal counselor and a set of courtly "caterpillars," and confronted with open revolt from his discontented barons, marks the line of development that leads from, say, *Tamburlaine* and *Selimus* on the one side, to *Woodstock, Edward II,* and *Richard II* on the other. From a loose rendition of heroic aspiration in an exotic setting, the emphasis has shifted towards a drama of ambition and disruption that anatomizes the ambivalent status of the Elizabethan peerage. In Lawrence Stone's analysis, a complex series of events was, by the 1590's, leading to a general failure of nerve among the aristocracy.[17] Two familiar symptoms of that failure emerge directly from the social drama of *2 Henry VI:* Suffolk's fierce, reflexive pride in his noble blood and connections at court, and York's desperate impulse to restore his family's lost eminence by reckless military adventures. Just as these are indices of a more general failure to govern, the one tragic figure in the plan is a governor, Good Duke Humphrey. He can fill the administrative vacuum that results from the defection of Suffolk and York, but he is powerless to resist their determination to destroy and replace him.

In terms of the continuities that I have set out to trace, the consequences of this changed setting — at least for the first three acts — are clear enough. The two characters who might have presented the strongest appeal to the heroic mood, Suffolk and York, are drastically reduced in stature, while Duke Humphrey suggests a new type of ideal ruler, the Ciceronian governor. Thus, if they are read as *exempla,* the social incidents that have just been listed serve to discount the value of ancestral name and martial fortitude, while laying stress on the importance of prudence, "a vertue that is occupied evermore, in searchyng out the truthe" and justice, "a vertue, gathered by long space, gevyng every one his awne, mindyng in all thynges, the common profite of our countrey."[18] The controlling image of Gloucester's judicial rectitude and expertise is established in a series of trial scenes, in which he pronounces variously upon the dispute between Peter and Horner (I.iii), the qualifications of York and Somerset for the French regency (I.iii), the fraudulent "miracle" invented by Saunder Simcox and his wife (II.i), the misdemeanors of Dame Eleanor (II.i), and, finally, the accusations that are brought against him at Bury St. Edmunds (III.i). By contrast, throughout the first four acts York's projected rise to eminence is less a matter of his own special abilities than of his systematic effort to subvert the principles thus established. His principal strategies, the alliance with the Nevilles and the manipulation of Jack Cade, exhibit a valor that has ceased to find expression in the open trial of warfare, while it seeks out the privacy of schemes and soliloquies. Similarly, Suffolk's pride in rank and title is exemplifed not in the martial deeds that would add to his family name, but rather in his illicit courtship of Queen Margaret, and his contemptuous exchanges with such "base" types as the humble petitioners ("Sir knave" and his "fellow") who mistakenly approach him in act one (I.iii.1–41), the angry Commons ("rude, unpolished hinds," "a sort of tinkers") who assail him after the murder of Gloucester (III.ii.270–276), and the pirates ("paltry, servile, abject drudges") who execute him shortly thereafter (IV.i.29–138). In so far as these contexts tend to deny the would-be hero his normal theater of operations — the battlefield and the tournament — the play as a whole may be said to embody "historical assessment" with a vengeance and, indeed, to mark a radical departure from the literary antecedents with which this study has been so much concerned. But there is a marked shift in emphasis within the play itself, one which serves to reopen the entire question of Suffolk's and York's value in a more hospitable setting.

The murder of Gloucester, which comes midway through the play, represents the most severe possible judgment on the ambitious nobles, and particularly Suffolk. At the same time, however, this event removes from the scene the one figure who embodies a thoroughgoing criticism of their personal aspirations. Instead of proceeding directly to their appointed miserable ends, therefore, both York and Suffolk enjoy a renewed vitality in the latter half of the play, as the social commentary, without Gloucester to interpret it, recedes into the background, and impinges less directly on the values of the two aristocrats. In effect, Shakespeare provides each of them with a new idiom and a new vision of nobility. The courtier, at his final parting with Margaret (III.ii), suddenly becomes an idealized and gracious amorist who measures the necessity of death against the permanence of love. York, the scheming Machiavel of the first three acts, reappears in the fifth as a visible embodiment of heroic authority, urging his claim to the throne on that

basis. The impact of these scenes depends, of course, on the fact that
they are set in an ambience so utterly different from that of *1 Henry
VI*. They take place not on a battlefield but in the court, where Suffolk
and York already stand judged as instances of "foul ambition." As a
result, both characters now appear from a double perspective. The
social stereotypes (corrupt courtier, rebellious baron) have been assimilated to more sympathetic theatrical roles, and, as the rhetorical
elaboration unfolds, those roles enlarge the stereotypes into examples of
personal ambition that cannot be adequately judged within a social order
that is itself deeply compromised. Neither of these characters, in the
hierarchical metaphor, "knows his place," and as a result each becomes
a far more interesting and problematic case than such professional caterpillars as Winchester and Buckingham. So Clifford's first response to
York in act five is one of puzzled amazement: "To Bedlam with him!
Is the man grown mad!" (V.i.131). The dramatist has discovered,
however distantly, a radical form of tragic irony: when heroic and
aristocratic values are transferred from the purely martial world of Talbot
and Joan into a court where the nobility are "brave halfe paces between
a throne and a people," they may appear as inherently anarchic even
though they are still admirable in themselves. It is Shakespeare's tentative acknowledgment of this predicament with respect to Suffolk and,
more especially, York that makes them truly represent the crisis of the
aristocracy in *2 Henry VI*.

This transition from a drama of mordant social commentary to a
more idealized and sympathetic portrayal of heroic aspiration poses
some large problems of interpretation. The easiest way of dealing with
them is to postulate that Shakespeare began by experimenting with a
form like Rossiter's "morality of state," but found that it involved
rejecting an old ideal without adequately providing for a new one, and
so returned to the conventional formulas of heroical-historical drama in
the closing acts. I do not offer this hypothesis because I think that the
transition is clumsy or fortuitous. Quite the contrary: in using an analysis
of courtly intrigues and political failures to define the conditions that
permit — perhaps even necessitate — the rise of a new "Prince," Shakespeare was only discovering for himself the underlying configurations
of *Il Principe*. But it should be quite clear that the critique of Suffolk
and York that is sustained by Gloucester never begins to generate a

vision of the aristocratic life which convincingly supplants their own. Hence, after Gloucester's death, the reassertion of order and stability, such as it is, can only be accomplished by one of them. That is the crucial difference between *2 Henry VI* and *Richard II,* a play which it closely resembles in many respects. In *2 Henry VI,* the analysis of decay in the state is still predicated on the conception of the body politic and the ideal ruler that is common to all heroical-historical drama: the warrior prince leading his feudal ranks in wars of conquest. *Richard II* also shows what happens when aristocratic caterpillars corrupt the royal court and threaten the anointed body of the king; but in the later play the caterpillars are seen within the whole "garden" of the state, a type of Eden that evolves according to its own higher moral laws, while the "body" of the king, like the body of Christ, figures the health of the entire commonweal. As long as it remained uninformed by such a sacramental conception of politics and kingship, the social ethos of *2 Henry VI* was bound finally to accommodate the same contentious aristocrats whom it set out to criticize. The only real gain (if one can call it that) lay in the dramatist's perception, which was to carry over into *3 Henry VI* and *Richard III,* that the whole humanistic ideal of the hero king necessarily contained the seeds of its own deterioration.

This interdependence between the play's ethical criticism and its heroic themes is firmly established in the opening scene, which seems to me one of the finest in the play. It begins with the ceremonial addresses of Suffolk and Margaret, which usher in the style of courtly posturing and decadent "magnificence" that was adumbrated at the close of *1 Henry VI*:

> *Queen.* Great King of England, and my gracious lord,
> The mutual conference that my mind hath had
> By day, by night, waking, and in my dreams,
> In courtly company, or at my beads,
> With you mine alderliefest sovereign,
> Makes me the bolder to salute my king
> With ruder terms, such as my wit affords,
> And over joy of heart doth minister.

(I.i.24–31)

As soon as the royal couple and their favorite depart, Gloucester duly measures the ugly substance that this Petrarchan shadow conceals against the great achievements of the era that has just passed:

> Brave peers of England, pillars of the state,
> To you Duke Humphrey must unload his grief —
> Your grief, the common grief of all the land.
> What! did my brother Henry spend his youth,
> His valour, coin, and people, in the wars?
> Did he so often lodge in open field,
> In winter's cold, and summer's parching heat,
> To conquer France, his true inheritance?
> And did my brother Bedford toil his wits,
> To keep by policy what Henry got?
>
> .   .   .   .   .   .
>
> Or hath mine uncle Beaufort and myself,
> With all the learned Council of the realm,
> Studied so long, sat in the Council House
> Early and late, debating to and fro
> How France and Frenchmen might be kept in awe?
>
> .   .   .   .   .
>
> O peers of England! shameful is this league,
> Fatal this marriage, cancelling your fame,
> Blotting your names from books of memory,
> Razing the characters of your renown,
> Defacing monuments of conquer'd France,
> Undoing all, as all had never been!
>
> (I.i.74–83; 87–91; 97–102)

Gloucester is a type of the Renaissance governor whom humanists like Ascham and Eloyt saw as supplanting such medieval *chevaliers* as Talbot, and his tone here is hardly bellicose. It would be impossible to find, among the earlier histories, a more balanced portrayal of the ideal ruler through humanistic topics. The emphasis falls on fortitude ("Did he so often lodge in open field/In winter's cold and summer's parching heat") and prudence ("And did my brother Bedford toil his wits,/To keep by policy what Henry got"). Both these virtues are put in the service of Henry's patrimony, "his true inheritance." By exemplifying them, Henry's peers all achieved an honored place in the registers of fame. Gloucester is ideally suited to witness the decay of this high tradition in the ambience of Henry's court, but, as the survivor, along with Salisbury and Beaufort, of a departed order, he is powerless to do anything about it. In this scene, as elsewhere, he shows his frustration and impotence by abrupt fits of choler and sadness, which are relieved only by unexplained silences and departures.

Hence it is York who, at the conclusion of the scene, ventures to translate Gloucester's themes into action, although he does so in a radically new context.

> Anjou and Maine are given to the French;
> Paris is lost; the state of Normandy
> Stands on a tickle point now they are gone;
> Suffolk concluded on the articles,
> The peers agreed, and Henry was well pleas'd
> To change two dukedoms for a duke's fair daughter.
> I cannot blame them all: what is't to them?
> 'Tis thine they give away, and not their own.
>
> .   .   .   .   .
>
> A day will come when York shall claim his own;
> And therefore I will take the Nevils' parts
> And make a show of love to proud Duke Humphrey,
> And when I spy advantage, claim the crown,
> For that's the golden mark I seek to hit.
> Nor shall proud Lancaster usurp my right,
> Nor hold the sceptre in his childish fist,
> Nor wear the diadem upon his head,
> Whose church-like humour fits not for a crown.
> Then, York, be still awhile, till time do serve:
> Watch thou, and wake when others be asleep,
> To pry into the secrets of the state;
> Till Henry surfeit in the joys of love,

With his new bride and England's dear-bought queen,
And Humphrey with the peers be fall'n at jars:
Then will I raise aloft the milk-white rose,
With whose sweet smell the air shall be perfum'd,
And in my standard bear the arms of York,
To grapple with the house of Lancaster;
And force perforce I'll make him yield the crown,
Whose bookish rule hath pulled fair England down.

                                        (I.i.215–222; 240–260)

The tone and imagery of this passage, which recall Marlowe's Machiavellian Duke of Guise, could hardly be farther from Gloucester's.
This flippant, mercantile appraisal of "his own" inheritance makes it
clear that York is alive to the ancestral values of *1 Henry VI* only in a
very limited way. Nevertheless, it should already be apparent that York
is not, finally, going to be the mere villain of the piece, for he is only
measuring himself against the humanistic standards that Gloucester has
just invoked. Like the Henry of noble memory, York is ready to "grapple"
in the field while others surfeit in the joys of love; like Bedford, York
will use his wits "To pry into the secrets of the state," and like all the
learned Council of the realm he will watch and wake "when others be
asleep." If their aim was to secure Henry's true inheritance, York would
only "claim his own"; if they erected characters of renown, York will
"raise aloft the milk-white rose."

   This transition from Gloucester's highminded critique of Henry's
court to York's half ironic reassertion of the *topoi* on which he bases
that critique foreshadows the basic design of the entire play. As the
portrayal of social corruption broadens and unfolds, Margaret, Suffolk,
and their new allies continue to beguile Henry with games of courtly
makebelieve, and Gloucester continues to expose their foul practices
wherever he can. His effectiveness, however, is always limited by his
reliance on purely judicial procedures (he assures his wife that he "must
offend" before he can "be attainted" [II.iv.59]), and he is finally sacrificed to his own faith in legal rectitude.

   By the beginning of the fourth act the homiletic moral, "Virtue is
chok'd with foul Ambition" (III.i.143), has virtually been played out:
it is concluded by the expulsion of Suffolk and the eschatological

horrors of Winchester's demise. It is just at this point that York, who has been mostly in the wings up to now, determines to raise aloft the milk-white rose and purge Henry's court of its corrupted elements. For York alone, of all the decadent aristocrats, has still managed to preserve some semblance of the antique pattern of heroical worth that was established by Henry V. Hence he alone can raise himself from the status of a symptom of courtly viciousness in the earlier acts to that of a judgment on it in the later ones.

York's reappearance in the fifth act occasions Shakespeare's second experiment in reformulating the idiom and topics of *Tamburlaine*. At first sight, the result may appear to be rather less controlled and successful than the portrayal of Joan in *1 Henry VI*.

> Ah! sancta majestas, who'd not buy thee dear?
> Let them obey that knows not how to rule;
> This hand was made to handle nought but gold:
> I cannot give due action to my words,
> Except a sword or sceptre balance it.

> King did I call thee? No, thou art not king;
> Not fit to govern and rule multitudes,
> Which dar'st not, no, nor canst not rule a traitor.
> That head of thine doth not become a crown;
> Thy hand is made to grasp a palmer's staff,
> And not to grace an awful princely sceptre.
> That gold must round engirt these brows of mine,
> Whose smile and frown, like to Achilles' spear,
> Is able with the change to kill and cure.
> Here is a hand to hold a sceptre up,
> And with the same to act controlling laws.
> Give place: by heaven, thou shalt rule no more
> O'er him whom heaven created for thy ruler.

(V.i.5–9; 93–105)

In the pure Marlovian version the heroic exemplar urges his right to rule, as here, without reference to parentage or ancestry; and it is no accident that York does not once mention his hereditary claims in this final act. It is rather the controlling image of the awful "brows" dispensing life and death that figures, as it does in *1 Tamburlaine,* the transmutation of *virtù* into a natural right to rule.[19]

> [*Mena.*] Pale of complexion, wrought in him with passion,
>   Thirsting with sovereignty, with love of arms,
>   His lofty brows in folds do figure death,
>   And in their smoothness amity and life.
>
> (*1 Tamb.,* II.i.19–22)

Insofar as Shakespeare has ventured to reproduce the effect of Marlowe's verse here, he comes out a clear second best. The aptness of the formulas, in the later play, lies rather in the implied suggestion that York himself does not measure up to the original ideal. A phrase such as "who'd not buy thee dear," which recalls the commercial imagery of York's first soliloquy, reminds us that his sense of his own worth is limited by his preoccupation with material rewards, and that he cannot imagine what the real cost of his actions will be. The charge that Henry "dar'st not, no, nor canst not rule a traitor," with its heavy unconscious irony, only serves to focus the confusions that arise when what is almost entirely a literary conception of sovereignty is invoked within an established political system. Such confusions can be clarified but they can hardly be resolved here: so long as traitors even less admirable than York are free to wreak havoc on Henry's kingdom, he is free to argue that his apparent lawlessness amounts to a superior definition of nobility.

York's ambivalent status as both remedy and cause of the decay in Henry's court is epitomized by the connection between his lofty aspirations and the peasants' revolt engineered during his absence in act four. While he is in Ireland, Jack Cade and his followers also weigh the claims of *noblesse de robe* and *noblesse d'épée,* and reach similar conclusions:

> *Bev.* O miserable age! Virtue is not regarded in handicraftsmen.
> *Hol.* The nobility think scorn to go in leather aprons.
> *Bev.* Nay, more; the King's Council are no good workmen.
> *Hol.* True; and yet it is said, "Labour in thy vocation": which is
>   as much to say as, "Let the magistrates be labouring men";
>   and therefore should we be magistrates.

> *Bev.* Thou hast hit it; for there's no better sign of a brave mind
> than a hard hand.
>
> (IV.ii.10–20)

The relevance of this burlesque to the main plot is assured by its place
within York's own strategy. York is Jack Cade's silent partner, and he
begins his own campaign only after Cade's revolt is under way. Cade
himself ensures that the connection is not forgotten by imitating his
patron's claims to royal ancestry (IV.ii.37–50), his intention to purge
Henry's court of "false caterpillars" (IV.iv.36; see also IV.ii.61–67;
IV.vii.28–30), his detestation of all things French (IV.ii.159–165), his
admiring recollection of Henry V (IV.ii.149–152), his distaste for
"bookish rule" (IV.ii.81–104), his insistence on martial eminence as
requisite for aristocratic station (IV.vii.76), and his easy association of
martial bravery and material prosperity (IV.ii.61–72). These details are
set, moreover, within a continuous parody of the conventional formulas
for heroic self-assertion. As in the comedy of *1 Henry VI*, the favorite
joke consists in puncturing the would-be hero's set speeches by irreverent
asides that specify social realities:

> *Cade.* My father was a Mortimer, —
> *But.* [*Aside.*] He was an honest man, and a good bricklayer.
> *Cade.* My mother a Plantagenet, —
> *But.* [*Aside.*] I knew her well; she was a midwife.
> *Cade.* My wife descended of the Lacies, —
> *But.* [*Aside.*] She was, indeed, a pedlar's daughter, and sold many
> laces.
>
> (IV.ii.37–44)

by outlandish attempts at magnificence:

> [*Cade.*] Wither, garden; and be henceforth a burying-place to all
> that do dwell in this house, because the unconquer'd soul
> of Cade is fled.
>
> (IV.x.62–64)

and by reductive detail:

> *Cade.* Iden, farewell; and be proud of thy victory. Tell Kent from
> me, she hath lost her best man, and exhort all the world to
> be cowards. . . .
>
> (IV.x.71–73)

The vitality of these scenes, as with any exercise in mock-heroic, stems
from their bringing widely disparate elements into a momentary comic
equilibrium; and it is to Shakespeare's purpose that two of those elements — Richard Plantagenet, lineal heir to the House of York, and
Jack Cade, clothier of Kent — are set in the most improbable proximity
to one another. When Stafford's brother exclaims "Jack Cade, the Duke
of York hath taught you this" (IV.ii.147), one may take his words in
the broadest sense. York sets Cade an example, or, in theatrical terms,
teaches him a part; and Cade plays it to the hilt, not wisely but too well.
Measuring Cade's performance in act four against his patron's in act
five, one learns to judge York's ideals by their consequences within the
social order. The point is not simply that the audience now sees the
meaning of the accusation that York is "treasonable"; it has also been
made clear that in a body politic where the specialty of rule is constantly violated, York's claims to sovereignty assume a special validity.
When he exclaims

> King did I call thee? No, thou art not king;
> Nor fit to govern and rule multitudes,
> Which dar'st not, no, nor canst not rule a traitor.
>
> (V.i.93–95)

he stands exposed as both the cause and the remedy of the condition he
describes. If the paradox is not a facile one, that is in part because it is
rooted in the whole series of ironic parallels and contrasts between York
and Cade: York is disruptive and ambitious — but by Cade's standards
he is not anarchic; his hereditary claim to the throne is so distant as
to make his motives suspect, but it is hardly an outright fraud; he
acquiesces in the murder of Humphrey and demands the imprisonment

of Margaret's new favorite, Somerset, but he does not advocate the wholesale execution of "scholars, lawyers, courtiers, gentlemen," and other "false caterpillars" (IV.iv.35–36). In effect he epitomizes the ambiguous place of heroic virtue in a court that is weak and corrupt, has forfeited its claims to authority, but still believes in order.

Shakespeare's success with Jack Cade, Suffolk, and York indicates that he continued to rely on the popular historical drama for his significant character roles. If York represents another imitation of Tamburlaine, his protégé descends from "such conceits as clownage keeps in pay," the would-be soliders of the subplot such as Hempstring and Halterstick in *Horestes,* or Strumbo and Trompart in *Locrine.* The parting of Margaret and Suffolk quickly develops its own special idiom, but it is controlled by the conventional formulas of curse, lament, and complaint to fortune appropriate to a *Mirror*-like tragedy of thwarted ambition. All of these rhetorical materials are, of course, refashioned to suit Shakespeare's picture of Henry's court; but they were nevertheless ready at hand to illustrate why the fragmentation of that court was a more complicated event than the ethical categories of the opening scenes would suggest. Such a tradition can also be limiting; in this case it was perhaps less helpful with Gloucester than with the other principals. He stands for political rectitude, but he cannot compete imaginatively with Suffolk and York. When he next appears, it will be as a prophet, John of Gaunt, who stands outside the arena of political life.

In the last play of the trilogy, the heroic example shifts violently towards the anarchic. Two of its principal spokesmen, Young Clifford and York's son Richard, are in fact already audible by the close of *2 Henry VI.* Here is Young Clifford speaking over the body of his father:

> Henceforth I will not have to do with pity:
> Meet I an infant of the house of York,
> Into as many gobbets will I cut it
> As wild Medea young Absyrtus did:
> In cruelty will I seek out my fame.

(V.ii.56–60)

Henceforth the emphasis will fall upon the destructiveness of uncontrolled heroic wrath, and Seneca will join Marlowe as a presiding inspiration.

3 Henry VI

Civil war was not a popular theme in the Elizabethan playhouse. Despite the timeliness of the subject and the playwrights' eagerness to advertise their moral utility, the conjunction of a God-ordained English magistrate, a treasonable usurper, and a populace in arms carried political overtones that were altogether too uncomfortable for the popular companies to manage. The legal difficulties of the Lord Chamberlain's Men over the despotism scenes in *Richard II* are too well known to rehearse here; and Queen Elizabeth's celebrated remark on that occasion can be taken as a firm royal endorsement to the hundred and sixty-odd "Documents of Control" reprinted by E. K. Chambers.[20] Small wonder that most playwrights elected to circumvent by as wide a margin as possible the nightmares of deposition and murder that comprised so much of English history in the fifteenth century. Entries in the *Annals of English Drama* for the years 1580–1590 show about fifteen histories set in classical times or exotic locales; of these, twelve depict wars of conquest, two deal with civil wars, but in a setting (Republican Rome) where no sanctity was attached to hereditary succession, and one, *The Battle of Alcazar,* can only be described as an uncontrolled melange of Senecan tragedy, Marlovian ambition, and warmed-over moral commonplaces. Along with these titles there are two English histories, *The Famous Victories of Henry V* and *Edward III,* which treat wars of conquest, and one two-part play of uncertain date, *The Troublesome Reign of King John,* which does not treat a domestic rebellion.[21]

This rough tabulation will serve to recall that Shakespeare's decision to dramatize the latter part of Henry's reign, a decision which he probably reached sometime in or before 1590, must have led him to take a fresh look at the theater of the 1580's. Any recension of the events that followed the battle of St. Albans would presumably have had to include the outright murder not only of King Henry VI, but also of his son Prince Edward, the "legitimate" pretender York, and his youngest son, the Earl of Rutland. Such materials plainly demanded a less equivocal attitude towards heroic violence than the playwright had hitherto displayed: for it would have been utterly unthinkable to endow the "agents" that stood behind these legendary atrocities with orthodox humanistic ideals. In *1 Henry VI* Shakespeare had contrasted a civilized and purified picture of martial fortitude to its base counterpart, the fake unnatural valor of Joan La Pucelle. *2 Henry VI* takes a more ambivalent view of the aspiring mind; but in so far as York's ambitions are supported by his royal ancestry and martial pre-eminence, and by the manifest weaknesses of Henry's court, his role can still be formulated in terms of humanistic values common to the popular drama and Elizabethan politics.[22] Moreover, once civil war erupts on the battlefield itself, Shakespeare is careful to scale down the proportions of York's aggression. His climactic encounter is not with the king, but with the king's champion Clifford, and both of these parties respectfully place their dispute within the decorum of a chivalric trial by combat:

> *Clif.*   What seest thou in me, York? Why dost thou pause?
> *York.*   With thy brave bearing should I be in love,
>   But that thou art so fast mine enemy.
> *Clif.*   Nor should thy prowess want praise and esteem,
>   But that 'tis shown ignobly and in treason.
> *York.*   So let it help me now against thy sword
>   As I in justice and true right express it.
> *Clif.*   My soul and body on the action both!
> *York.*   A dreadful lay! Address thee instantly.
> *Clif.*   *La fin couronne les oeuvres.*
>   [*They fight, and Clifford falls and dies.*]
> *York.*   Thus war hath given thee peace, for thou art still.
>   Peace with his soul, heaven, if it be thy will!
>   (*2 Henry VI,* V.ii.19–30)

The very different image of heroic character that is to predominate in *3 Henry VI* is already apparent in the first few lines of the play, which, like the second scene of *Macbeth,* probe the uncertain boundaries that divide acts of war from crimes of blood. York's stirring account of his army's victory over Clifford, Stafford, and the "great Lord of Northumberland,/Whose war-like ears could never brook retreat" (I.i.4–5) finds its gruesome sequel in the reports of his assembled family. Edward announces that "Lord Stafford's father, Duke of Buckingham,/Is either slain or wounded dangerous" and invites his father to "behold his blood" (10–11; 13). His brother Falconbridge adds to this "the Earl of Wiltshire's blood" (14). Richard rounds off the demonstration by throwing down the Duke of Somerset's head, and concluding "Thus do I hope to shake King Henry's head" (20). Such relish of violence and bloodshed places York's struggle to attain his "right" in rather a new perspective. His wish to "raise aloft the milk-white rose" (2 *Henry VI*, I.ii.255) now appears as an unrelenting compulsion to slaughter all the House of Lancaster. Hence, one is not surprised to discover later in this scene that the Lancastrians themselves now act from motives of revenge rather than the feudal loyalties displayed in the last act of 2 *Henry VI*. There is to be no more talk of "praise and esteem," or of "justice and true right." When Young Clifford meets York, and is himself challenged to personal combat, Northumberland advises him that "It is war's prize to take all vantages;/And ten to one is no impeach of valor" (I.iv.59–60). Not surprisingly, the play's chief oratorical forms are the *vituperatio* and the lament. Within these set speech types the formulaic virtues of a noble ancestry, strength and beauty, courage and wisdom are continually "reversed," in keeping with the regular procedures of rhetorical invective, into their opposites: congenital viciousness, deformity and ugliness, brutality and cunning.

If the play as a whole is to be seen as anything more than a nihilistic bloodbath of tragedy and revenge, it is necessary to keep in mind the vision of aristocratic ideals and public order that makes the implicit contrast to these "reversals." For the transition from 2 *Henry VI* to 3 *Henry VI* marks the dramatist's continuing discovery of an historical process that followed naturally from the extension of heroic ideals into Tudor politics. An analysis of aristocratic corruption portends the rise of a new "prince," one who still identifies himself with the traditional values of hereditary nobility, strength, and courage, although he presses his claims with an unexampled show of ruthlessness and cunning. He offers the hope of a return to a nobler age; but the very act of violence that brings about his accession foreshadows the utter dissolution of all aristocratic values and social obligations until, finally, the torrent of revenge and civil war gives rise to a new Machiavel, and a last parody of heroic *virtù*. In *Richard II* and *Julius Caesar* the entire conception receives its mature expression. There the workings of retribution and expiation finally permit one to infer some principle of order beyond the mere anarchy of civil war. But the characters of *3 Henry VI* inhabit a less hopeful world. Except for the momentary flicker of King Henry's prophecy over young Harry Richmond, there is only the ceaseless deterioration of aristocratic idealism into uncontrolled violence and brutality. Although its end cannot be foreseen, its source can be discovered in that original encounter between York and Old Clifford.

When Warwick, early in the first scene, remarks to Northumberland, Westmoreland, and Young Clifford, "You forget/That we are those which chas'd you from the field/And slew your fathers" (I.i.89–91), it is clear from the preceding dialogue that he merely intends to remind them that they are no longer in any position to enforce Henry's title to the crown. Their reply, however, puts a radically different construction on his allusion:

> *Nor.* Yes, Warwick, I remember it to my grief;
> And, by his soul, thou and thy house shall rue it.
> *West.* Plantagenet, of thee and these thy sons,
> Thy kinsmen and thy friends, I'll have more lives
> Than drops of blood were in my father's veins.
> *Clif.* Urge it no more; lest that, instead of words,
> I send thee, Warwick, such a messenger
> As shall revenge his death before I stir.
>
> (I.i.93–100)

With these words, the battle of St. Albans is transformed, *ex post facto*, from the open, chivalric test enacted by York and Old Clifford into a personal tragedy involving the violation of family pieties. Indeed, the political origins of this conflict — the deposition and murder of Richard II, the weakness of the Lancastrian title, the attainder of York's father for treason — are scarcely mentioned after the brief debate in the opening scene that is defiantly sidetracked by the three aggrieved sons. Even the gentle king passes quickly over the public allegiance that is properly due to him, and seeks to arouse more visceral sentiments:

Earl of Northumberland, he slew thy father,
And thine, Lord Clifford; and you both have vow'd revenge
On him, his sons, his favourites, and his friends.

(I.i.54–56)

When Henry does allow himself to be persuaded, for moral as well as
practical reasons, to reach a compromise, he is at once deserted not only
by his followers, but also by his queen, who seeks nothing less than
"utter ruin of the House of York" (I.i.261). The subsequent murder of
York at the hands of Clifford and Margaret duly ensures that his three
sons also will act in a spirit of filial revenge. The aggrieved children,
like Pyrrhus in Seneca's *Troades* and in Ovid,[23] find that the death of
their heroic fathers demands to be remembered as a crime of violence;
and in keeping with the time-honored logic of revenge, their filial pas-
sions enjoin them to seek retribution in kind. The premise at work here
is succinctly formulated by Young Clifford at the close of *2 Henry VI*:
"York not our old men spares,/No more will I their babes" (V.ii.
51–52); similarly, to pursue the classical instance, the son of Achilles
determines to become the murderer of Astyanax.

The playwright's mastery of these unfamiliar materials is apparent
from the consistency with which he places the breakdown of personal
ideals in their apposite historical contexts. If *3 Henry VI* does not degenerate into a pseudopolitical revenge tragedy like *The Battle of
Alcazar,* it is because all of its important characters have, in effect, a
double role. Each is conceived both as a member of an aggrieved family
and as a participant in a complex political struggle. York is a legitimate
claimant to the throne, but he is also the father of young Rutland; Clifford is champion of the royalist cause but also, like Northumberland,
Oxford (see III.iii.101–107), and Westmoreland, he is son to a slain
father; Warwick is a "Proud setter up and puller down of kings" (III.
iii.157), but he is also son to the "stabb'd" Old Salisbury (II.vi.30) and
brother to younger Salisbury,[24] who dies in battle crying "Warwick,
revenge! Brother, revenge my death!" (II.iii.19); Margaret is the Yorkist
queen, but she is also mother of the disinherited Prince Henry, and the
outraged wife of his "unnatural" father King Henry (I.i.225); finally,
the three sons of York achieve sovereignty and impose order at the end,
but the deeds by which they acquire and maintain the crown are those

of avenging sons and unnatural brothers. As in *2 Henry VI,* only on a universal scale, the public status and obligations of these characters are measured against the increasingly dubious claims of their personal ideals. Familial honor, hitherto a counterweight to uncontrolled ambition and reckless personal ideals, now becomes the source of new atrocities. The sundering of honor and politics is nowhere more apparent than in this play, where every attempt to invoke a political compromise is frustrated by the demand for personal revenge, until one finally arrives at the hollow pretense of "country's peace and brothers' loves" (V.vii.36) that concludes the action even as it foreshadows the frauds and fratricides of *Richard III.*

It is the repentant *"Son that hath kill'd his father"* (II.v.54 S.D.) and *"Father that hath kill'd his son"* (II.v.78 S.D.) who epitomize the chaos that results when personal revenges are projected into the arena of history. Here the public role of each figure (the Son was "press'd forth" by the king, the Father fights on the Yorkist side) fades into utter insignificance before the magnitude of the family tragedy. And, at the same time, the futility of seeking retribution for the "crimes" of war is implicit in the very situation: these bereaved mothers will "ne'er be satisfied" (II.v.106). For the participants, deeds of violence committed in battle are finally anonymous — indeed, they are the more tragic for being so. Both parties "knew not what they did." The ultimate result of such "Erroneous, mutinous, and unnatural" quarrels (90) is not the satisfaction of accomplished revenge, but the discovery of utter bereavement. "I'll bear thee hence," says the lamenting Son, "where I may weep my fill" (113); and the Father adds,

> . . . let them fight that will,
> For I have murder'd where I should not kill.

> (121–122)

The tragic perception of the Son and Father depends, of course, upon the unique irony of their situation. Had father met father, the episode might have become a simple restatement of the main plot, in which the sons find their revenges by destroying one another. Hence, the spirit of lucidity in which they can acknowledge that a father and a son have been "murder'd" (not simply "kill'd"), and still forswear war for lamentation, necessarily is unavailable to the principal antagonists in this conflict. For Clifford and Margaret, Richard and his brothers, a public act of violence against any member of the family can only be construed as a personal crime, to be revenged by what Othello would call an "honorable murder." Richard speaks for all of them when he urges his brothers to forgo the "passion" of lament for the *consolatio* of revenge (II.i.79–88).

To arrive at a more detailed estimate of the play's politics, one must again turn to its dramatic format and rhetorical designs. As an historical revenge play, *3 Henry VI* finds its operative conceptions of human character in the set topics of rhetorical invective. York's great *vituperatio* of Margaret (I.iv.111–168), the Lancastrian queen who has learned to play the Amazon, enumerates the significant "topics" of revenge drama by reversing all the set commonplaces of demonstrative oratory. The despised "She-wolf of France" whose father is "not so wealthy as an English yeoman" (I.iv.111, 123), has exchanged her feminine *bona animi,* modesty and "government" (132), for the impudent ferocity of an "Amazonian trull" (114). Her grotesque display of "courage" can only be understood as an inexplicable deviation from nature, a relinquishment of human identity for the unchanging "vizard" (116) of the actor.

> 'Tis beauty that doth oft make women proud;
> But God he knows thy share thereof is small.
> 'Tis virtue that does make them most admir'd;
> The contrary doth make thee wonder'd at.
> 'Tis government that makes them seem divine;
> The want thereof makes thee abominable.
> Thou art as opposite to every good
> As the Antipodes are unto us,
> Or as the south to the Septentrion.
>
> (128–136)

The descriptive figures amplify this reversal of the civilized into the barbarous through stock epithets like the "outdoing" comparison to "tigers of Hyrcania" (155), and the celebrated "tiger's heart wrapp'd in a woman's hide" (137). Elsewhere in the play, these formulas for an unnatural revenge are reproduced in a wide variety of situations, usually in tiny pieces of invective interspersed throughout the dialogue, and occasionally in longer set speeches, but almost always with reference to Clifford or Richard. Local instances would include epithets like "cruel child-killer," "crook-back," and "foul misshapen stigmatic" (II.ii.112, 96, 136), as well as more extended figures such as Rutland's comparison of Clifford to a "pent-up lion" (I.iii.12–15) or Henry's picture of Richard as an "indigest, deformed lump" (V.vi.51), and lengthy pieces of invective such as Margaret's portrayal of Richard and his brothers as "bloody cannibals," "butchers," and "deathsmen" (V.v.59, 61, 65). All these examples (and more could be cited) point back to the elementary definitions of humanity invoked in York's address to Margaret. Together they present a composite image of the revenging son who determines to reproduce the original "crime" by destroying still another family: the playwright has come full circle from the idealistic wish of Old York and Young Talbot simply to "die in pride." His leading characters have become, in effect, the base, unnatural monsters that the Herculean hero originally set out to destroy.

The conception is not entirely original with *3 Henry VI*. The overarching transition from lofty epic deeds to downright savagery and murder is adumbrated in the Induction scene of *The Spanish Tragedy,* where the fallen courtier Don Andrea is transported away from the field of battle, past the Elysian abode of "wounded Hector" and "Achilles' Myrmidons," via Hades to the earthly theater of Revenge.[25] And the same contrast is treated more extensively, if less coherently, in Peele's *Battle of Alcazar.* Within this broad framework Clifford and Queen Margaret would resemble the paragons of Senecan cruelty, Atreus and Medea, each of whom satisfies a passion for revenge by tormenting an afflicted father with the death of his only child. The Senecan analogy is made explicit when Clifford vows to emulate "wild Medea" at the close of *2 Henry VI* (V.ii.59). Other allusions, of a fairly specific nature, can occasionally be heard as well. The napkin dipped in Rutland's blood, which Margaret uses to torment York in I.iv, was perhaps inspired by *The Spanish Tragedy,* while several lines in that scene suggest the influence of Kyd's *Soliman and Perseda.*[26] Like all these plays, *3 Henry VI* uses the materials of Senecan revenge tragedy to create an ambience in which the heroic pursuit of honor is released from the pieties that ordinarily regulate even bloodshed and violence. In so far as the play that results is one where dukes, princes, and kings are slaughtered without regard to their high political status, it is apparent that the logic of the revenge play is being used as a kind of general metaphor for civil war, and the individual miscreants are, accordingly, judged with far greater severity in this play than in the more psychological dramas of Seneca and Kyd.

The revenge-play format, however, is only a part of the total design of *3 Henry VI,* which, like *The Jew of Malta,* moves through its isolated revenges to wholesale aggressions on the very fabric of society. Emerging from an environment in which the *lex talionis* enjoins men to violate all moral and political obligations, the youngest son of York determines to disregard the very fraternal ties that hold together his own house. His decision to act as "myself alone" is paralleled partly by Edward's self-regarding exercise of his royal prerogatives and partly by Clarence's temporary abjuration of his two brothers. But it was inevitable, given the Tudor myth about Richard, that he should exemplify the final declension from revenger to Machiavel. The two types were commonly associated by such moralists as Gentillet, who portrays the legendary Italian "delectation, pleasure, and contentment" in revenge that is exacted "after some strange and barbarous fashion." [27] For a dramatist writing in 1590, the Machiavel and revenger of the popular stage would already have intersected in *The Jew of Malta.* So far as one can judge from the corrupt text in which that play survives, Marlowe's hero represents a transmutation of Kyd's impassioned revengers along lines that suggest, in some respects, Shakespeare's subsequent treatment of Richard III.[28] For both Barabas and Richard are, at bottom, social and moral outcasts whose malice towards the individuals who have injured them evolves into an anarchic revolt against all those who are of "better person" than themselves. The crucial point of resemblance is evident in Barabas' soliloquy after his brethren have left him to meditate upon his afflictions.

[*2nd Jew.*] Farewell, Barabas.

Exeunt.

Bar.   Ay, fare you well,
         See the simplicity of these base slaves,
         Who—for the villains have no wit themselves—

> Think me to be a senseless lump of clay
> That will with every water wash to dirt.
> No, Barabas is born to better chance
> And framed of finer mold than common men
> That measure nought but by the present time.
> A reaching thought will search his deepest wits
> And cast with cunning for the time to come.
>
> (*Jew*, I.ii.214–223)

The Shakespearian sequel to this comes in the third act of *3 Henry VI*, as Richard's brothers bid him farewell:

> [*King Ed.*] Lords, use her honourably.
>
> *Exeunt all but Richard.*
>
> *Rich.*   Ay, Edward will use women honourably.
>   Would he were wasted, marrow, bones, and all. . . .
>
> (III.ii.123–125)

For the next seventy lines this "valiant crook-back prodigy" (I.iv.75) unfolds his elaborate meditation on the ambitions of nature's outcast. Like Barabas, he owes his aggressiveness in part to an inbred "deformity" that excludes him from any conventional place in human society, coupled with his unique talents for succeeding on his own terms. For Marlowe's hero, this role proves something of a dead end. After completing his devilish revenges on Ferneze's son Lodowick, Barabas simply continues to devise schemes to outwit and exploit his Christian antagonists. Almost apologetically, Barabas soliloquizes, "I must confess we come not to be kings" (I.i.127), as if he were explaining why his Machiavellian talents must be confined to the limited possibilities offered by the corrupt citizenry of Malta. Richard, however, emerges from a world of heroic ambition, and he can see beyond the possibilities of ceaseless revenge to the "golden time" (III.ii.127) of personal sovereignty, when the "misshap'd trunk that bears this head" will "Be round impaled with a glorious crown" (III.ii.170–171). Accordingly, his soliloquy concludes with a final allusion to Marlowe's hyperbole, refashioned to suit the worthy examples set for himself by this heroic Machiavel:

I'll drown more sailors than the Mermaid shall;
I'll slay more gazers than the basilisk;
I'll play the orator as well as Nestor,
Deceive more slily than Ulysses could,
And, like a Sinon, take another Troy.
I can add colours to the chameleon,
Change shapes with Proteus for advantages,
And set the murderous Machiavel to school.
Can I do this, and cannot get a crown?
Tut! were it further off, I'll pluck it down.

(III.ii.186–195)

The rhetorical frame is still that of *Tamburlaine*. Richard will "outdo" the beauty of the Mermaid, the eloquence of Nestor, the prudence of Ulysses, and the deadly might of the basilisk. If the joke is obvious enough, it should also be clear that Shakespeare's mock-heroics have come of age. This is neither a country girl dabbling in witchcraft and sham heroics nor a clothier of Kent leading a peasants' revolt. Richard speaks as a Renaissance prince, and he chooses his examples with a due sense of decorum: Proteus was a god of epic tradition; Nestor, Ulysses, and Sinon decided the most important battle of legendary history; and Machiavelli had undertaken to explain the revolutions of fortune, in antiquity and in the present, through a dispassionate analysis of power politics. Richard's aspiration to outdo the celebrated Greeks and their modern apologist gives a final, ironic turn of the screw to the humanistic pursuit of fame and honor. Perhaps the emulation of Hector and Hercules, Aeneas and Achilles, which has by now made anarchy out of the social and political order, was ill conceived from the start. For if one judges by the criterion of practical efficacy, such fame as these worthies achieved may amount to no more than a mere escutcheon, a dubious memorial to their grinning honor. Hence Richard can turn the very formulas of rhetorical invective to his own advantage, arguing that it is precisely those qualities which make a man despicable in the world of copybook humanism that best qualify him for an earthly crown. Beneath the parody, there are only two features of Marlowe's original conception that remain intact: the drive towards absolute pre-eminence, and the ability to kill without remorse.

Even Sir Walter Raleigh, whose *History of the World* (1612) is a monument to the enduring hold of providential configurations on the Elizabethan imagination, would, one supposes, have had difficulty discerning the hand of the Almighty in this terrifying exposure of secular values. *3 Henry VI* pictures human history as the visible effect of uncontrolled revenge and cynical Machiavellian ambition, a final anarchic distortion of heroic ideals. And alongside that picture, as if in some final effort to counter the moral bankruptcy of these "honorable murders" by invoking Elizabethan convictions about the sacramental nature of kingship and the role of Providence in human affairs, Shakespeare intermittently draws our attention to the choric figure of the "gentle king." I have left Henry to the end, because he poses a melancholy counterstatement to the themes I have been pursuing. His character is a projection of orthodox pieties about politics and history as they appear when divorced from any power to put them into effect. And he discovers, beneath the erratic reversals of *3 Henry VI,* an invitation to meditate on the fragility of his ideals before the repeated incursions of "sour Adversity" (III.i.24). When the exiled king re-enters *"disguised with a prayer book"* (III.i.12 S.D.) after the Battle of Towton, it is only to learn that the sacred oath of allegiance rendered unto a king is without meaning for the "simple men" (82) who take it. Later, before the battle of Coventry, Henry is further instructed in the relation between moral virtue and political power:

> *Exe.* The doubt is that he will seduce the rest.
> *K. Hen.* That's not my fear; my meed hath got me fame:
> I have not stopp'd mine ears to their demands,
> Nor posted off their suits with slow delays;
> My pity hath been balm to heal their wounds,
> My mildness hath allay'd their swelling griefs,
> My mercy dried their water-flowing tears;
> I have not been desirous of their wealth,
> Nor much oppress'd them with great subsidies,
> Nor forward of revenge, though they much err'd.
> Then why should they love Edward more than me?
> No, Exeter, these graces challenge grace;

And, when the lion fawns upon the lamb,
The lamb will never cease to follow him.

Shout within, "A York! A York!"

(IV.viii.37–50)

In the face of these grim realities Henry is intermittently drawn towards a retreat from the history that circumscribes his existence. The tragedy of the nameless Father and Son is counterpointed by his picture of a timeless pastoral idyll in which he would "be no better than a homely swain" (II.v.22). Later he resolves that he will "conquer Fortune's spite/By living low where Fortune cannot hurt me" and urges the Protectorship on Warwick, who is "fortunate" in all his deeds (IV.vi.19–20, 25). As even Warwick falls before the rising Yorkists, Henry can only retreat further from his own history, first into "patience," finally into the receding vistas of prophecy. In a gracious gesture towards the Tudor myth, Shakespeare has him bless young Henry Richmond (IV.vi.67–76). But Henry's last glimpse into the future takes place under less promising auspices:

> [*Hen.*] And if the rest be true which I have heard,
>   Thou cam'st —
> *Rich.*   I'll hear no more: die, prophet, in thy speech.
>
> *Stabs him.*
>
>   For this, amongst the rest, was I ordain'd.
>
> (V.vi.55–58)

This final, symbolic encounter surely intimates that Henry's benign vision of Richmond's "peaceful majesty" must be deferred to a world radically different from that of *Henry VI.*

5 The Tradition of Fame and the Arts of Policy: *Richard III* and *1 Henry IV*

1 Henry VI opens with a lament for Henry V, the hero-king who was "too famous to live long." As Elizabethan audiences were soon to learn, he was also too famous to be buried and forgotten. In *1 Henry IV* Shakespeare had already begun to reassemble the legend that is forfeited in the earlier cycle, and *Henry V*, while it is uncompromisingly severe in its repudiation of the French chivalric style, remains the only play that he could have written with Hall's *Union* in one hand and Erasmus' *Institutio Principis* in the other. In itself, this revival of the hero-king is hardly surprising. The figure, like the theatrical conventions that secured his popularity, was an indestructible part of Shakespeare's world. The student of English drama in the seventeenth century, following this figure through the plays of Dryden and his contemporaries, is bound to be more impressed by his resilience and adaptability than by his occasional disappearance into the stereotypes of political orthodoxy. The problem at hand, once again, has rather to do with the peculiar adjustments that ensue when the heroic pattern is assimilated to English social convention. The later histories challenge our attention because they resume that problem and, more particularly, because they suggest a new way of looking at it. Where *Henry VI* chronicles the attrition of the chivalric legacy throughout the fifteenth century, the later histories presuppose that the legend of the hero-king has a life of its own, a currency in popular belief that will outlast any number of "vile politicians." For a legendary ideal is liable to persist indefinitely, as Machiavelli recognized, once it passes into the mythology of statecraft: whatever the Prince himself may come to know or believe, it is still required that he identify himself to the world through the rituals of chivalry.

Thus the early trilogy will stand as "heroical" literature in a sense which does not apply to the histories that follow. Whatever their peculiar misdeeds and betrayals, the principal figures of *Henry VI* all can give their personal assent to the heroic traditions that secure their public identities. True, Richard, Duke of Gloucester, introduces himself as an aspirant "Machiavel"; but the imagery and tone of his exposition are still controlled by the conventions of Marlovian conqueror-drama. Machiavelli would not have recognized it. Richard III, Henry Bolingbroke, and his son Hal inhabit a world that is considerably less assured about its relationship to the ideal past of epic and romance. They participate in the rituals of chivalry and courtly display, but they do not, and cannot, wholly identify themselves with what they have come to recognize as a political myth. Even Henry V, on the eve of Agincourt, acknowledges that the identity which "Ceremony" confers does not square with his deepest intuitions about himself. Like his father, he has to live with the knowledge that the formal attributes of "majesty" are, in effect, a special "person" or "presence" which must always be kept "fresh and new" (*1 Henry IV*, III.ii.56, 55). The crux of the problem, as Richard III discovers on the eve of Bosworth Field, lies in the relation of this "person" to the man who keeps it. "Everyone sees what you appear to be," Machiavelli reminds his new prince; "few really know what you are." [2] So much may be clear; but then, who does know what this new prince really is? How, if tradition does not tell him, can he know himself?

It is evident that Shakespeare comes to reappraise the heroic tradition and its significance in English history by way of these dilemmas. To pursue them through *Richard III* and *1 Henry IV*, the two plays that actually try to resolve them, is to gain a fuller sense both of the values which underlie *Henry VI* and of the conceptual limits within which the trilogy is enclosed. In *1 Henry VI* Shakespeare sets forth the criteria that differentiate heroic ceremony from mere "bravery." In *Richard III* he begins with a consummate impersonator, and proceeds to raise the larger problem of whether artifice and "form" can be taken as trustworthy determinants of a ruler's true nature. The critique that results strikes at the very notion of exemplary behavior. If the proper style really can be mastered by a self-professed "villain," what is there to prevent an unbroken chain of cynical princes and gullible subjects? In *Henry VI* the problem of authenticity can finally be resolved only by reference to ancestry and nurture. Talbot's rectitude is guaranteed because he is a Talbot; the Bastard's infamy is immanent in the circumstances of his birth. When these conventions break down in the succession of generations around which the trilogy is organized, there is nowhere to turn. The interested spectator can only try to weigh one man's pretensions against another's. The prince can only try to suit his performance to his audience's expectations. In *1 Henry IV* Shakespeare takes this erosion of traditional standards for granted, as a fact of political life, and thereby secures the freedom to redefine the incentives that lead a prince to elect the chivalric vocation. What Young Talbot inherits, Hal chooses for himself; and the reasoning that underlies his choice comprises, in turn, the fullest available justification for the heroic ideals of *Henry VI*.

Richard III

When Richard announces, "I am determined to prove a villain" (I.i.30), he is paying his farewell to the noble occupations of love and war and entering a more devious theater of operations, one in which he is the trickster and his antagonists are the gulls. As A. P. Rossiter has said, he is the companion of Barabas and Volpone, a "murderous practical joker" who "inhabits a world where everyone deserves everything he can do to them." [3] His evident amusement at being unsuited to play the courtier at Edward's triumphs seems calculated to stress the essential incongruity: what is this vicious, ironic comedian doing in a serious play about English history? Unlike his predecessors in the earlier trilogy, and the plays that stand behind them, Richard possesses no vision of aristocratic honor to establish his significance as a humanistic example. Nor can he be adequately described (although it is becoming customary to do so) as simply an admonitory stereotype of political ambition. The limitations of that idea are aptly summarized in Coleridge's wise and penetrating comment on the play:

As, in the last [*Richard III*], Shakespeare has painted a man where ambition is the channel in which the ruling impulse runs, so, in the first [*Richard II*], he has given us a character, under the name of Bolingbroke, or Henry IV., where ambition itself, conjoined unquestionably with great talents, is the ruling impulse. In Richard III. the pride of intellect makes use of ambition as its means; in Bolingbroke the gratification of ambition is the end, and talents are the means.[4]

If Richard were ambitious in the manner of Henry Bolingbroke — or his own father York — his character would present no special difficulty. But "pride of intellect" is less easily accounted for, in an historical framework, than heroic aspiration or ordinary political canniness.

The conception must have seemed novel even to the enthusiastic audiences who applauded Burbage's rendition of the part. There was little in the sixteenth-century portrayals of Richard that would have prepared them for it. The monster who emerges from Sir Thomas More's *History of King Richard III* is a creature of popular demonology conceived in a spirit of classical irony. As court propagandist for Henry Richmond's son, More took pains to preserve the Tudor myth about the Yorkist Antichrist who was born with hair and teeth and grew up to kill the babes in the Tower; as an urbane humanist historian he kept the legendary monster under control by treating his aspirations as an elaborate, grotesque joke. Consequently, "The History of King Richard III" occupies a special place in the pages of Grafton, Hall, and Holinshed. Rather than a loose collection of historical episodes, it constitutes a polished piece of rhetorical invective, designed to set forth its object as a hopeless case of depravity and deformity. For a playwright such material would seem to offer meager alternatives. Thomas Legge manfully tried to recreate Richard as a weak and vicious tyrant in the neo-Senecan play *Richardus Tertius* (1579). Ten years later, writing for a popular rather than a university audience, the anonymous author of *The True Tragedy of Richard III* simply ignored More altogether and, like Colley Cibber some hundred and ten years later, cast Richard as a Marlovian conqueror with an anguished conscience. Shakespeare took a third course. In effect, he preserved the myth about Richard's monstrosity, but he transferred More's alert sense of irony to Richard himself. In the *History* it is the witty and sophisticated narrator who characterizes Richard and Buckingham as mere actors, wondered at by a populace that can only regard them as figures in some private charade; in the play it is the hero himself who eagerly cultivates the role of stage manager and elicits his audience's unanimous acclaim. In theatrical terms, the youngest son of York happily assumes the role of a villain — a lineal descendant of the Vice, the clown, and the comic Machiavel, in whom the desire to entertain, to maximize the possibilities for comic impersonation and verbal wit, is always ascendant.

How was it that Shakespeare, in recounting the final, ghastly aftermath of *Henry VI,* took such a figure for his hero? And what are the connections between the play's comedy and its sombre historical backdrop? Such questions as these do not loom very large in recent criticism of the play. It is rather the explicitly moral dimension of Richard's character that has attracted the most attention from the historically minded criticism of this century. The classic account of the "modern" Richard is set forth in the chapter on Shakespeare's villains in E. E. Stoll's *Shakespeare Studies: Historical and Comparative in Method.*[5] By Stoll's reckoning all of Shakespeare's great villains personify one side of a traditional Christian dualism, projecting the eternal struggle between good and evil onto the secular stage through such historical analogues as the Vice, the Machiavel, and the Senecan badman. The villainies of a character like Richard can thus be taken as a self-fulfilling exercise in anarchy and evil, utterly divorced from any plausible human motivations. More specialized studies, particularly those of Bernard Spivack, Mario Praz, and F. L. Lucas, along with Wolfgang Clemen's magisterial *Kommentar zu Shakespeares Richard III,* have all tended to confirm the hypothesis.[6] The play may be taken, in other words, as part revenge drama, with Margaret as Divine Nemesis, and part morality, with Richard as "the formal vice, Iniquity" (III.i.82). As such it will appear not to be a history, in the sense that I have been using the term, but rather a tragedy, more precisely, a tragedy that now and again affords glimpses, through Margaret's elaborate choric laments and Richard's crisis of conscience, into the formal configurations and traditional homiletics of Christian historiography. This reading offers the surest guide to the moral scaffolding of the piece — but it takes the risk of reducing the adroit theatrical intellect that delighted Lamb, Hazlitt, and generations of playgoers, to a mere cipher in a providential scheme. It exposes the ethical confusions implicit in the eighteenth- and nineteenth-century idealizations of Richard's character, but it fails to account for the intellectual brilliance that prompted them in the first place.

I recur to the play's comedy because it bears directly on many of the topics that occupied the previous chapter. The jokes originate, it will be recalled, in *3 Henry VI*, with Richard's mock-heroic promise to emulate and outdo the most successful orators of antiquity, Ulysses, Nestor, and Sinon, and the godlike pattern of quick-change artistry, Proteus. If he opens *Richard III* by formulating his ideal in less spacious phrases, the shift in tone, from classical allusion to unvarnished assertion, only serves to underscore the irony of his original citations: "villains" — clowns, parasites, time-servers, men who live by their tongues — have a way of insinuating themselves into history and epic, genres where they cut an unlikely figure just as the "unfashionable" Richard looks out of place at Edward's triumph. In public, however, Richard is still careful to keep decorum, with the result that the humanistic history of *Henry VI* repeats itself in this play: only it repeats itself as farce. For much of the first four acts, Richard flaunts his "pride of intellect" by mimicking the visible forms of aristocratic and heroic virtue as if they were just so many parts to be learned. Speaking through his mouthpiece Buckingham, he makes the sternest appraisal of that "base declension and loathed bigamy" (III.ii.189) which would disqualify Edward's lineage from the throne. He can be a courtly lover like Suffolk (I.ii), a loyal brother in adversity like Warwick (I.iii), and a forthright, plainspeaking counselor like Gloucester (I.iii). When occasion demands, he proves as stirring a martial orator as Talbot (V.iii), and an even more pious recluse than Henry VI (III.vii). In the civilized world of the court these postures serve Shakespeare's "slave of nature" just as the armor and curtle-axe that Tamburlaine puts on serves Marlowe's hero: they are the "adjuncts" by which he establishes his claims to that high status which his birth had apparently denied him. Richard, however, never dreams of suggesting that the outward forms of nobility should fit the man beneath; indeed he is quite explicit to the contrary. He becomes a lover to frustrate the ends of love, a counselor to inhibit the exercise of good counsel, and a patriot to subvert the *respublica*.

Where Marlowe's aspirant hero selects one commonplace definition of nobility and lives it out, Shakespeare's aspirant villain selects them all, but views each in the reductive light of satire.

Beneath his Protean transformations there is a stable, unchanging Richard, but he is identifiable not so much as a moral stereotype as an extension of Marlowe's belief in the efficacy of the individual will to shape the world by its own force of character. In Richard's case the conception has all been channelled into "pride of intellect"; but the pride, the core of heroic self-assertion, remains intact. Hence the curious fact that this "villain" never stoops to such mere devices as the forged letters, shuffled corpses, and poisoned rapiers that are the stock in trade of his predecessors Barabas and Lorenzo. As if in deference to the more lofty decorum of an historical action, he engages his enemies at first hand; and even as they are tricked by his imitations of virtue, they are tried, tempted, and overcome by his comic assault on their ethical defenses. Invariably the success of his impersonations depends on the victim's inability to distinguish the false from the genuine article. As the scourge of whatever God stands behind Margaret's unremitting moral calculus, Richard tempts each inhabitant of this "dark monarchy" with the illusion of virtue best calculated to elicit his personal failing: Clarence's blind adherence to fraternal ties (which had led him to rejoin Edward after taking the sacrament to fight for Warwick); Anne's readiness to forgive Richard his murders at Tewkesbury — if they were all for love; Hastings' fatuous satisfaction at the execution of his ancient enemies, Dorset, Rivers, and Grey; and, finally, Buckingham's naive supposition that usurpation can be compacted by a gentlemen's agreement. Like *Tamburlaine,* much of *Richard III* is about the intrinsic superiority of a natural virtue for sovereignty in a corrupt world; only it views the phenomenon through parody and impersonation rather than aristocratic idealism. By so doing, the play finally calls into question the whole notion of a "public" aristocratic style of life based on humanistic ideals.

If the comedy were not so relentlessly mock-heroic, if Richard had made his way to the throne by forged letters and poisoned rapiers, presumably the conclusion would have shown us Wily Beguiled, as in "the farce of the old English humour, the terribly serious, even savage comic humour" that T.S. Eliot associates with *The Jew of Malta*.[7] But

Shakespeare's intention was not to produce a bloody farce contrived by "God your only jig-maker," nor was he interested (as was the author of *The True Tragedy*) in casting Richmond as a bold and bloody revenger. It may be, as Hamlet says, that "the enginer/Hoist with his own petar" (III.iv.206–207) provides the most entertaining of ironies; but Richard is not permitted to continue as an "engineer" beyond the fourth act. Beneath the brilliant impersonations that decorate its surface, *Richard III* moves inexorably towards the consummation of the Tudor myth about English history; and as if to preclude any ambiguity on this point, the final act externalizes the moral constituents of the myth in the most uncompromising terms. The battleground shifts from the guilt ridden court to Bosworth Field, and the representatives of good and evil, Richmond and Richard, are presented as two sides of a stable polarity.

This movement into a fully providential vision of history does not depend, however, on Richard's simply being reduced to a figure in a pattern. The externalization of moral values on the plane of national history is exactly paralleled, and extended into an individual conscience, when Richard looks within himself. As the lights burn blue, he at last begins to apprehend inexorable processes of historical *time* ("It is now dead midnight" [180]) moving towards their appointed end. Now his "villainies" reappear to him as sins, all crying out for the moment of judgment:

> Perjury, perjury, in the highest degree,
> Murder, stern murder, in the direst degree,
> All several sins, all used in each degree,
> Throng to the bar, crying all, "Guilty! guilty!"
>
> (V.iii.197–200)

The villain who would be king discovers what it means to be a "murderer" in a providential universe, and his astute mockery of what the world admires as virtue now returns to mock him as well: "Fool, of thyself speak well. Fool, do not flatter" (193). It has frequently been argued that Shakespeare was trying, at this point, to do something for which he was not yet prepared: to portray the conscience of an earlier Macbeth, a murderer tormented by self-knowledge. But there is another way of taking these lines. For what has always been denied by Richard's postures and calculations — as it is denied here — is just that core of personal honor, or "worth," which would have left him with a self to know. Had he ever possessed it, his recognition that "I am I" might indeed have foreshadowed the tragic ironies that result when Othello and Macbeth, as well as lesser men (like Claudius and Laertes), confront themselves. Instead we get a momentary glimpse into the hall of mirrors where Machiavelli's player king must look for self-knowledge. "Everyone sees what you appear to be, few really know what you are." Having made his "person" solely the creature of his audiences' expectations, Richard finds it impossible to know what he is, or to imagine what he might have been. On the one hand there is the most austere of moral appraisals, on the other, flattery; but no recollection of, or any meaning for, the performance itself.

No one would question that Richard's sudden apprehension of his own past shows, to borrow Coleridge's words again, "the dreadful consequences of placing the moral in subordination to the intellectual." Whether Shakespeare was able to convey this lesson "at the same time that he taught the superiority of moral greatness" [8] is rather more problematic. In order to establish Richmond in his special role as God's Captain, Shakespeare found it necessary to expunge all traces of what his audience would have recognized as "heroic" from the character; and readers ever since have noted the relative flatness of Richard's conqueror.[9] Richmond's final prayer, of course, has a way of disarming this criticism: one would not wish to be among those "traitors" who do not say "Amen." But the very fact that Shakespeare found it appropriate to go to this extreme indicates the extent of his disillusionment with the tradition of fame. Conventional ideas of personal worth enter this play only as brittle parodies: for Richard they are springes to catch woodcocks; for Shakespeare, the bait of falsehood by which he takes his carp of truth. Small wonder that Richmond elects to say a prayer rather than celebrate his triumph.

The prayer celebrates a paradise regained. Not a "paradise within thee happier far," to be sure, but nonetheless one in which God's Captain chooses piety over all those uncertain virtues that would elicit the last infirmity of a noble mind. This study has dealt, for the most part, with a narrow range of theatrical conventions and rhetorical strategies; but Shakespeare's experience with humanist history, at least in its wider implications, was scarcely an isolated phenomenon. The high regard of his own generation for the moral value of worthy *exempla* is captured in the stanzas that Fame addresses to Fortune in Drayton's *Legend of Robert, Duke of Normandy*:

> But I alone the Herald am of Heaven,
> Whose spacious Kingdome stretcheth farre and wide,
> Through ev'ry Coast upon the light'ning driven,
> As on the Sunne-beames, gloriously I ride,
> By them I mount, and downe by them I slide,
>   I register the Worlds long-during houres,
>   And know the hie Will of th'immortall powers.[10]

It is this Christianized *Fama* who presides at the death of Talbot in *1 Henry VI*. Shakespeare, more farsighted than his predecessors, seems to have recognized from the start that what she has to offer should never be confused with mere worldly success: it is rather a formal, humanistic *consolatio*, one that gives a permanent, didactic significance to the apparent failures of history.

Yet no one in the early histories ever learns from Talbot's example. Instead, the characters who succeed him drift further and further towards the Machiavellian premise that fame is the creature of earthly fortune.[11] Richard of course becomes the most eloquent spokesman for this point of view, urging his father, his brother, and finally himself, on towards the crown

> Within whose circuit is Elysium
> And all that poets feign of bliss and joy.

(I.ii.29–31)

The moral and political confusions that necessarily result are perhaps nowhere more explicit than in the scene where Sir John Montgomery declares to York's son Edward:

> What talk you of debating? In few words:
> If you'll not here proclaim yourself our King,

> I'll leave you to your fortune and be gone
> To keep them back that come to succour you.
> Why shall we fight, if you pretend no title?

(IV.vii.53–57)

It is an easy leap from here to the logic that openly refutes any attempt to distinguish between legitimate aspiration and brazen fakery:

> Treason doth never prosper, what's the reason?
> For if it prosper, none dare call it Treason.[12]

Richard III, then, comes to embody Shakespeare's severest appraisal of the quest for earthly fame, and, by extension, of the humanistic values which support that quest. The high permanence of fame is invoked only once in the play, and that occasion provides, I believe, the exception that proves the rule.

> *Prince.* I do not like the Tower, of any place.
>   Did Julius Caesar build that place, my lord?
> *Buck.* He did, my gracious lord, begin that place,
>   Which, since, succeeding ages have re-edified.
> *Prince.* Is it upon record, or else reported
>   Successively from age to age, he built it?
> *Buck.* Upon record, my gracious lord.
> *Prince.* But say, my lord, it were not regist'red,
>   Methinks the truth should live from age to age,
>   As 'twere retailed to all posterity,
>   Even to the general all-ending day.
> *Rich.* [*Aside*] So wise so young, they say do never live long.
> *Prince.* What say you, uncle?
> *Rich.* I say, without characters fame lives long.
>   [*Aside.*] Thus, like the formal Vice, Iniquity,
>   I moralize two meanings in one word.
> *Prince.* That Julius Caesar was a famous man:
>   With what his valor did enrich his wit,
>   His wit set down to make his valor live.
>   Death makes no conquest of this conqueror,

> For now he lives in fame, though not in life.
> I'll tell you what, my cousin Buckingham —
> *Buck.* What, my gracious lord?
> *Prince.* An if I live until I be a man,
> I'll win our ancient right in France again
> Or die a soldier as I lived a king.
> *Rich.* [*Aside.*] Short summers lightly have a forward
> spring.
>
> (III.i.68–94)

It is hardly necessary to expound Richard's cryptic "meanings" in order to appreciate the ironies of the situation. This is the one case where the rule given earlier — that "everyone deserves everything he can do to them" — does not apply. The young prince inquires whether Julius Caesar indeed began the building of the Tower of London. His faith in the enduring, worldly efficacy of his grammar-school training in the humanities ("Death makes no conquest of this conqueror") and his eagerness to "win our ancient right in France again" can only be a source of private amusement to his uncle, the callous veteran of *2* and *3 Henry VI*. It was also, one supposes, the focus of more poignant ironies for the bookish young playwright who had already measured the distance between Talbot and Gloucester. Youth is betrayed by the "formal Vice, Iniquity"; the Tower is not a "monument" — it is a charnel house.

The irony, of course, includes Richard as well. Despite his efforts to falsify the account, his own infamy is assured "Even to the general all-ending day," not because of what chroniclers will set "upon record" — but because "murder will out." The playwright's idea of history, like his ideals of personal "worth," has undergone a drastic transformation. Coming to terms with one historical tradition, Shakespeare arrives at another, which we may tentatively identify as Christian and providential.

1 Henry IV

In dedicating *The Prince* to Lorenzo the Magnificent, Machiavelli pauses to explain why it is that "a man of humble and obscure condition" should venture to "discuss and direct the government of princes."

. . . for in the same way that landscape painters station themselves in the valleys in order to draw mountains or high ground,
and ascend an eminence in order to get a good view of the plains,
so it is necessary to be a prince to know thoroughly the nature of
the people, and one of the populace to know the nature of princes.[13]

The treatise that follows is, technically speaking, still another "mirror
for princes" and it observes the same format as most of its predecessors
in the genre.[14] There is, however, an immense difference between
Machiavelli's perspective on the ordinary humanistic virtues and that of,
say, Erasmus; and the difference goes far deeper than the Italian's occasional cynicism about the value of earthly fame. Machiavelli recog-
nizes that it is still necessary for a Renaissance ruler to exemplify courage and wisdom, strength and beauty, and the glory of his family name;
but not because the prince knows that these are simply the natural attributes of the highest type of man in society, and his own birthright besides. Rather, it is only in this way that he can be known as a "prince"
by "the populace" who enfranchise him. With such an analysis we have
moved irrevocably beyond the feudal dream of "Christian service and
true chivalry," yet have stopped short of the hypocritical charades that
do service for politics in *Richard III.* Before one even puts the question,
"Is the prince honest or is he a hypocrite?" there is, it seems, a prior
determination to be made: What makes someone a prince? If we postulate, as Machiavelli seems to be doing here, that a man is a prince because the populace acknowledges him to be one, then the whole problem of "acting" like a prince is not so much a matter of the prince's
personal morality as it is a condition of his very existence.

Tudor humanists knew perfectly well that their efforts to popularize
the cult of fame ran counter to the hierarchical rigidities of medieval
feudalism. They were always loyal to their Cyruses and Alexanders, and
they were always eager to emphasize the importance of *res gestae* in
the lives of kings and statesmen; but they were hardly prepared to say
that the admiration which such worthies received actually constituted
their license to rule. Great men pursue fame because they are stirred
by the example of other great men. "Had Achilles never lived," Heywood surmises, "Alexander had never conquered the whole world." The
recommendation that rulers lead exemplary lives, in the full rhetorical

sense of the term, might serve political purposes — it marked out a respectable path for ambition to follow — but it was never meant to constitute a political claim. The allegiance of ordinary men was taken for granted; sovereigns sought the admiration of posterity. In the court, it is true, the arts of securing reputation are refined into a kind of theatrical performance that consciously tries to impress its audience.

> And if he happen moreover to be one to shew feates of Chivalrie in open sights, at tilt, turney, or *Joco di canne,* or in any other exercise of the person, remembring the place where he is, and in presence of whom, he shall provide before hand to be in his armour no lesse handsom and sightly than sure, and feede the eyes of the lookers on with all thinges that hee shall thinke may give a good grace, and shall doe his best to get him a horse set out with faire harnesse and sightly trappings, and to have proper devises, apt posies, and wittie inventions that may draw unto him the eyes of the lookers on as the Adamant stone doth yron.[15]

Castiglione's courtier can openly cultivate such effects because he is enjoined to perform only for members of his own aristocratic caste ("remembring the place where he is, and in presence of whom"), who will see in his performance the ritualistic affirmation of values that are shared by all its members. Like the "choyse of the nobility of Greece" who "personated" the deeds of Jupiter before Achilles, they confirm their social identities by acting out ideal patterns of human behavior among themselves. But what is the fate of this theatrical performance, and the exemplary values that it is meant to embody, when the old audience deteriorates and a new one emerges in its stead, as it does in *Richard II*? The prince must now perform, whether he wishes to or not, before those men "of humble and obscure condition" who line the streets of London to appraise the style of Richard and Bolingbroke. It is they who "know the nature of princes."

In a general way, Bolingbroke has only inherited the ethical problem that figures so prominently in all the histories that follow *Tamburlaine*: does chivalry cease to be chivalry when it becomes a means of securing power and privilege? Only now it is a problem that the ruler necessarily discovers for himself, and answers by himself. Is it possible to "personate" majesty on demand, so to speak, and yet remain majestic in one-self? No doubt many Elizabethans would have insisted that the question ought to be put as it is at the end of *Richard III*: after such knowledge, what forgiveness? But if the need to "act" like a king is simply a matter of political necessity, such a verdict may be premature. Machiavelli's purportedly amoral analysis of "How a prince must act in order to gain reputation" in chapter 21 of *The Prince* has the virtue of forcing the question into the open without prejudging it. When he observes that "Nothing causes a prince to be so much esteemed as great enterprises and giving proof of prowess," he is not, of course, thinking about poster-ity. The prince should know that these "great things" will keep "his sub-jects' minds uncertain and astonished, and occupied in watching their result." [16] Yet he never draws the inference, so characteristic of the stage "Machiavel," that *cose grandi* are mere "toys" for those in the know. Instead, he scrupulously refrains from deciding whether the prince ought to retain his native love of excellence, or put himself wholly in the service of a "Machiavellian" cynicism. Evidently, this is a matter wherein the prince must decide for himself.

If *1 Henry IV* is taken to be a play about Prince Hal's choice of chivalry over vanity[17] — and of course it is many things besides — its real originality lies, I believe, in its readiness to confront such questions as these. The Bolingbrokes know that *res gestae* afford the only means by which they can be recognized as princes; and they know that they must perform, in the new state which Bolingbroke has helped to create, not in the company of a select group of peers, but rather before the undifferentiated company of "men" whose opinion helped Henry Boling-broke to the crown. The king's instructions to his son and heir indicate clearly enough how the value of fame is both enhanced and debased in such a situation.

> Had I so lavish of my presence been,
> So common-hackney'd in the eyes of men,
> So stale and cheap to vulgar company,
> Opinion, that did help me to the crown,
> Had still kept loyal to possession
> And left me in reputeless banishment,
> A fellow of no mark nor likelihood.

By being seldom seen, I could not stir
But, like a comet, I was wond'red at;
That men would tell their children, "This is he!"
Others would say, "Where? Which is Bolingbroke?"
And then I stole all courtesy from heaven,
And dress'd myself in such humility
That I did pluck allegiance from men's hearts,
Loud shouts and salutations from their mouths
Even in the presence of the crowned King.
Thus did I keep my person fresh and new,
My presence, like a robe pontifical,
Ne'er seen but wond'red at; and so my state,
Seldom but sumptuous, show'd like a feast
And won by rareness such solemnity.

(III.ii.39–59)

Considered as advice to a prince, this is sound Machiavellian doctrine.
Despite the obvious ironies, it shows a political grasp that is beyond
the range of Hotspur and Falstaff alike. Considered as the personal
testimony of a crowned king, it is damning. For Bolingbroke, as the
metaphor of disguise suggests, has followed his own advice too well:
he cannot believe in the postures that he recommends. The accession
of a "modern" political consciousness has brought hypocrisy in its wake.
At the battle of Shrewsbury Field, he will be so lavish of his presence,
which has ceased to hold any intrinsic value for him, as to outfit a whole
brigade of counterfeit kings. His expertise in manipulating appearances,
great as it is, leaves him the servant rather than the master of the
"person" he has so assiduously cultivated.

   Thus Bolingbroke's account of how to wear the garment of majesty
can hardly be said to make Hal's prospects any clearer. Instead, it only
complicates them, bringing him face to face with the whole problem of
motive. It cannot suffice that he should simply turn from vanity to
chivalry, nor can his dilemma be reduced to the question of legitimacy,
"How is the true prince to be known?" For the answers to that question,
crucial as they are, only serve to introduce the more compelling inquiry
that follows from Bolingbroke's advice: "How does the true prince
come to know himself? What is he actually made of?"

If the play does offer any answers to these questions, they must be sought in Hal's early soliloquy, which closely parallels the lines already quoted from his father's subsequent advice to him:

> If all the year were playing holidays,
> To sport would be as tedious as to work;
> But when they seldom come, they wish'd-for come,
> And nothing pleaseth but rare accidents.
> So, when this loose behaviour I throw off
> And pay the debt I never promised,
> By how much better than my word I am,
> By so much shall I falsify men's hopes;
> And, like bright metal on a sullen ground,
> My reformation, glitt'ring o'er my fault,
> Shall show more goodly and attract more eyes
> Than that which hath no foil to set it off.
> I'll so offend to make offence a skill,
> Redeeming time when men think least I will.

199 - 212

(I.ii.228–241)

The lines fall naturally into the meditative frame of an unrhymed Shakespearian sonnet, moving from the relaxed commonplaces of the first quatrain into a deepening awareness of the way in which the rhythms of "holiday" and "work" bear on Hal's princely vocation. Like his father, Hal knows that he can realize his full political identity only through those tricks of perspective that are to make him the observed of all observers. Here, however, the prince's sense of the way he will appear to the populace is confirmed not only by an inbred aristocratic sense of occasion, but also by Hal's personal delight in anticipating the arrival of his own maturity. He cannot know how his reformation will be viewed by others except by reference to his own untutored feelings: if his personal pleasure in "holiday" comes from its "accidental" rarity, it only follows that his return from holiday will be no less pleasing (to others, now) just because it too is at once natural and unexpected. What deflects the suspicion that Hal is dealing in appearances *per se* is the virtual identity of the politician's sense of timing (the gift of selecting the right perspectives in which to be viewed) and the "natural" feelings that accompany the transition from youth to maturity in pastoral comedy. At this level the speech looks beyond the social distinctions that separate the prince and the populace, and into a realm where both can respond to a natural, festive image of order-in-variety. As in his earlier use of the sun metaphor, Hal assimilates his own drive towards a mature identity to other natural successions that "please" while they are "wond'red at," just because they are "wish'd-for" and "wanted" (I.ii. 224–225). The implicit contrast, of course, is to the "comet" Bolingbroke, who is "wond'red at" precisely because the man himself is so difficult to identify. Hal's advantage, which is beyond any power of contrivance, lies in his ability to ground the requisite theatrical effects in spontaneous human needs and feelings that he shares with his audience. What pleases him will be pleasing to them.

As a professional politician, Bolingbroke will try to convince his truant son that pleasing the populace is a full-time job; but unrelieved "work" of any sort, Hal decides, is as "tedious" for the performer as it is for his onlookers. (The intuition is confirmed by his experience with the youthful apprentice, Francis the drawer.) If, however, one reserves youth for play, then work, when the time comes for it, will share in the attractiveness of sport. His reformation will "show more goodly" not because its theatrical effect has been calculated in advance, but because it will possess the "rare" spontaneity of "play" — because the performer, in this case, will appreciate that chivalry is not only a trade, but also a test, a rite of passage that still elicits the prince's native relish of virtue in action.

By insisting that the aristocratic life be freed from the domain of "work," Hal not only restores the prince's integrity, he also manages to redefine the intrinsic political value of chivalry in a world where everything has its market price. When Hal promises to "pay the debt I never promised" he tacitly acknowledges that he has an obligation to justify his claim to the throne. As the financial metaphor implies, his pursuit of glory cannot simply be a matter of "sport." But he still exempts that obligation from the closed political economy that entangles the other principles. In Bolingbroke's scheme of values, the worth of a prince's reputation is suspiciously akin to the parcel of a reckoning. When he complains that Hal is making himself "cheap" by vile participation, he implies that he is debasing the value of the royal coinage. And when

he contrasts Hal to Hotspur, it is clearly the latter's industry in accumu-
lating *res gestae* that he has in mind. Unlike these industrious apprentices,
the prodigal "sun" has managed to stay free of any indentures or "bar-
gains." Like his father, Hal "knows at what time to promise, and when
to pay" (IV.iii.53), but he means to falsify men's hopes by how much
"better" he is than his word — and the adjective is to be taken in a
qualitative sense here. When the obligation falls due, he will render
payment in "bright metal," and the pun (mettle/metal, gold) manages
beautifully the transition from Bolingbroke's new state to a golden
world of princely chivalry and aristocratic magnificence. When the day
of reckoning arrives — "Thou owest God a death" (V.i.127) — it is
Bolingbroke who renders "counterfeit royals" faster than the Douglas
can spend them. His son remains, as Falstaff says, "essentially mad
[made?] without seeming so" (II.iv.541), out of that bright metal which,
when it is stamped with the king's image, is the coin of the realm.

Bolingbroke's error is to let the heroic life become a mere creature
of political expedience. Hotspur's error is to suppose that the pursuit
of honor betrays its purposes when it is given any social valuation what-
soever. He is exasperated by Glendower's courtly manners. He cannot
bear to hear Vernon praise Hal's fine chivalric style, which he regards
as "vanities," and "trim." And he makes a point, when they meet at
Shrewsbury Field, of dispensing altogether with compliment and title.

> *Hot.*   If I mistake not, thou art Harry Monmouth.
> *Prince.* Thou speak'st as if I would deny my name.
> *Hot.*   My name is Harry Percy.
> *Prince.*   Why, then I see
>   A very valiant rebel of the name.
>   I am the Prince of Wales.
>
>   (V.iv.59–63)

He is a Tamburlaine who has no need of Theridamas and Zenocrate,
the one truly "democratic" warrior in all the heroical histories. His
ardent refusal to exchange "a world of figures" for "the form of what
he should attend" (I.iii.209–210) inevitably calls into question Hal's
attention to chivalric custom; and it impinges as well on the more

general effort, which I have been following through all the preceding chapters, to discover a productive relationship between literary and social conventions.

The obvious criticism here is that Hotspur's quest for glory has social implications whether he realizes it or not. Quarreling over the spoils in advance, calling for the "indentures," he reveals himself as yet another honorable soldier turned mercenary. In general, though, he gives his undivided loyalty to the disembodied "honor" that dwells upon the pale-faced moon, or in the "bottom of the deep." That is his tragedy: pursuing it, he pursues something that can never be attained, and so requires a life of unrequited exertions. The cruelest irony of the play is that Henry Bolingbroke and Hotspur should converge in portraying the heroic life as the ceaseless accumulation of "proud titles," unrelieved by moments of social occasion or self-fulfilment. "Even as I was then is Percy now" (III.iii.96). A terrible sense of futility invests Hotspur's dying words, especially if the listener expects to hear of any lasting fame that he has won:

> O Harry, thou hast robb'd me of my youth!
> I better brook the loss of brittle life
> Than those proud titles thou hast won of me.
> They wound my thoughts worse than thy sword my flesh.
> But thoughts the slaves of life, and life time's fool,
> And time, that takes survey of all the world,
> Must have a stop.

(V.iv.77–83)

"Robb'd" — his memory cannot penetrate beyond the store of proud titles he has accumulated. In Hal's terms, Hotspur has never been young. The natural variations of youth and maturity, and the whole idea of "holiday" are utterly foreign to him. His time of youth, sleeping and waking, has been apprenticed to that "nature" which

> Wills us to wear ourselves and never rest
> Until we reach the ripest fruit of all . . .

(1 Tamburlaine, II.vii.26–27)

He did not "spend that shortness basely" (V.ii.83), like the thriftless prodigal, but invested it all in those titles that now pass on to Prince Hal. He is the slave of time because he cannot regulate his life by those conventions that allow the "loftie image" of heroic aspiration to find its completion in human history. Without specific expectations there can be no fulfilment and, finally, no lasting memory. Life just stops.

Under Hal's stewardship those "proud titles" will be transmuted into an enduring social form — the Prince of Wales — and eventually into a pattern for posterity to recall. Shakespeare's histories begin in memory and end in myth. *I Henry IV* does not recover the myth; it recovers the conditions that make it possible in the first place. To distinguish Hal's sense of the heroic life from the more restrictive versions embodied by Bolingbroke and Hotspur is to return, finally, to the commonplace wisdom of humanistic theory, as it came to be interpreted on the popular stage. A great man's deeds can be exemplary only if they are animated by a relish of excellence in itself; yet this "heroical" temper still has to realize itself through the forms and conventions that mark out a particular stretch of human history. Hal's peculiar task is to discover these things for himself. He stands outside the paradigm of example and emulation with which I began. Where the Talbots inherit a code of behavior that prescribes their duties and inspires their courage, Hal's only clear legacy is his father's dubious recommendation that he conform to the example set by Hotspur and himself. That Hal should labor under such a liability is not surprising. Shakespeare's scepticism about the power of a heroic tradition to renew itself by example accumulates steadily throughout *Henry VI,* until it finally emerges as a central theme in the early tetralogy; and it is no less evident, of course, in many of the plays that follow the later one. What is remarkable is that Hal should turn the liability into an asset. By insisting on his freedom from heroic tradition he restores the opportunity to claim it freely, and so to remake it in his own image: "Henry V, too famous to live long."

Notes, Works Cited, and Index

Notes

1   Premises of Heroical-Historical Drama, 1587–1592

1. Max M. Reese, *The Cease of Majesty* (London, 1961), p. 66.
2. John Dover Wilson, ed., *1 Henry VI* (Cambridge, 1952), p. xxvii ("Introduction"). While Wilson's remark refers specifically to *2 Henry VI,* it represents his approach to the other two plays in the trilogy as well. See also Edmond Malone, ed., *The Plays and Poems of William Shakespeare* (London, 1790), VI, 381–400 ("A Dissertation on the THREE PARTS OF KING HENRY VI"); T. M. Raysor, ed., *Coleridge's Shakespearean Criticism* (rev. ed., London, 1960), I, 127 ("Notes on the History Plays"); Allison Gaw, *The Origin and Development of 1 Henry VI in Relation to Shakespeare, Marlowe, Peele, and Greene* (Los Angeles, 1926).
3. E. M. W. Tillyard, *Shakespeare's History Plays* (New York, 1946); Lily B. Campbell, *Shakespeare's "Histories": Mirrors of Elizabethan Policy* (San Marino, Calif., 1947); Irving Ribner, *The English History Play in the Age of Shakespeare* (rev. ed., London, 1965); and M. M. Reese, *The Cease of Majesty,* cited above. While it is, I think, fair to put Professor Ribner in this company, I should add that *The English History Play* does insist on the relevance of Marlowe and the popular heroic drama to Shakespeare's histories, and that it has many useful things to say about humanist historiography in the Renaissance.
4. *Marlowe and the Early Shakespeare* (Oxford, 1953), pp. 104–131.
5. *An Apology for Actors,* quoted from the photographic facsimile prepared by Richard H. Perkinson (New York, 1941), sig. B3^r–B4^r.
6. Cited from the text in G. Gregory Smith, ed., *Elizabethan Critical Essays* (Oxford, 1904), I, 179.
7. See Eugene Waith, *The Herculean Hero* (New York, 1962). The phrase is taken from Kenneth Clark's *The Nude* (New York, 1956), p. 190; it is cited by Waith on p. 17.
8. See, for example, Cicero, *De officiis,* ed. and trans. Walter Miller (London, 1913), pp. 62–63; Pierre de la Primaudaye, *The French Academie,* trans. T.B. (London, 1586), *STC* 15233, sig. S7^r–S8^v.
9. *The Arte of English Poesie,* ed. Gladys Willcock and Alice Walker (Cambridge, 1936), pp. 35–36.
10. For further discussion of these topics, see chapter 2 below; Robin G. Collingwood, *The Idea of History* (Oxford, 1946), pp. 14–45; and J. B. Bury, *The Ancient Greek Historians* (London, 1909), pp. 242–259.

11. *An Apology for Poetry* in *Elizabethan Critical Essays*, I, 169, 168.

12. *The Arte of English Poesie*, p. 41. The idea goes back at least as far as Plato's pronouncement that "we can admit no poetry into our city save only hymns to the gods and praises of good men." *The Republic*, ed. and trans. Paul Shorey (London, 1935), II, 465. The origins of the conflation of history and rhetoric in antiquity are discussed in B. L. Ullman, "History and Tragedy," *Transactions of the American Philosophical Association*, 73 (1942), 25–53; and F. W. Walbank, "History and Tragedy," *Historia*, IX (1960), 216–234.

13. Cited from George Lyman Kittredge, ed., *The Complete Works of Shakespeare* (Boston, 1936). All passages quoted from Shakespeare in my text are taken from this edition unless otherwise indicated (i.e., in the case of *Henry VI* and *Richard III*).

14. *A Discourse of English Poetry* (London, 1586), STC 25172, sig. D3ᵛ. (I cite the original text because the emendations of this passage in Smith, *Elizabethan Critical Essays* seem to me unnecessary.)

15. Anthony Munday (?) in Silvianus, *A Second and Third Blast of Retrait from Plaies and Theaters* (London, 1580), STC 21677, sig. H3ʳ.

16. Stephen Gosson, *Plays Confuted in Five Actions* (London, 1582), STC 12095, sig. D5ᵛ–D5ʳ.

17. See Wolfgang Clemen, *English Tragedy before Shakespeare*, trans. T. S. Dorsch (London, 1961), for an account of the "set" speech in earlier Elizabethan drama. For a general discussion of the function of panegyric and lament in heroic literature, see C. M. Bowra, *Heroic Poetry* (London, 1952), pp. 8–17.

18. *Pierce Pennilesse His Supplication to the Divell*, quoted from the *Works*, ed. Ronald B. McKerrow (corrected reprint, Oxford, 1958), I, 212.

19. All citations from *1 Henry VI* in my text refer to the edition of Andrew S. Cairncross (London, 1962).

20. With the exception of *1 Henry VI* and *Edmond Ironside*, all dates are taken from Alfred Harbage's *Annals of English Drama*, revised by Samuel S. Schoenbaum (London, 1964). As Irving Ribner notes in *The English History Play*, pp. 211–242, most commentators would now date *Edmond Ironside* at about 1590, despite the later date given in the *Annals*. Hence I include it here. *The Wars of Cyrus* was not written for the popular stage, but I have listed it because it was evidently revised (for popular production?) in imitation of *1 Tamburlaine*. See the edition of J. P. Brawner (Urbana, Ill., 1942), pp. 10–38.

21. *Discoveries*, cited from Charles H. Herford and Percy and Evelyn Simpson, eds., *Ben Jonson*, VIII (Oxford, 1947), 587.

22. The Admiral's Men evidently produced several of the heroical histories that Heywood recalls. Philip Henslowe's *Diary*, ed. R. A. Foakes and R. T. Rickert (Cambridge, 1961), records the production of a *Troilus and Cressida* by Chettle and Dekker in 1599 (pp. 106, 107, 118, 121), as well as two anonymous cycles: *1 and 2 Caesar and Pompey* in 1594–95 (pp. 25, 26, 27, 28, 30), and *1 and 2 Hercules* in 1595 (p. 28 ff.). If these entries are grouped with some fifteen or so lost plays from the 1590's whose titles refer to the martial exploits — the wars, conquest, battle, or siege — undertaken by some celebrated warrior prince, it seems clear that the form enjoyed a theatrical vogue that outlasted its literary maturity by some years.

23. See *The Herculean Hero*, pp. 60–87.

24. With the exception of this stage direction, which is quoted directly from the 1593 octavo of *Tamburlaine*, all citations from Marlowe in my text refer to Irving Ribner, ed., *The Complete Plays of Christopher Marlowe* (New York, 1963).

25. *An Apology for Poetry* in *Elizabethan Critical Essays*, I, 161.

26. See, for example, Lily B. Campbell, *Shakespeare's "Histories,"* pp. 3–116; Alfred Harbage, *As They Liked It* (New York, 1947), pp. 152–162.

27. The passage itself is largely based on a contemporary textbook in up-to-date military strategy, Paul Ives' *Practise of Fortification*. See Paul Kocher, *Christopher Marlowe, A Study of His Thought, Learning, and Character* (Chapel Hill, North Carolina, 1946), pp. 248–255.

28. See Arthur Ferguson, *The Indian Summer of English Chivalry* (Durham, N.C., 1960).

29. See *Shakespeare's History Plays*, pp. 59–70; *The English History Play*, pp. 305–312. The adulatory "court play" that emerges as a distinctive response to Elizabeth's own brand of absolutism is treated in David Bevington, *Tudor Drama and Politics* (Cambridge, Mass., 1968), pp. 168–186.

30. Reprinted in John Griffiths, *The Two Books of Homilies Appointed to Be Read in Churches* (Oxford, 1859), pp. 550–598.

31. *An Apology for Actors*, sig. F3^r–F4^v.

32. *Pierce Pennilesse*, in *Works*, ed. McKerrow, I, 213.

33. Edited by Andrew S. Cairncross (London, 1957). All citations from *2 Henry VI* in my text refer to this edition.

34. See *Woodstock: A Moral History* (London, 1946), pp. 1–76.

35. *Woodstock*, p. 6.

36. *Woodstock*, p. 9.

37. *The English History Play*, pp. 28–29. See also Irving Ribner, "The Morality Roots of the Tudor History Play," *Tulane Studies in English*, IV (1954), 21–43.

38. The best account of the transition from morality drama to the major Elizabethan genres is David Bevington's *From Mankind to Marlowe* (Cambridge, Mass., 1962), especially pp. 152–262. On the relationship between the "estate satire" of the moralities and the later city comedy, see Alan Dessen, "The Alchemist: Jonson's Estates Play" in *Renaissance Drama,* VII (1964), 35–54.

2   The Rhetorical Basis of the Popular History

1. Ed. Laurence Michel (New Haven, 1958), p. 68.

2. See Frank S. Fussner, *The Historical Revolution* (New York, 1962), *passim*.

3. See in particular Herschel Baker, *The Race of Time* (Toronto, 1967), pp. 73–96; also Bernard Weinberg, *A History of Literary Criticism in the Italian Renaissance* (Chicago, 1961), I, 40–45.

4. *The Prose Works,* ed. J. A. St. John (London, 1888), III, 518 (*Familiar Letters, XXVI*). Cited in Baker, *Race of Time,* p. 89.

5. See *The Idea of History* (Oxford, 1946), pp. 14–45 ("Greco-Roman Historiography"). Collingwood uses the term "substantialism" to describe this metaphysical principle (*ibid.,* pp. 20–21, 42–45). The impact of classical historiography, in both its "substantialist" and its "humanistic" aspects, is the subject of an article by Irving Ribner which anticipates the present line of argument in several respects: "The Idea of History in Marlowe's *Tamburlaine,*" *ELH, XX* (1953), 251–266. Briefly, my approach differs from his in its concern with rhetorical procedures and in its emphasis on the relevance of classical historiography to Elizabethan writers other than Marlowe; but any reader who is interested in these things will find his article very useful.

6. *History of the Peloponnesian War,* ed. and trans. Charles Forster Smith (London, 1928), I, 41. Thucydides is defending the use of interpolated speeches and the "absence of the fabulous" in his narrative.

7. See the comments of Tacitus' editor Henry Furneaux in Tacitus, *Annalium ab excessu divi Augusti libri* (Oxford, 1896), I, 19–28.

8. Collingwood, *Idea of History,* p. 44.

9. *Cornelii Taciti Annalium libri I–IV, edited . . . for the use of schools and junior students* (Oxford, 1886), p. 3. Cited by Collingwood, *Idea of History,* p. 39.

10. Collingwood, *Idea of History,* p. 44.

11. See *The "Art" of Rhetoric,* ed. and trans. John Henry Freese (London, 1926), pp. 3–33; and Sister Miriam Joseph, *Shakespeare's Use of the Arts of Language* (New York, 1947), p. 19.

12. *Mimesis*, trans. Willard R. Trask (Princeton, 1953), p. 39.

13. *Mimesis*, p. 40.

14. See *Mimesis*, pp. 37–40.

15. *The Enduring Monument* (Chapel Hill, 1962), p. 77. See also Duane Stuart, *Epochs of Greek and Roman Biography* (Berkeley, 1928).

16. *An Apology for Poetry* in *Elizabethan Critical Essays*, ed. G. Gregory Smith (Oxford, 1904), I, 160.

17. Ed. and trans. John C. Rolfe (Cambridge, Mass., 1935), I, 132–133.

18. *European Literature and the Latin Middle Ages*, trans. Willard R. Trask (New York, 1953), p. 70. A useful supplement to Curtius' account is R. R. Bolgar, *The Classical Heritage and Its Beneficiaries* (Cambridge, 1954), which treats the pedagogical disciplines and institutions through which a "topical" system of reading classical literature in commonplace anthologies was transmitted to the Renaissance. See in particular pp. 265–379, and the passage quoted below, note 39.

19. See E. M. Sanford, "The Study of Ancient History in the Middle Ages," *Journal of the History of Ideas*, V (1944), 21–43.

20. The *Progymnasmata* exists in several editions and translations: (1) The original Greek text may be consulted in Hugo Rabe, ed., *Rhetores Graeci*, X (Leipzig, 1926), 1–51. (2) Between 1507 and 1680 there were ten different translations of Aphthonius into Latin and, by the count of Donald L. Clark ("The Rise and Fall of Progymnasmata in Sixteenth and Seventeenth Century Grammar Schools," *Speech Monographs*, XIX [1952], 259–263), no less than 114 different printings. The most widely used of these was the *Aphthonii Progymnasmata Partim a Rodolpho Agricola, partim a Johanne Maria Catanaeo Latinate, donata cum Scholis Reinhardi Lorichii* (Marburg, 1542; rev. 1546). The extensive scholia and supplementary exercises make this edition many times larger than the "Greek Aphthonius." All passages cited from Aphthonius in my text are found in the 1636 reprint of this edition, *STC* 706.1, on deposit at the Houghton Library of Harvard University and hereafter cited as *Progymnasmata*. No modern edition or translation of the "Latin Aphthonius" exists, and all translations from Latin to English in my text are my own. (3) While there is no translation into English of the "Latin Aphthonius," Richard Rainolde's *Foundacion of Rhetorike* (1563) is a free adaptation of parts of the 1542 edition into English; and (4) Ray Nadeau has translated the "Greek Aphthonius" into English in *Speech Monographs*, XIX (1952), 264–285. For further discussion of this work, one may consult Donald L. Clark's detailed account of it in *John Milton at St. Paul's School* (New York, 1948), pp. 230–249; Thomas W. Baldwin, *William Shakespeare's Small Latine and Lesse Greeke*

(Urbana, Ill., 1944), II, *passim*; Virgil K. Whitaker, *Shakespeare's Use of Learning* (San Marino, Calif., 1953), pp. 32–35; R. R. Bolgar, *The Classical Heritage*, pp. 38–39; and F. R. Johnson's introduction to the *Foundacion of Rhetorike* (New York, 1945).

21. Aphthonius, *Progymnasmata*, sig. K8^r–P1^r. Study of (or instruction from) the *Rhetorica ad C. Herennium* and Quintilian would provide further practice in these topics. See Harry Caplan, ed. and trans., *Ad C. Herennium de ratione dicendi* (Cambridge, Mass., 1954), pp. 172–183; Harold E. Butler, ed. and trans., *The Institutio Oratoria of Quintilian* (New York, 1921), I, 464–479. For an account of the importance of the *Ad Herennium* and Quintilian in Elizabethan grammar school training, see Baldwin, *Small Latine*, II, 69–108, 197–237.

22. See Morton W. Bloomfield, "A Preliminary List of Incipits of Latin Works on the Virtues and Vices, Mainly of the Thirteenth, Fourteenth, and Fifteenth Centuries," *Traditio*, XI (1955), 260–379; Lester K. Born, "The Perfect Prince: A Study in Thirteenth- and Fourteenth-Century Ideals," *Speculum*, III (1928), 470–504, and Born's Introduction to Erasmus' *The Education of a Christian Prince* (New York, 1936); John E. Mason, *Gentlefolk in the Making: Studies in the History of English Courtesy Literature and Related Topics from 1531 to 1774* (Philadelphia, 1935); and John M. Major, *Sir Thomas Elyot and Renaissance Humanism* (Lincoln, Neb., 1964), pp. 39–170.

23. *Progymnasmata*, sig. L1^v.

24. In *European Literature and the Latin Middle Ages*, pp. 162–165, Curtius discusses the importance of the "outdoing *topos*" in late classical and medieval panegyric.

25. *Progymnasmata*, sig. Q8^v–S4^v. Compare Quintilian, III, 390–395; also see the discussion of *conformatio* (personification) in the *Ad Herennium*, pp. 398–401.

26. See Wolfgang Clemen, *English Tragedy before Shakespeare*, trans. T. S. Dorsch (London, 1961), pp. 211–286.

27. *Progymnasmata*, sig. S4^v–T6^r; compare the *Ad Herennium*, pp. 356–359, 386–387; also Quintilian, III, 249 (cited by Lorich) and 399; and Curtius, *European Literature and the Latin Middle Ages*, p. 69.

28. *Progymnasmata*, sig. L3^v–P1^r.

29. *Progymnasmata*, sig. S4^v.

30. *Progymnasmata*, sig. Q8^v.

31. *Progymnasmata*, sig. S7^v.

32. *Progymnasmata*, sig. O7^r.

33. *Progymnasmata*, sig. O7^r: "ut statim intelligi posset, qualis is esset

qui tantum in discrimen Romanum nomen adduxerit, primum ipsum ducem ex descriptionis loco depinxit his verbis."

34. *Progymnasmata,* sig. O8ᵛ. The passage from Livy will be found in Benjamin O. Foster, ed. and trans., *Livy* (London, 1929), V, 10–13.

35. For further drills, similar to the one just discussed, see, for example, Aphthonius' exercise analyzing a passage from Livy for practice in construing *bona corporis,* sig. L5ᵛ. The treatment of *exemplum* (or *paradigma*) in Susenbrotus and Erasmus, which is discussed below, likewise involves the analysis of historical — and literary — materials into rhetorical forms. See Joannes Susenbrotus, *Epitome Troporum ac Schematum* (London, 1562), *STC* 23437, sig. G5ʳ–G6ᵛ; and Desiderius Erasmus, *On Copia of Words and Ideas,* trans. Donald B. King and Herbert David Rix (Milwaukee, 1963), pp. 68–76.

36. Cited above, note 35. I have used the University Microfilms copy of the edition printed at London in 1562.

37. Susenbrotus, sig. G5ʳ.

38. See Allan H. Gilbert, ed., *Literary Criticism: Plato to Dryden* (Detroit, 1962), pp. 459–461.

39. See *The Classical Heritage,* pp. 274–275, and p. 365, which summarizes the end result of the "notebook method" of learning set forth in Erasmus' *Copia*: "A few hundred pages of Cicero and Demosthenes, a few hundred lines of Virgil and Homer, with extracts from the historians and the elegiac poets, and perhaps a tragedy by Euripides or a comedy by Terence, came to represent the sum total of the Graeco-Roman legacy for all but a chosen few classical scholars."

40. *Copia* (cited above, note 35), p. 68.

41. *Copia,* pp. 68–76.

42. See Ruth Kelso, *The Doctrine of the English Gentleman in the Sixteenth Century* (Urbana, Ill., 1929), pp. 133–134; and Fritz Caspari, *Humanism and the Social Order in Tudor England* (Chicago, 1954), pp. 89–90.

43. Ed. Foster Watson (London, 1907), p. 281 (Book III, chapter 25: "Of Experience, whiche have preceded oure tyme, with a defence of Histories").

44. Ed. Gladys Willcock and Alice Walker (Cambridge, 1936), pp. 39–41.

45. See *English Tragedy before Shakespeare, passim,* and especially pp. 21–56. The persistence and reformulation of the "topics" through the Middle Ages is treated by Curtius in *European Literature and the Latin Middle Ages,* pp. 79–105 ("Topics"); Clemen's chapter on "The Dramatic Lament and Its Forms" in *English Tragedy,* pp. 211–252, illustrates how the received

"lament *topoi*" influenced the style and content of one set speech form in earlier Elizabethan drama.

46. *Mimesis*, p. 38. Henry A. Kelly's forthcoming study of providential themes in English historiography in the Middle Ages and the Renaissance examines the prose chronicles in great detail and concludes by questioning the degree to which any of the English historians' occasional citations to Providence were integrated into the total design of the works themselves. See Henry A. Kelly, "Providential Themes in English Historiography," Ph.D. diss., Harvard University (1965).

47. For a general account of the range and variety of English commonplace books in the sixteenth century see William G. Crane, *Wit and Rhetoric in the Renaissance* (New York, 1937), pp. 33–48. Donald L. Clark, *John Milton at St. Paul's School*, pp. 217–226, supplements Crane's account; see also Charles R. Baskerville, "Taverner's *Garden of Wisdom* and the *Apophthegmata* of Erasmus," *Studies in Philology*, XXIX (1932), 149–159.

48. The extent of the commerce between dramatic characters and the anecdotal biographies of the commonplace books may be suggested by a rough statistical example: the eleven worthies treated in Udall's translation of the *Apophtegmata* (cited below, note 49) find their way into the short *titles* of twenty-three plays listed for the years 1550–1600 in Alfred Harbage's *Annals of English Drama*, revised by Samuel S. Schoenbaum (London, 1964). That such collections were, in fact, used by dramatists should be clear from the ensuing discussion of *Cambises* and *Tamburlaine*.

49. The first edition, *Apophtegmatum, sive scite dictorum libri sex* (Basel, 1531), was a loose redaction in six books of the apothegms that Plutarch had addressed to Trajan. The fourth edition, printed in 1532, added two more books derived from Diogenes Laertes' *Lives and Sayings of the Philosophers*. In 1542 Nicholas Udall's translation of books III and IV of Erasmus' eight was published as *Apophthegmes, that is to saie, prompte, quicke, wittie and sentencious sayinges, of certain Emperours, Kynges, Capitaines, Philosophers, and Oratours . . . Excisum typis Richard Grafton* (London, 1542), STC 10443. All citations from the *Apophtegmata* in my text refer to the copy of Udall's translation on deposit in the Houghton Library, Harvard University (hereafter cited as *Apophthegmes*). The only modern edition of the *Apophtegmata* is that in Erasmus, *Opera omnia* (London, 1962), IV, 93–380. The 1564 edition of Udall's translation has been edited by Robert Roberts (Boston, Lincolnshire, England, 1877). For its use in the grammar schools, see Baldwin, *Small Latine*, II, 307–309, and Clark, *John Milton at St. Paul's School*, pp. 216–226.

50. *Apophthegmes*, sig. Z7^v.

51. *Apophthegmes*, sig. Z5^r.

52. *Apophthegmes*, sig. Z5^r.

53. See, for example, *Apophthegmes*, sig. Z6^r.

54. *Apophthegmes*, sig. **3^v.

55. *Apophthegmes*, sig. *7^v.

56. *Apophthegmes*, sig. *7^v.

57. *Apophthegmes*, sig. **6^r.

58. *From Mankind to Marlowe* (Cambridge, 1962), pp. 175–176.

59. I have borrowed the phrase from Bevington's review of unflattering appraisals of the moral interlude, *From Mankind to Marlowe*, p. 2.

60. John S. Farmer, ed., *The Dramatic Writings of Richard Edwards, Thomas Norton, and Thomas Sackville* (London, 1906), p. 79. In "*Damon and Pythias* and Renaissance Theories of Tragedy," *English Studies*, XXXIX (1958), 200–207, William A. Armstrong shows that Edwards (rather confusedly) regarded his *exemplum* as a "tragedy."

61. Cited from the edition of Ronald B. McKerrow (Oxford, 1909), lines 1937–1942.

62. Cited from the edition of Ronald B. McKerrow (Oxford, 1911), lines 1194–1195.

63. *The Medieval Heritage of Elizabethan Tragedy* (corrected reprint, Oxford, 1962), p. 267. See also W. A. Armstrong, "The Background and Sources of Preston's *Cambises*," *English Studies*, XXXI (1950), 129–131.

64. *The Second Booke of the Garden of Wysedom*, STC 23713 (London, 1539), sig. C4^v.

65. Cited from the text in Charles R. Baskerville, Virgil B. Heltzel, and Arthur H. Nethercot, eds., *Elizabethan and Stuart Plays* (New York, 1934). All citations to *Cambises* in my text are from this edition.

66. *The Herculean Hero* (London, 1962), p. 62.

67. The most thorough discussion of Marlowe's sources is still that of Una Ellis-Fermor in her edition of *Tamburlaine the Great* (London, 1930), pp. 17–61. Marlowe's use of Le Roy is dealt with in Hallet Smith's "Tamburlaine and the Renaissance," *Elizabethan Studies and Other Essays in Honor of George F. Reynolds* (Boulder, Colo., 1945), pp. 126–132.

68. Translated by T. B. (London, 1586). The compiler indicates the nature of his collection by recommending it for "the varietie of excellent sayings and examples wherewith it is replenished"; sig. *2^r.

69. Translated by Thomas Fortescue (London, 1571), STC 17849, sig. X3^v–X3^r.

70. Translated by R. A[shley] (London, 1594), STC 15488, sig. VI^v.

71. Ernest Talbert, *The Problem of Order* (Chapel Hill, N.C., 1962) dis-

cusses the presentation of Virtues in Tudor pageantry on pp. 79–88. See also R. C. Strong and J. A. Van Dorsten, *Leicester's Triumph* (London, 1964), p. 98.

72. See *The Herculean Hero*, pp. 70–87, for a reading of the play as an exposition of character.

73. *Induction to Tragedy* (University, La., 1939), pp. 48–105.

74. Menaphon's description of Tamburlaine is an extremely accurate formal *effictio*. See, for example, the *Ad Herennium*, pp. 386–387. Curtius treats the beauty-of-rulers *topos* in *European Literature and the Latin Middle Ages*, pp. 180–182.

75. Thomas Wilson, *The Arte of Rhetorique* (London, 1553), facsimile reproduction prepared by Robert Bowers (Gainesville, Fla., 1962), p. 25.

76. Stephen Gosson, *Plays Confuted in Five Actions*, (London, 1582) sig. C6^r.

77. For a discussion of "magnificence" as it applies to *Tamburlaine*, see below, pp. 117–118.

3   "Parentage" and "Deeds": The Heroic Example from *Tamburlaine* to *3 Henry VI*

1. The best recent survey of the subject is Lawrence Stone's *The Crisis of the Aristocracy: 1558–1641* (Oxford, 1965), particularly pp. 129–196. The classic study of the problem, of which Stone's work is a refinement, is, of course, R. H. Tawney's "The Rise of the Gentry, 1558–1640," *Economic History Review*, XI (1941), 1–38. In *Tudor Drama and Politics* (Cambridge, Mass., 1968), pp. 213–215, David Bevington discusses some connections between *Tamburlaine* and the social attitudes of its audience.

2. Besides the studies referred to in chapter 1, note 29, see Stone, *Crisis of the Aristocracy*, pp. 21–64 ("The Peerage in Society") and pp. 65–128 ("The Inflation of Honours"); see also Ruth Kelso, *The Doctrine of the English Gentleman in the Sixteenth Century* (Urbana, Ill., 1929), pp. 31–41 ("The Theory of the Favored Class").

3. *The French Academie*, trans. T. B. (London, 1586), sig. S7^r–S8^v.

4. Lodowick Bryskett, *A Discourse of Civil Life; Containing the Ethike Part of Morall Philosophie* (London, 1606), STC 3958, sig. Ff3^r. For a general survey of this virtue as it is used by one early Elizabethan playwright, see William O. Harris, *Skelton's Magnyfycence and the Cardinal Virtue Tradition* (Chapel Hill, N.C., 1965).

5. See *The Doctrine of the English Gentleman in the Sixteenth Century*, pp. 18–30 ("What Is a Gentleman?"), and J. E. Mason, *Gentlefolk in the Making* (Philadelphia, 1935), *passim*.

6. See Mason, *Gentlefolk in the Making*, pp. 9–12; and John M. Major, *Sir Thomas Elyot and Renaissance Humanism* (Lincoln, Neb., 1964), pp. 39–170.

7. *Middle-Class Culture in Elizabethan England* (Chapel Hill, N.C., 1935), pp. 121–169.

8. *The Crisis of the Aristocracy*, p. 156.

9. *Shakespeare's Audience* (New York, 1941), pp. 11–14. The examples of disorderly conduct in the playhouse cited below are taken from pp. 102–104.

10. Ed. W. W. Greg (Oxford, 1926). All citations from *Alphonsus* in my text refer to this edition.

11. Ed. John Dover Wilson (Oxford, 1910).

12. Ed. W. W. Greg (Oxford, 1907). All citations from *The Battle of Alcazar* in my text refer to this edition.

13. Ed. Ronald B. McKerrow (Oxford, 1907). All citations from *Locrine* in my text refer to this edition.

14. All citations from *3 Henry VI* in my text refer to the edition of Andrew S. Cairncross (London, 1964).

15. See Irving Ribner, "Greene's Attack on Marlowe: Some Light on *Alphonsus* and *Selimus*," *Studies in Philology*, LII (1955), 162–171, and W. A. Armstrong, " 'Tamburlaine' and 'The Wounds of Civil War,' " *Notes and Queries*, N.S., V (1958), 381–383.

16. See *The Arte of English Poesie*, ed. Gladys Willcock and Alice Walker (Cambridge, 1936), p. 42.

17. Cited from the text prepared by Geoffrey Bullough in *Narrative and Dramatic Sources of Shakespeare*, IV (New York, 1962). All citations from *The Famous Victories* in my text refer to Bullough's edition.

18. Ed. W. W. Greg (Oxford, 1911). All citations from *Edward I* in my text refer to this edition.

19. As in *Henry V*, II.ii. Compare Stone, *Crisis of the Aristocracy*, pp. 267–268.

20. Ed. W. W. Greg (Oxford, 1929). All citations from *The True Tragedy of Richard III* in my text refer to this edition.

21. See *Chapman's Homer*, ed. Allardyce Nicoll (New York, 1956), I, 52, 228, 349.

22. See Josephine W. Bennett, *The Evolution of "The Faerie Queene"*

(Chicago, 1942), pp. 61–79; Edwin Greenlaw, *Studies in Spenser's Historical Allegory* (Baltimore, 1932), pp. 1–58; and Arthur B. Ferguson, *The Indian Summer of English Chivalry* (Durham, N.C., 1960).

23. Ed. Eleanore Boswell (Oxford, 1927). All citations from *Edmond Ironside* in my text refer to this edition.

24. All citations from *Edward III* refer to the text in *The Shakespeare Apocrypha*, ed. Charles F. Tucker Brooke (Oxford, 1908), pp. 67–103.

25. Stone, *Crisis of the Aristocracy*, p. 591.

26. *A Discourse upon the Meanes of Wel Governing*, trans. Simon Patericke (London, 1602), STC 11743 sig. T1ʳ.

27. Gentillet, *Discourse*, sig. T1ʳ.

28. *Elizabethan Revenge Tragedy* (Princeton, 1940), p. 102.

29. Ed. W. Bang (Oxford, 1908).

30. Compare, for example, *Locrine*, lines 1722–1756, and *The Battle of Alcazar*, lines 1389–1409.

31. *The Medieval Heritage of Elizabethan Tragedy* (corrected reprint, Oxford, 1963), p. 410.

32. See, for example, lines 398, 448–449, 1976–1977, 1995–1998.

33. Richard Sylvester, ed., *The History of King Richard III*, in the Yale edition of the *Works*, II (1963), 8.

34. Cited from the edition of G. Blakemore Evans (Baltimore, 1959). All citations from *Richard III* in my text refer to this edition.

4   The Hero in History: A Reading of *Henry VI*

1. *The Plays and Poems of William Shakespeare*, ed. Edmond Malone (London, 1790), VI, 381 ("A Dissertation on the THE THREE PARTS OF KING HENRY VI") — hereafter cited as "Malone."

2. Malone, p. 382.

3. Peter Alexander, *Shakespeare's Henry VI and Richard III* (Cambridge, 1929); Madeleine Doran, *Henry VI, Parts II and III: Their Relation to the Contention and the True Tragedy* (Iowa City, Iowa, 1928). A sophisticated reformulation of Malone's position is set forth in Charles T. Prouty, *The Contention and Shakespeare's 2 Henry VI* (New Haven, 1954). The case for joint authorship is argued in John Dover Wilson's introductions to *1* and *2 Henry VI* (Cambridge, 1952), pp. xxi–l and pp. vii–liii respectively. For a rebuttal of Wilson's argument, see Leo Kirschbaum, "The Authorship of *1 Henry VI*," *Publications of the Modern Language Association*, LXVII (1952), 809–822.

4. *Lectures on Dramatic Art and Literature,* trans. John Black (rev. ed., London, 1904), pp. 419–440.

5. A pioneering study of the thematic structure of *Henry VI* and other plays is Hereward T. Price's, "Construction in Shakespeare," *University of Michigan Contributions in Modern Philology,* XVII (1951).

6. E. M. W. Tillyard, *Shakespeare's History Plays* (New York, 1946), p. 158.

7. Arthur C. Sprague, *Shakespeare's Histories, Plays for the Stage* (London, 1964), p. 116. For an extensive and often illuminating interpretation of this scene, see Sigurd Burckhardt, *Shakespearean Meanings* (Princeton, 1968), pp. 47–77.

8. Irving Ribner, *The English History Play* (rev. ed., London, 1965), p. 95.

9. Among the critical commentaries on the three plays, the best treatments of these topics are J. P. Brockbank, "The Frame of Disorder — *Henry VI*" in *Early Shakespeare,* ed. John Russell Brown and Bernard Harris (London, 1961), pp. 73–99; and the chapters on *Henry VI* in A. C. Hamilton's *The Early Shakespeare* (San Marino, California, 1967), pp. 9–62. On the use of formal rhetoric, see Gladys Willcock, "Language and Poetry in Shakespeare's Early Plays," *Proceedings of the British Academy,* XL (1954), 103–117; and generally, Ernest Talbert, *Elizabethan Drama and Shakespeare's Early Plays* (Chapel Hill, N.C., 1963), pp. 161–234.

10. See chapter 1, pp. 29–33. Salisbury's comment as Winchester, Buckingham, and Somerset depart in the opening scene of *2 Henry VI* is frequently cited as if it were an audible reminder of subterranean morality conventions: "Pride went before, Ambition follows him./While these do labour for their own preferment,/Behooves it us to labour for the realm" (179–181). Here, to be sure, good and evil counselors are given allegorical tags and evaluated in terms of their disposition towards "the realm." But Salisbury's little "allegory" is simply a variation on a familiar Elizabethan proverb, "Pride goes before, and shame (ambition) comes after," (Tilley P 576), which suggests a further, Biblical parallel: "Pride goes before destruction and an high minde before the fal" (Prov. xvi:8, cited from the "Bishops Bible," *STC* 2107). In so far as these proverbs embody veiled prophecies, they accord with the larger sequence of prophecy and fulfilment through which Shakespeare usually suggests the workings of fate or Providence in these plays. See Cairncross' note at I.i.179, and, more generally, Wolfgang Clemen, "Anticipation and Foreboding in Shakespeare's Early Histories," *Shakespeare Survey,* VI (1953), 25–35.

11. Malone, VI, 383. Among the criticism on *1 Henry VI,* I have also

made use of David Bevington's introduction to the text edited by himself for the Pelican Shakespeare (Baltimore, 1966). Lawrence Ryan's edition for the Signet Shakespeare (New York, 1967) appeared after this study was well underway, but I was pleased to find that our interpretations of *1 Henry VI* are alike on many points.

12. Baltimore, 1940; Durham, N.C., 1960. Also see Curtis Watson, *Shakespeare and the Renaissance Concept of Honor* (Princeton, 1960).

13. The association of the Vice, glamorous "new customs," and Roman Catholic ritual and ornament is a common theme in moral interludes through the 1550's and 1560's; among extant texts it occurs as late as Ulpian Fulwell's *Like Will to Like* (1568), which was reissued in 1587.

14. See Rossiter's persuasive arguments in his introduction to *Woodstock*, pp. 47–72. There are scenes at court in *The Famous Victories of Henry V* and *A Looking Glass for London and England*, but these are not on the scale of those in *2 Henry VI*.

15. A. B. Grosart, ed., *The Works of Fulke Greville* (Blackburn, Lancashire, 1870), IV, 189 ("The Life of the Renowned Sir Philip Sidney").

16. Arthur Sherbo, ed., *Johnson on Shakespeare*, in the Yale edition of the *Works*, VIII (1968), 612.

17. See *The Crisis of the Aristocracy*, especially pp. 21–64, 164–188, 199–272, 385–504.

18. Thomas Wilson, *The Arte of Rhetorique*, ed. Robert Bowers (Gainesville, Fla., 1962), p. 46.

19. Compare *1 Tamburlaine*, II.v.60–64, III.ii.71–75.

20. *The Elizabethan Stage* (Oxford, 1923), IV, 259–345 (Appendix D).

21. E. A. J. Honigman would move the date of Shakespeare's *King John* back to 1590–91. See the introduction to his edition of *King John* (London, 1954), pp. xliii–lix.

22. Throughout the sixteenth century, as Stone makes clear, "The object of rebellion was to free the king from evil advisers" (p. 267), not "usurpation" *per se*. York observes this convention when he demands the removal of Somerset; then he violates it in the assertion of his "right" to the crown.

23. Shakespeare's familiarity with the lament of Hecuba in book XIII of the *Metamorphoses* is well known. See Baldwin, *Small Latine*, II, 193–194. It is less certain that he knew the *Troades*, but see John W. Cunliffe, *The Influence of Seneca on Elizabethan Tragedy* (London, 1893), p. 79, and K. Koeppel, "Shakespeares *Richard III* und Senecas *Troades*," *Shakespeare-Jahrbuch*, XLVII (1911), 188–190.

24. Cairncross' note at II.iii.15 explains that this anonymous "brother" must be Young Salisbury.

25. Thomas Kyd, *The Spanish Tragedy,* ed. Philip Edwards (Cambridge, Mass., 1959), I.i.48–49.

26. See Cairncross' introduction, pp. xvi–xvii, and his notes at I.iv.84, 152; and *The Spanish Tragedy,* ed. Philip Edwards, II.v. 51–52 and note.

27. *A Discourse upon the Meanes of Wel Governing,* trans. Simon Patericke (London, 1602), *STC* 11743, sig. Q5^r.

28. The title page of the Quarto states that *The True Tragedy* "was sundrie times acted by the Right Honourable the Earle of Pembroke his servants." If, as Chambers suggests (*William Shakespeare* [Oxford, 1930], I, 49–50), Pembroke's company was an offshoot of an "amalgamation" of Strange's Men and the Admiral's Men, Shakespeare would probably have had a working acquaintance with the mutations of revenge tragedy discussed below in connection with *3 Henry VI: The Spanish Tragedy* and *The Jew of Malta* were both in Strange's repertory by 1592 at the latest. If he indeed acted in those plays, and others which are "recalled" in *Henry VI,* there would appear to be a fairly obvious explanation for the profusion of verbal parallels that has prompted so much speculation about the authorship of the trilogy. Here, as elsewhere, hard evidence is lacking.

5   The Tradition of Fame and the Arts of Policy: *Richard III* and *1 Henry IV*

1. See J. H. Walter's introduction to the text of *Henry V* edited by himself for the New Arden Shakespeare (London, 1954), pp. xiv–xviii. Walter's treatment of the play as it relates to humanistic conceptions of the ideal ruler is thorough and well documented; therefore I have not felt that it was necessary to discuss it in this concluding chapter.

2. Max Lerner, ed., *The Prince and the Discourses* (New York, 1950). Quotations from *The Prince* in my text are based on (but do not always exactly correspond to) this translation.

3. *Angel with Horns and Other Shakespearian Lectures* (London, 1961), p. 16.

4. Thomas M. Raysor, ed., *Coleridge's Shakespearean Criticism* (rev. ed., London, 1960), II, 141 (the Lectures of 1811–12).

5. New York, 1927, pp. 337–403.

6. *Shakespeare and the Allegory of Evil* (New York, 1958); "Machiavelli and the Elizabethans," *Proceedings of the British Academy,* XIV (1928),

49–97; *Seneca and Elizabethan Tragedy* (Cambridge, 1922); *Kommentar zu Shakespeares Richard III* (Göttingen, 1957). The *Kommentar* has been translated and abridged by Jean Bonheim, *A Commentary on Shakespeare's Richard III* (London, 1968).

7. *Selected Essays 1917–1932* (New York, 1938), p. 5.

8. *Shakespearean Criticism*, I, 205; II, 165.

9. See the discussion of this scene in Clemen's *Kommentar*, pp. 311–315.

10. J. William Hebel, ed., *Works*, II (Oxford, 1932), 391. The passage is cited in Edward O. Benjamin, "Fame, Poetry, and the Order of History in the Literature of the English Renaissance," *Studies in the Renaissance*, VI (1959), 64–84.

11. The text most frequently cited in this regard by seventeenth-century historians was the comment on Caesar in chapter 10 of the *Discourses*: "Nor let any one be deceived by the glory of that Caesar who has been so much celebrated by writers; for those who praised him were corrupted by his fortune, and frightened by the long duration of the empire that was maintained under his name, and which did not permit writers to speak of him with freedom" (*The Prince and the Discourses*, ed. Max Lerner, p. 142). Shakespeare may have had it in mind while writing the exchange (discussed below) between Richard and Prince Edward concerning the permanence of Caesar's fame. See Benjamin, "Fame, Poetry, and the Order of History" for citations of this passage.

12. Sir John Harington, *The Letters and Epigrams*, ed. Norman E. McClure (Philadelphia, 1926), p. 164.

13. *The Prince*, p. 4.

14. See Allan H. Gilbert, *Machiavelli's "Prince" and Its Forerunners* (Durham, N.C., 1938).

15. *The Book of the Courtier*, trans. Sir Thomas Hoby, ed. W. D. and W. B. Drayton Henderson (London, 1928), p. 96.

16. *The Prince*, pp. 81–82.

17. See, in particular, John Dover Wilson, *The Fortunes of Falstaff* (New York, 1944), and E. M. W. Tillyard, *Shakespeare's History Plays* (New York, 1946), pp. 264–303. I have also drawn on C. L. Barber's essay, "Rule and Misrule in *1 Henry IV*" in *Shakespeare's Festive Comedy* (Princeton, 1959), pp. 192–221.

Works Cited

Ad C. Herennium de ratione dicendi, ed. and trans. Harry Caplan. Cambridge, Mass.: Harvard University Press, 1954.

Alexander, Peter. *Shakespeare's Henry VI and Richard III*. Cambridge: Cambridge University Press, 1929.

Aphthonius. *Aphthonii Progymnastmata Partim a Rodolpho Agricola . . . cum Scholis Reinhardi Lorichii*. London, 1636.

Aristotle. *The "Art" of Rhetoric*, ed. and trans. John Henry Freese. London: W. Heinemann, 1926.

Armstrong, W. A. "The Background and Sources of Preston's *Cambises*," *English Studies*, XXXI (1950), 129–131.

———. "*Damon and Pythias* and Renaissance Theories of Tragedy," *English Studies*, XXXIX (1958), 200–207.

———. " 'Tamburlaine' and 'The Wounds of Civil War,' " *Notes and Queries*, N.S., V (1958), 381–383.

Auerbach, Erich. *Mimesis: The Representation of Reality in Western Literature*, trans. Willard R. Trask. Princeton: Princeton University Press, 1953.

Baldwin, Thomas W. *William Shakespeare's Small Latine and Lesse Greeke*, 2 vols. Urbana, Ill.: University of Illinois Press, 1944.

Baker, Herschel. *The Race of Time: Three Lectures on Renaissance Historiography*. Toronto: University of Toronto Press, 1967.

Baker, Howard. *Induction to Tragedy: A Study in a Development of Form in Gorboduc, The Spanish Tragedy, and Titus Andronicus*. University, La.: Louisiana State University Press, 1939.

Barber, C. L. *Shakespeare's Festive Comedy: A Study of Dramatic Form and Its Relationship to Social Custom*. Princeton: Princeton University Press, 1959.

Baskerville, C. R., Virgil B. Heltzell, and Arthur Nethercot, eds., *Elizabethan and Stuart Plays*. New York: Henry Holt, 1934.

Baskerville, Charles R. "Taverner's *Garden of Wisdom* and the *Apophthegmata* of Erasmus," *Studies in Philology*, XXIV (1932), 149–159.

Benjamin, Edward O. "Fame, Poetry, and the Order of History in the Literature of the English Renaissance," *Studies in the Renaissance*, VI (1959), 64–84.

Bennett, Josephine. *The Evolution of "The Faerie Queene."* Chicago: University of Chicago Press, 1942.

Bevington, David M. *From Mankind to Marlowe: Growth of Structure in the Popular Drama of Tudor England.* Cambridge, Mass.: Harvard University Press, 1962.

————. *Tudor Drama and Politics: A Critical Approach to Topical Meaning.* Cambridge, Mass.: Harvard University Press, 1968.

Bloomfield, Morton W. "A Preliminary List of Incipits of Latin Works on the Virtues and Vices, Mainly of the Thirteenth, Fourteenth, and Fifteenth Centuries," *Traditio, XI* (1955), 260–379.

Bolgar, R. R. *The Classical Heritage and Its Beneficiaries.* Cambridge: Cambridge University Press, 1954.

Born, Lester K. "The Perfect Prince: A Study in Thirteenth- and Fourteenth-Century Ideals," *Speculum, III* (1928), 470–504.

Bowers, Fredson. *Elizabethan Revenge Tragedy.* Princeton: Princeton University Press, 1940.

Bowra, C. M. *Heroic Poetry.* London: Macmillan, 1952.

Brockbank, J. P. "The Frame of Disorder — *Henry VI*" in *Early Shakespeare,* ed. J. R. Brown and Bernard Harris. London: Edward Arnold, 1961.

Brooke, Charles F. Tucker, ed., *The Shakespeare Apocrypha.* Oxford: Oxford University Press, 1908.

Bryskett, Lodowick. *A Discourse of Civill Life.* London, 1606.

Bullough, Geoffrey. *Narrative and Dramatic Sources of Shakespeare,* 5 vols. New York: Columbia University Press, 1957–64.

Burckhardt, Sigurd. *Shakespearian Meanings.* Princeton: Princeton University Press, 1968.

Bury, Joseph B. *The Ancient Greek Historians.* London: Macmillan, 1909.

Campbell, Lily B. *Shakespeare's "Histories": Mirrors of Elizabethan Policy.* San Marino, Calif.: Huntington Library Publications, 1947.

Caspari, Fritz. *Humanism and the Social Order in Tudor England.* Chicago: University of Chicago Press, 1954.

Castiglione, Baldassare. *The Book of the Courtier,* trans. Sir Thomas Hoby, ed. W. D. Rouse and W. B. Drayton Henderson. London: J. M. Dent, 1928.

Chambers, E. K. *The Elizabethan Stage,* 4 vols. Oxford: Oxford University Press, 1923.

————. *William Shakespeare,* 2 vols. Oxford: Oxford University Press, 1930.

Chapman, George. *Chapman's Homer,* ed. Allardyce Nicoll, 2 vols. New York: Pantheon Books, 1956.

Cicero. *De officiis,* ed. and trans. Walter Miller. London: W. Heinemann, 1913.

Clark, Donald L. *John Milton at St. Paul's School: A Study of Ancient Rhetoric in English Renaissance Education.* New York: Columbia University Press, 1948.

———. "The Rise and Fall of Progymnasmata in Sixteenth and Seventeenth Century Grammar Schools," *Speech Monographs,* XXIX (1952), 259–263.

Clark, Kenneth. *The Nude: A Study in Ideal Form.* New York: Pantheon Books, 1956.

Clemen, Wolfgang. "Anticipation and Foreboding in Shakespeare's Early Histories," *Shakespeare Survey,* VI (1953), 25–35.

———. *English Tragedy before Shakespeare: The Development of Dramatic Speech,* trans. T. S. Dorsch. London: Methuen, 1961.

———. *Kommentar zu Shakespeares Richard III; Interpretation eines Dramas.* Gottingen: Vandenhoek and Ruprecht, 1957.

Coleridge, S. T. *Coleridge's Shakespearean Criticism,* ed. T. M. Raysor, 2 vols., rev. ed. London: J. M. Dent, 1960.

Collingwood, Robin G. *The Idea of History.* Oxford: Oxford University Press, 1946.

Crane, William G. *Wit and Rhetoric in the Renaissance: The Formal Basis of Elizabethan Prose Style.* New York: Columbia University Press, 1937.

Cunliffe, John W. *The Influence of Seneca on Elizabethan Tragedy.* London: Macmillan, 1893.

Curtius, Ernst Robert. *European Literature in the Latin Middle Ages,* trans. Willard R. Trask. New York: Pantheon Books, 1953.

Daniel, Samuel. *The Civil Wars,* ed. Laurence Michel. New Haven: Yale University Press, 1958.

Dessen, Alan. *"The Alchemist:* Johnson's Estates Play," *Renaissance Drama,* VII (1964), 35–54.

Doran, Madeleine. *Henry VI, Parts II and III: Their Relation to The Contention and The True Tragedy.* Iowa City, Iowa: University of Iowa Humanistic Studies, 1928.

Drayton, Michael. *The Works of Michael Drayton,* ed. J. William Hebel, 5 vols. Oxford: Oxford University Press, 1931–1941.

Edmond Ironside, ed. Eleanore Boswell. Oxford: Malone Society, 1927.

Edwards, Richard. *The Dramatic Writings of Richard Edwards, Thomas Norton and Thomas Sackville,* ed. John S. Farmer. London: Early English Drama Society, 1906.

Eliot, T. S. *Selected Essays, 1917–1932.* New York: Harcourt Brace, 1938.

Elyot, Sir Thomas. *The Boke Named the Governour,* ed. Foster Watson. London: J. M. Dent, 1907.

Erasmus, Desiderius. *Apophthegemes,* trans. Nicholas Udall. London, 1542.

————. *The Education of a Christian Prince,* ed. and trans. Lester K. Born. New York: Columbia University Press, 1936.

————. *On Copia of Words and Ideas,* trans. Donald B. King and Herbert David Rix. Milwaukee: Marquette University Press, 1963.

————. *Opera omnia, Emendatiora et Auctoria, ad optimas editiones,* 11 vols. 1703–1706; reprinted London: Gregg Press, 1962.

Farnham, Willard. *The Medieval Heritage of Elizabethan Tragedy.* 1936; reprinted Oxford: Basil Blackwell, 1963.

Ferguson, Arthur. *The Indian Summer of English Chivalry: Studies in the Decline and Transformation of Chivalric Idealism.* Durham, N.C.: Duke University Press, 1960.

Foakes, R. A. and R. T. Rickert, eds., *Henslowe's Diary.* Cambridge: Cambridge University Press, 1961.

Fussner, Frank S. *The Historical Revolution: English Historical Writing and Thought 1580–1640.* New York: Columbia University Press, 1962.

Gaw, Allison. *The Origin and Development of 1 Henry VI in Relation to Shakespeare, Marlowe, Peele, and Greene.* Los Angeles: University of Southern California Studies, 1926.

Gentillet, Innocent. *A Discourse upon the Meanes of Wel Governing,* trans. Simon Patericke. London, 1602.

Gilbert, Allan H., ed., *Literary Criticism: Plato to Dryden.* 1940; reprinted Detroit: Wayne State University Press, 1962.

————. *Machiavelli's "Prince" and Its Forerunners; The Prince as a Typical Book de Regimine Principum.* Durham, N.C.: Duke University Press, 1938.

Gosson, Stephen. *Playes Confuted in Five Actions.* London, 1582.

Greene, Robert (?). *Alphonsus King of Aragon,* ed. W. W. Greg. Oxford: Malone Society, 1926.

———— (?). *Locrine,* ed. Ronald B. McKerrow. Oxford: Malone Society, 1907.

Greenlaw, Edwin. *Studies in Spenser's Historical Allegory.* Baltimore: Johns Hopkins Press, 1932.

Greville, Fulke (Lord Brooke). *The Works of Fulke Greville,* ed. A. B. Grosart, 4 vols. Blackburn, Lancashire, 1870.

Griffiths, John, ed., *The Two Books of Homilies Appointed to Be Read in Churches.* Oxford, 1859.

Hamilton, A. C. *The Early Shakespeare*. San Marino, Calif.: Huntington Library Publications, 1967.

Harbage, Alfred. *Annals of English Drama, 975–1700*, rev. Samuel S. Schoenbaum. London: Methuen, 1964.

——. *As They Liked It: A Study of Shakespeare's Moral Artistry*. New York: Macmillan, 1947.

——. *Shakespeare's Audience*. New York: Columbia University Press, 1941.

Hardison, O. B. *The Enduring Monument*. Chapel Hill, N.C.: University of North Carolina Press, 1962.

Harington, Sir John. *The Letters and Epigrams*, ed. Norman E. McClure. Philadelphia: University of Pennsylvania Press, 1926.

Harris, William O. *Skelton's Magnyfycence and the Cardinal Virtue Tradition*. Chapel Hill, N.C.: University of North Carolina Press, 1965.

Heywood, Thomas. *An Apology for Actors*, ed. Richard H. Perkinson. New York: Scholar's facsimiles and reprints, 1941.

Johnson, Samuel. *Johnson on Shakespeare*, ed. Arthur Sherbo, 2 vols. New Haven: Yale University Press, 1968.

Jonson, Ben. *Ben Jonson*, ed. Charles H. Herford and Percy and Evelyn Simpson, 12 vols. Oxford: Oxford University Press, 1925–1952.

Kelly, Henry A. "Providential Themes in English Historiography." Ph.D. diss., Harvard University, 1965.

Kelso, Ruth. *The Doctrine of the English Gentleman in the Sixteenth Century, with a Bibliographical List of Treatises on the Gentleman and Related Subjects Published in Europe to 1625*. Urbana, Ill.: University of Illinois Press, 1929.

Kirschbaum, Leo. "The Authorship of *1 Henry VI*," *Publications of the Modern Language Association*, LXVII (1952), 809–822.

Kocher, Paul. *Christopher Marlowe: A Study of His Thought, Learning, and Character*. Chapel Hill, N.C.: University of North Carolina Press, 1946.

Koeppel, K. "Shakespeares *Richard III* und Senecas *Troades*," *Shakespeare-Jahrbuch*, XLVII (1911), 188–190.

Kyd, Thomas. *The Spanish Tragedy*, ed. Philip Edwards. Cambridge, Mass.: Harvard University Press, 1959.

La Primaudaye, Pierre de. *The French Academie*, trans. T.B. London, 1586.

Le Roy, Louis. *The Variety of Things*, trans. R. A[shley]. London, 1594.

Livy. *Ab urbe condita*, ed. and trans. Benjamin O. Foster *et al.*, 14 vols. London: W. Heinemann, 1919–1959.

Lodge, Thomas (?). *The Wounds of Civil War*, ed. John Dover Wilson. Oxford: Malone Society, 1910.

Lucas, F. L. *Seneca and Elizabethan Tragedy.* Cambridge: Cambridge University Press, 1922.

Machiavelli, Niccolò. *The Prince and the Discourses,* ed. Max Lerner. New York: Modern Library, 1950.

Major, John M. *Sir Thomas Elyot and Renaissance Humanism.* Lincoln, Neb.: University of Nebraska Press, 1964.

Marlowe, Christopher. *The Complete Plays of Christopher Marlowe,* ed. Irving Ribner. New York: Odyssey, 1963.

————. *Tamburlaine the Great,* ed. Una Ellis-Fermor. London: Methuen, 1930.

Mason, John E. *Gentlefolk in the Making: Studies in the History of Courtesy Literature and Related Topics from 1531 to 1774.* Philadelphia: University of Pennsylvania Press, 1935.

Mexia, Pedro. *The Foreste,* trans. Thomas Fortescue. London, 1571.

Milton, John. *The Prose Works,* ed. J. A. St. John, 5 vols. London, 1888.

Miriam Joseph, Sister. *Shakespeare's Use of the Arts of Language.* New York: Columbia University Press, 1947.

More, Thomas. *The History of King Richard III,* ed. Richard Sylvester. New Haven: Yale University Press, 1963.

Nashe, Thomas. *The Works of Thomas Nashe,* ed. Ronald B. McKerrow, 5 vols. 1910; reprinted Oxford: Basil Blackwell, 1958.

Painter, Sidney. *French Chivalry: Chivalric Ideas and Practices in Medieval France.* Baltimore: Johns Hopkins Press, 1940.

Peele, George (?). *The Battle of Alcazar,* ed. W. W. Greg. Oxford: Malone Society, 1907.

————. *Edward I,* ed. W. W. Greg. Oxford: Malone Society, 1911.

Phillips, John. *The Play of Patient Grissel,* ed. Ronald B. McKerrow. Oxford: Malone Society, 1909.

Plato. *The Republic,* ed. and trans. Paul Shorey. London: W. Heinemann, 1935.

Praz, Mario. "Machiavelli and the Elizabethans," *Proceedings of the British Academy,* XIV (1928), 49–97.

Price, Hereward T. "Construction in Shakespeare," *University of Michigan Contributions in Modern Philology,* XVII (1951).

Prouty, Charles T. *The Contention and Shakespeare's 2 Henry VI: A Comparative Study.* New Haven: Yale University Press, 1954.

Puttenham, George. *The Arte of English Poesie,* ed. Gladys D. Willcock and Alice Walker. Cambridge: Cambridge University Press, 1936.

Quintilian. *Institutio oratoria,* ed. and trans. Harold E. Butler, 4 vols. New York: G. P. Putnam, 1921–1922.

R.B. *Appius and Virginia*, ed. Ronald B. McKerrow. Oxford: Malone Society, 1911.

Reese, Max M. *The Cease of Majesty: A Study of Shakespeare's History Plays*. London: Edward Arnold, 1961.

Ribner, Irving. *The English History Play in the Age of Shakespeare*. Rev. ed., London: Methuen, 1965.

———. "Greene's Attack on Marlowe: Some Light on *Alphonsus* and *Selimus*," *Studies in Philology*, LII (1955), 162–171.

———. "The Morality Roots of the Tudor History Play," *Tulane Studies in English*, IV (1954), 21–34.

———. "The Idea of History in Marlowe's *Tamburlaine*," *ELH*, XX (1953), 251–266.

Rossiter, A. P. *Angel with Horns and Other Shakespearian Lectures*. London: Longman's, 1961.

Sanford, E. M. "The Study of Ancient History in the Middle Ages," *Journal of the History of Ideas*, V (1944), 21–43.

Schlegel, A. W. *Lectures on Dramatic Art and Literature*, trans. John Black. London: G. Bell, 1904.

Selimus, ed. W. Bang. Oxford: Malone Society, 1908.

Shakespeare, William. *The Plays and Poems of William Shakespeare*, ed. Edmond Malone, 10 vols. London, 1790.

———. *The Complete Works of Shakespeare*, ed. George Lyman Kittredge. Boston: Ginn, 1936.

———. *King Henry V*, ed. J. H. Walter. London: Methuen, 1954.

———. *The First Part of King Henry VI*, ed. David M. Bevington. Baltimore: Penguin Books, 1966.

———. *The First Part of King Henry VI*, ed. Andrew S. Cairncross. London: Methuen, 1962.

———. *The First Part of King Henry VI*, ed. John Dover Wilson. Cambridge: Cambridge University Press, 1952.

———. *King Henry VI, Part One*, ed. Lawrence V. Ryan. New York: New American Library, 1967.

———. *The Second Part of King Henry VI*, ed. Andrew S. Cairncross. London: Methuen, 1957.

———. *The Second Part of King Henry VI*, ed. John Dover Wilson. Cambridge: Cambridge University Press, 1952.

———. *The Third Part of King Henry VI*, ed. Andrew S. Cairncross. London: Methuen, 1964.

———. *King John*, ed. E. A. J. Honigman. London: Methuen, 1954.

————. *Richard III,* ed. G. Blakemore Evans. Baltimore: Penguin Books, 1959.

Silvianus. *A Second and Third Blast of Retrait from Plaies and Theaters.* London, 1580.

Smith, G. Gregory, ed., *Elizabethan Critical Essays,* 2 vols. Oxford: Oxford University Press, 1904.

Smith, Hallet. "Tamburlaine and the Renaissance," *Elizabethan Studies and Other Esays in Honor of George F. Reynolds.* Boulder, Colo.: University of Colorado Press, 1945.

Spivack, Bernard. *Shakespeare and the Allegory of Evil: the History of a Metaphor in Relation to His Major Villains.* New York: Columbia University Press, 1958.

Sprague, Arthur. *Shakespeare's Histories: Plays for the Stage.* London: The Society for Theater Research, 1964.

Stoll, E. E. *Shakespeare Studies: Historical and Comparative in Method.* New York: Macmillan, 1927.

Stone, Lawrence. *The Crisis of the Aristocracy: 1558–1641.* Oxford: Oxford University Press, 1965.

Strong, R. C. and J. A. Van Dorsten. *Leicester's Triumph.* London: Oxford University Press, 1964.

Stuart, Duane. *Epochs of Greek and Roman Biography.* Berkeley: University of California Press, 1928.

Suetonius. *Lives of the Caesars,* ed. and trans. John C. Rolfe. Cambridge, Mass.: Harvard University Press, 1935.

Tacitus. *Annalium ab excessu divi Augusti libri,* ed. Henry Furneaux. 2 vols. Oxford: Oxford University Press, 1896.

————. *Cornelii Taciti Annalium libri I–IV,* edited . . . *for the Use of Schools and Junior Students,* ed. Henry Furneaux. Oxford: Oxford University Press, 1886.

Talbert, Ernest. *Elizabethan Drama and Shakespeare's Early Plays: An Essay in Historical Criticism.* Chapel Hill, N.C.: University of North Carolina Press, 1963.

Taverner, Richard. *The Second Booke of the Garden of Wysedom.* London, 1539.

Tawney, R. H. "The Rise of the Gentry, 1558–1640," *Economic History Review,* XI (1941), 1–38.

Thucydides. *History of the Peloponnesian War,* ed. and trans. Charles F. Smith. London: W. Heinemann, 1928.

Tillyard, E. M. W. *Shakespeare's History Plays.* New York: Macmillan, 1946.

The True Tragedy of Richard III, ed. W. W. Greg. Oxford: Malone Society, 1929.

Ullman, B. L. "History and Tragedy," *Transactions of the American Philosophical Association*, LXXIII (1942), 25–53.

Waith, Eugene. *The Herculean Hero in Marlowe, Chapman, Shakespeare and Dryden*. New York: Columbia University Press, 1962.

Walbank, F. W. "History and Tragedy," *Historia*, IX (1960), 216–234.

The Wars of Cyrus, ed. J. P. Brawner. Urbana, Ill.: University of Illinois Press, 1942.

Watson, Curtis. *Shakespeare and the Renaissance Concept of Honor*. Princeton: Princeton University Press, 1960.

Webbe, William. *A Discourse of English Poetry*. London, 1586.

Weinberg, Bernard. *A History of Literary Criticism in the Italian Renaissance*, 2 vols. Chicago: University of Chicago Press, 1961.

Whitaker, Virgil. *Shakespeare's Use of Learning: An Inquiry into the Growth of His Mind and Art*. San Marino, Calif.: Huntington Library Publications, 1953.

Willcock, Gladys. "Language and Poetry in Shakespeare's Early Plays," *Proceedings of the British Academy*, XL (1954), 103–117.

Wilson, F. P. *Marlowe and the Early Shakespeare*. Oxford: Oxford University Press, 1953.

Wilson, John Dover. *The Fortunes of Falstaff*. New York: Macmillan, 1944.

Wilson, Thomas. *The Arte of Rhetorique*, ed. Robert Bowers. Gainesville, Fla.: Scholar's Facsimiles and Reprints, 1962.

Woodstock: A Moral History, ed. A. P. Rossiter. London: Chatto and Windus, 1946.

Wright, Louis B. *Middle-Class Culture in Elizabethan England*. Chapel Hill, N.C.: University of North Carolina Press, 1935.

Index

194 Index